PRAISE FOR

Decoding Your Dog

"What makes your dog tick? Do you wish he could talk? You don't
have to! *Decoding Your Dog* is all you need to speak the language,
thanks to a dream team of top veterinary behaviorists. This is one book
every dog lover needs to have, for a better-behaved companion who's
as tuned in to you as you can be to him."
— Dr. Marty Becker, author of Y̶___ ___ner's Manual

"This book confir̶___ ___ for decades, and
what young childr̶___ ___arts, as indisputable and
true . . . Dogs, each ___ ___ne of them, think, communicate, and feel. What the̶___ ___s what each and every blessed one of
us longs for too: to have ___arm heart to embrace us, a gentle hand to
guide us, and a loving teacher to show us the way."
— Sarah Hodgson, *Huffington Post*

"As a professional dog trainer, I am always searching for reputable resources that I can recommend to clients who want to further their understanding of canine behavior. I am overjoyed to add to my list *Decoding Your Dog,* which offers not only plenty of practical advice for
dog owners but also easy-to-follow explanations of the science behind
that advice."
— Laura Monaco Torelli, CPDT-KA, KPA CTP/Faculty

"Simply put, this is a book that I will be recommending to all dog owners, both those who need to correct problem behaviors for their dogs as well as those that want to prevent those behaviors from developing from the start."
— Lorie Huston, DVM, PetHealthCareGazette.com

"Behavioral problems often risk damaging the canine-human bond. Veterinary behaviorists are uniquely qualified to consider potential medical explanations while also understanding how to appropriately treat a wide array of behavior problems. This wonderful, practical book can help dog owners to ensure that their relationship lasts a lifetime. Highly recommended for anyone who loves a dog."
— Dr. Doug Aspros, 2013 president of the American Veterinary Medical Association

"The very best information to help your best friend from top veterinary behavioral experts. A must-buy for the caring dog owner. Two paws up!"
— Dr. Nicholas H. Dodman, director of the Animal Behavior Clinic at Tufts Cummings School of Veterinary Medicine and author of *The Well-Adjusted Dog*

Decoding Your Dog

 EXPLAINING COMMON DOG BEHAVIORS
AND HOW TO PREVENT
OR CHANGE UNWANTED ONES

American College of Veterinary Behaviorists
Edited by

Debra F. Horwitz, DVM, DACVB, and

John Ciribassi, DVM, DACVB

with STEVE DALE

MARINER BOOKS

HOUGHTON MIFFLIN HARCOURT

BOSTON   NEW YORK

First Mariner Books edition 2015

Copyright © 2014 by American College of Veterinary Behaviorists

www.hmhco.com

Library of Congress Cataloging-in-Publication Data is available.
ISBN 978-0-547-73891-8
ISBN 978-0-544-33460-1 (pbk.)

Book design by Victoria Hartman

Printed in the United States of America
DOC 10 9 8 7
4500783113

AUTHORS' NOTE: We, the editors and authors, believe that dogs are sentient
beings and should not be referred to by "it." In anecdotes about specific
dogs, we use whatever gender pronoun applies. When talking about dogs
in general, we alternate between "he" and "she" (the same pronoun
throughout an entire chapter), make the reference plural, or say something
like "your pet" or "your dog," because we believe dogs have a special place
in all our hearts and minds.

WHILE THIS BOOK IS BASED ON EXTENSIVE SCIENTIFIC RESEARCH AND
CONTAINS INSTRUCTIONS AND SAFETY PRECAUTIONS BASED ON THAT
RESEARCH AND ON CLINICAL EXPERIENCE, IT IS NOT INTENDED TO RE-
PLACE THE SERVICES OF A VETERINARY BEHAVIORIST. THE EDITORS, THE
AUTHORS, AND THE PUBLISHER DISCLAIM ANY RESPONSIBILITY FOR AD-
VERSE EFFECTS RESULTING DIRECTLY OR INDIRECTLY FROM INFORMA-
TION IN THIS BOOK.

We dedicate this book to Dr. R. K. Anderson, one of the founders of the American College of Veterinary Behaviorists. He was a man of great compassion and boundless energy and was an enthusiastic supporter of all his colleagues. RK taught all of us so much. While he will be greatly missed, his legacy of kindness and compassion to all living beings lives on.

CONTENTS

Acknowledgments   xi

Foreword by Victoria Stilwell   xv

Preface by Barbara L. Sherman   xvii

Introduction by Steve Dale   xxi

1. **Can't We Just Talk?**   1
   Learning to "Speak Dog"
   Jacqueline C. Neilson, DVM, DACVB

2. **Choosing Your New Best Friend**   16
   How to Find the Best Match for You and Your Puppy
   Meghan Elaine Herron, DVM, DACVB
   Patrick Yves Melese, MA, DVM, DACVB

3. **Creating a Mensa Dog**   38
   What Learning Really Is, and How Dogs Learn
   Katherine Albro Houpt, VMD, PhD, DACVB

4. **Housetraining 101**   59
   Do It Here, Do It Now
   Leslie Larson Cooper, DVM, DACVB

5. Tools of the Trade   83
   Humane and Safe Training Tools
   Lori Gaskins, DVM, DACVB

6. School Days   107
   Practical Advice on Getting from a Puppy to a Dog
   Gerrard Flannigan, MS, DVM, DACVB
   Ellen M. Lindell, VMD, DACVB

7. I Know They're Normal Behaviors, but How
   Do I Fix Them?   127
   Common Problems That Can Drive
   Any Dog Owner to Howl
   Jeannine Berger, DVM, DACVB
   Lore I. Haug, MS, DVM, DACVB

8. Lassie and Timmy: Kids and Dogs   150
   Creating a Family That Works
   Valarie V. Tynes, DVM, DACVB

9. All Dogs Need a Job   177
   How to Keep Your Dog Happy and Mentally Healthy
   Mary P. Klinck, DVM, DACVB

10. Aggression Unleashed: Do Dogs Mean to Be Mean?   199
    If Aggression Leads to More Aggression, How Do You Respond?
    Ilana Reisner, DVM, PhD, DACVB
    Stefanie Schwartz, MS, DVM, DACVB

11. Loyalty Gone Overboard: Separation Anxiety   235
    The "Velcro Dog" Dilemma
    E'Lise Christensen, DVM, DACVB
    Karen L. Overall, MA, VMD, PhD, DACVB, CAAB

12. I Know It's Going to Rain, and I Hate the Fourth of July   263
    Dogs Who Are Phobic About Sound
    Emily D. Levine, DVM, DACVB, MRCVS

13. Tail Chasing, Leg Licking—Can't You Stop?   281
    Compulsive Behaviors
    Melissa Bain, MS, DVM, DACVB
    Marsha Reich, DVM, DACVB

14. Dogs with an AARF Card: Growing Old with Grace   296
    Old Dogs Should Learn New Tricks
    Gary Landsberg, DVM, DACVB, DECAWBM (Behavior)

Conclusion   316
Appendix   318
Glossary   320
Recommended Resources   331
About the Editors   335
About the Authors   339
Members of the American College of
   Veterinary Behaviorists   348
Index   349

ACKNOWLEDGMENTS

From Debra F. Horwitz

This book never would have come to fruition without the dogged efforts and relentless commitment of many people. My deepest thanks go to my colleagues in the American College of Veterinary Behaviorists for being behind me the entire way and entrusting me with this important task. Their support, knowledge, and expertise power this book; I have learned from every one of you. Thank you to Steve Dale, who has been devoted to seeing that this book becomes a reality. He has stayed the course through all the ups and downs, taking our "ivory tower" prose and helping us put it into words to benefit pets and their people. Beth Adelman was "editing central" and kept all of us on track. We would have been lost without her. And finally, Jeff Kleinman of Folio Literary Management, our enthusiastic and intrepid agent who believed in this book from the start and kept us going through the rough patches, was always there with advice and an encouraging word.

Writing a book is bit like magic: so much goes unseen but is necessary to make it all look good. Our magic was created by the wonderful people at Houghton Mifflin Harcourt who made all this possible. We want to thank publisher Bruce Nichols, who believed in this concept, and Susan Canavan, our editor, who championed our book and saw its merits; without them this would never have happened. Thank you to Ashley Gilliam, our editorial assistant, who kept track of all the details; Michelle Bonanno in the publicity department for letting people know about our endeavor; Hannah Harlow for marketing and getting out the word; Michaela Sullivan for her outstanding cover design; and Lisa Glover for overseeing the copyediting of our words to perfection.

Dr. John Ciribassi, my coeditor, deserves a special thank you. He was a dream to work with. He never complained, was always so timely in his work, was never discouraged but cheerful beyond belief! When I asked him to do something, I could consider it done. Thank you, John; this would not have happened without you. You have been a wonderful friend and colleague; you are a neophyte editor no longer!

Finally, educating pet owners about behavior is a lifelong passion for me, supported and encouraged by my wonderful husband, Eugene, and our three grown children, Jeff, Laura, and Ben. My pets past and present have also helped. I have learned a great deal from them, including Oscar, my Westie, who currently shares our home. And, finally, my parents, who are no longer with me but always supported my passion even when "women didn't do veterinary medicine." Thanks, Mom and Dad.

From John Ciribassi

First and foremost I want to thank my wife, Elise, for giving me the time and space to pursue my dream of becoming a member of the American College of Veterinary Behaviorists (ACVB). Without her support, my career — and this book — would not have come to fulfillment. I also want to thank my children, Danielle and Rebekah, for putting up with their crabby father as he was preparing for the ACVB boards and for enduring countless dinners at home where Elise and I droned on about veterinary medicine. Thanks also go to my parents for giving me the means to achieve all that I have. And my four-legged children — Tyson, our Boxer, and Abby, our cat — have taught me more about animal behavior than any book or professor ever could.

I also want to express my eternal gratitude to Dr. Andrew Luescher, my mentor as I prepared for certification as a veterinary behaviorist. Without his patience and support there would have been no way for me to achieve what I have. His love and care of all creatures has been an inspiration.

Additional thanks to Steve Dale not only for his personal support of me as a veterinarian and behaviorist but also for his support of the veterinary profession and the pet-owning public. He has been a defender of animals locally, nationally, and internationally. I also thank him for bringing Beth Adelman on board for this project. She has kept everyone on track throughout the process and her insights into writing and animal behavior have greatly improved the quality of this book.

Finally, I want to thank my coeditor, Dr. Debbie Horwitz. I have long admired her talents as a behaviorist, a writer, and a speaker. This is the first book I have edited, and she has been behind me every step of the way and has been very patient with this neophyte. I could not have asked for a better person to work with on this, my inaugural literary endeavor.

From Steve Dale

I thank veterinary behaviorists for saving lives. Specifically, it was a veterinary behaviorist (and contributor to this book), Dr. Gary Landsberg, who helped spark the idea for this book. Dr. Debra Horwitz tailed me to ensure it would happen; she is as persistent on the trail as the best Bloodhound, never getting off track. And both she and Dr. John Ciribassi (whom I've called a friend for many years) "herded cats," rounding up their colleagues to contribute. I thank each and every "kitty" in the college for their insightful contributions.

Jeff Kleinman of Folio Literary Management was the real force to make this happen. Truly, without Jeff, no book — end of story. Of course, having a publisher helps (well, it's kind of necessary), and I thank our editor, Susan Canavan, at Houghton Mifflin Harcourt.

Beth Adelman compiled everything we needed for this book from contributors all over North America — no easy task. Beth also did the nitty-gritty editing. I have been in awe of Beth's talents for years and continue to be.

While I thank veterinary behaviorists for teaching me so much about the science of animal behavior, I've had several better teachers; they happened to have had four legs. One companion stands above all the rest. Without a dog named Chaser and an elevator that stalled between floors, I wouldn't be doing what I do today — but that's a story for another book.

I have a passion for this — passion lies within the heart. My heart will always beat most for my wife, Robin.

My dad, Bob, who loved animals, would never have believed that brilliant professional scientists would ever choose little ol' me. He died as the project was being conceived. I dedicate my contributions to his memory.

FOREWORD

I'm a dog trainer and behavior consultant — not a veterinary behaviorist. Although good dog trainers spend a lot of time dealing with canine behavioral issues and need to stay abreast of what the scientific community is continually discovering about how our canine companions think, feel, and learn, there is a difference between trainers and behaviorists. Good trainers rely on the medical and behavioral expertise of the veterinary and scientific community so that we too can use hard science to unpeel layer after layer of that unique and wonderful animal we call "man's best friend." This task is never ending, and we are constantly learning new and more-effective ways to harness the power of scientific knowledge in our work with dog owners on the ground.

Sadly, we live in an era when, as is the case with most generational shifts in thinking, there is a good deal of resistance when it comes to employing the concepts and ideologies that science is proving for us regarding our relationships with dogs. For decades, we relied on since-disproved theories of canine behavior to teach our dogs, and we ended up using misunderstood and misapplied concepts of domination and "alpha wolf" theory as the most natural and effective ways to control them. This put the emphasis on punishing dogs for misbehaving rather than teaching them what to do in different situations. But gradually we began to see the light: although dogs descended from wolves, dogs *are not* wolves, and they behave very differently. Dogs are not on a quest for world domination if left unchecked, and we don't need to be their dominant "pack leaders." Using harsh "teaching" techniques on dogs can, in fact, make many common behavioral issues much worse, or at least much more unpredictable — not to mention the fact that confrontational methods cause mistrust and compromise a dog's ability to learn and can damage the human–dog relationship.

Modern behavioral science has taught us that dominance and punishment are less effective and more dangerous than positive training philosophies, even for so-called red zone — or very aggressive — dogs, while conscience has told us that positive training also just *feels* more right. But in this debate over how best to build our relationships with dogs, proponents of the dominance- and punishment-based old-school training methods are not going quietly. There's too much money, history, and (mostly) pride at stake for them to reverse course and cross over from the "dark side," and that's a tough combination to overcome.

But fortunately for us (and dogs!), while you are free to not like what science tells you about a given topic, you can't really argue with it if the scientific research has been done carefully and methodically. You can certainly try, but chances are you'll be wrong.

The debate about training methods is over, and positive, force-free, reward-based training has been validated as the most effective, long-lasting, and humane choice by an outstanding scientific behavioral community that is made up in part of the very people who have contributed to this book.

As a dog trainer on TV and in private practice, I have dedicated my life to better understanding dogs, where they come from, how we got to where we are, and how best to give them the tools they need to succeed in our strange, domestic, human environment. Some of this is achieved by staying aware of common sense and our inner moral compass, but a lot of it also comes from understanding and assimilating what behavioral science tells us about our four-legged friends. Use the information you'll find in this book, as countless other positive trainers like me have done in our careers working with dogs, and you'll be building relationships the right way — relationships built on mutual trust, respect, and love instead of pain, fear, and intimidation.

Positively,

Victoria Stilwell — dog trainer, author, editor in chief of Positively.com, and host of *It's Me or the Dog*

PREFACE

The vision for this book arose from the collective desire of the American College of Veterinary Behaviorists to make available to dog owners scientifically correct information about dog behavior problems and to correct widespread misinformation about dog behavior. Each author of *Decoding Your Dog* is an ACVB member, expert at interpreting canine behavior.

Not a "bricks and mortar" institution, the ACVB (www.dacvb.org) is an organization of veterinarians with advanced training and experience in the field of applied animal behavior. Recognized by the American Veterinary Medical Association (www.avma.org) and founded in 1993, the ACVB certifies members, called "Diplomates," after they complete a rigorous training program. Required credentials include a veterinary degree followed by many years of education and training. In addition to intensive study, candidates applying for membership must publish in a scientific journal, manage hundreds of clinical cases in the field of veterinary behavior, write suitable case reports, and pass a rigorous written examination. Thus, the authors have advanced training and extensive experience in treating the behavior problems of dogs.

The editors of this book, Drs. Debra Horwitz and John Ciribassi, are experts and leaders in the field of veterinary behavior, with decades of combined experience. In their respective specialty practices, they have helped thousands of clients resolve their dogs' behavior problems. Dr. Horwitz, past president of the ACVB and 2012 Ceva Veterinarian of the Year, is author and editor of numerous books for veterinarians, focusing on how to treat pet behavior problems. Dr. Ciribassi, past president of the American Veterinary Society of Animal Behavior, is a popular speaker and author.

Steve Dale, a well-known pet journalist, radio and TV personality, and pet advocate, has assisted the editors and contributors. Steve has long emphasized the critical role of the veterinarian in solving pet behavior problems and the importance of behavior in the human-animal bond.

Behavior problems in our canine companions can erode the relationship we share. Even the closest ties, the deepest affection can be damaged. Behavior problems are common, reported by the majority of pet owners. And although some problems are minor, others have serious consequences. Without successful treatment, the result may be loss of the dog to a shelter or euthanasia. The goal of this book is to help you prevent or manage behavior problems so that you and your dog can live in harmony together.

The authors will recommend first that if you note a change in your pet's behavior, consult with your dog's veterinarian, to be certain that a medical problem is not contributing to it. Your veterinarian may be able to help, or he or she may refer you to an ACVB Diplomate or other qualified behavioral professional, such as a Certified Applied Animal Behaviorist. (See Recommended Resources at the end of this book.) The following pages will show you how to interpret your dog's behavior and to work with your veterinarian or specialist to manage or prevent specific behavior problems. Solving canine behavior problems is a bit like solving a mystery. Veterinary behaviorists need to know *who, when, where, why,* and *what,* to best manage the problem. For example: *Who* is the dog with the problem? (In multidog households it might not be so obvious.) *When* does the problem occur? *Where* does the problem occur? *Why* does your dog exhibit the problem behavior? *What* is your goal?

I think the authors would agree that, in a sense, this book was written by our patients — the dogs we have observed or treated for behavior problems, whose voices we have heard, whose signals we have witnessed. The dogs expressed themselves not in words but in flashes of the tail, flicks of the ear, hard stares at strangers. Most importantly, they have communicated to us through subtle signs of anxiety, fear, and conflict. The chapters in this book, written by ACVB members, interpret these signals.

Decoding Your Dog will help you to best understand your dog, based on his or her behavior, and prevent or manage behavior problems that create conflict. If you live with a dog, this book will be an invaluable guide.

BARBARA L. SHERMAN, MSc, PhD, DVM, DACVB
Past President, American College of Veterinary Behaviorists

INTRODUCTION

Veterinary behaviorists are like superheroes. When pet owners feel they have nowhere else to turn, these superheroes swoop in and save the day. Better put, they save lives.

These veterinary superheroes are an exclusive club; it's not easy to join their ranks. To become board certified in veterinary behavior, a person must be a graduate veterinarian and have undergone at least one year of general practice. They must then take formal training in behavioral medicine by completing a residency training program that lasts three to five years, during which they see behavior cases, do research, and publish their findings. The final hurdle in becoming a board-certified veterinary behaviorist is passing a two-day examination.

This book reveals the true identities of these superheroes. Of course, many veterinary behaviorists have appeared individually on television and radio, and they've been quoted when reporters know they are the "real deal." Veterinary behaviorists have written books, but until now those have mostly been textbooks or articles in peer-reviewed journals — which others (me included) have then communicated to the general public.

Veterinary behaviorists preach the gospel of science, and everything they do is based on it. Often, it's veterinary behaviorists who conduct that science in the first place. If you want to know what a dog is barking about, ask a dog. If you want to know why that dog is barking, ask a veterinary behaviorist.

The concept for this book was hatched at the Western Veterinary Conference, in a hallway at the Mandalay Bay Hotel, when I and a contributor to this book, veterinary behaviorist Dr. Gary Landsberg, commiserated. The ongoing perpetuation of antiquated and seemingly made-up notions to explain dog behavior frustrated us both. We agreed that it was about time for another perspective to be offered — one based on science.

"Follow the science" is what legendary veterinary behaviorist the late Dr. R. K. Anderson often said. Dr. Anderson, the original "cookie pusher," was among the first to demonstrate success using positive reinforcement techniques. A few years back, I told Dr. Anderson, "It seems that motivation might be a more effective means to teach dogs than intimidation."

His response: "You just graduated! It's that simple!"

Another simple premise offered repeatedly throughout these pages: instead of focusing on what the dog has done wrong, reward what the dog does right.

Sadly, dogs lose their home and some die when these simple suggestions are not followed, or when well-meaning dog owners follow misguided advice, such as "You must be dominant to show your dog who is the boss." When the human-animal bond is fractured, that's when the dog is vulnerable.

Just as there is often something that can be done to help with heart or kidney disease, dealing with behavior is a matter of making an appropriate diagnosis, followed by suitable treatment advice from qualified professionals.

With an army of only about sixty ACVB specialists (as of the writing of this book) and growing, veterinary behaviorists can't personally touch every dog. But many Diplomates (what these specialists are called) do speak around the world and write in journals, so for years their influence has touched veterinarians, veterinary technicians, dog trainers, and certified dog behavior consultants — who all touch many more people.

In *Decoding Your Dog*, veterinary behaviorists will now touch you and your pet directly. Keeping it simple, these veterinary behavior superheroes love dogs — and the science to help them. Understanding dog behavior is fascinating. And when you better understand your dog, you may be able to prevent problems altogether. Or if they do occur, following the advice outlined here, you can help your dog — or know when and where to find qualified help. I know you and your best friends can only benefit.

STEVE DALE

Can't We Just Talk?

Learning to "Speak Dog"

Jacqueline C. Neilson, DVM, DACVB

Lady looked so sweet curled up in her bed that her new owner, Kate, couldn't help herself; she just had to kiss her dog. As Kate approached the dog bed, Lady's body stiffened ever so slightly and her head dropped about half an inch. Her neck extended forward and her tongue flicked up to lick her nose. Lady's dreamy gaze intensified to a hard stare, focused on Kate. But Kate was sure Lady would enjoy a little attention and continued to approach. After all, Lady had been in the shelter for several weeks before she was adopted and their first week together had been great. Lady really seemed to enjoy all the petting.

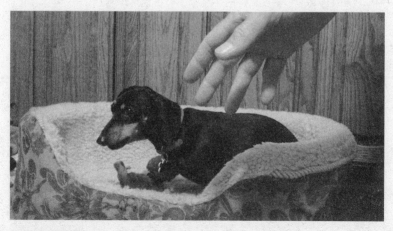

This dog's ears, eyes, and body posture all say she is feeling afraid.
Jacqueline Neilson

As Kate got closer, she heard a low rumble; Lady's upper lip trembled and lifted slightly. When Kate bent over to kiss Lady, Lady made a horrible guttural sound, lifted off the dog bed, and threw herself, mouth open and teeth snapping, toward Kate. Kate pulled back, shocked. It was all over within seconds. While Kate wasn't physically hurt, emotionally she was devastated. What type of monster had she adopted? Could she live with a dog who showed such unpredictable aggression?

Ignoring the signs of aggression will often result in a bite or attempted bite.
Jacqueline Neilson

Some variation of this scene plays out in living rooms across the country every day. It may be between the dog and a person or between two people. Yes, people snap at each other too — except we usually use angry words rather than our teeth to communicate. But we are expressing the same idea. The reason for all this discord is usually a lack of communication, a misunderstanding, or expectations that haven't been met.

Despite the way things seemed to Kate, Lady was not being unpredictable. In fact, she'd said everything she could possibly say in dog language to tell Kate not to kiss her: the stiffening of her body, the hard stare, the snarl, the growl — this is dog language for *"Stop! I'm not comfortable with this."* The problem was that Kate didn't get the message in time to change her behavior, *and* Kate thought Lady would like attention when Lady really didn't want it.

Ultimately, we'd all like our dogs to be able to enjoy and accept all the attention we want to lavish on them. Certainly, there are steps Kate can take to bring Lady closer to that goal. However, part of that process involves Kate becoming a better "listener" — and with dogs, a big part of listening is observing. Learning to be a better listener is something that can help us all build better relationships with our pets.

Facts, Not Fiction

Lassie is perhaps the ultimate fantasy of a dog who understands everything we say and communicates with uncanny clarity. Yes, there was a real dog (actually, several dogs) who played the role of Lassie, but the stories were all fiction. Despite that, many people expect their dog to be able to communicate the way Lassie did.

Dogs are primarily nonverbal communicators, while humans are primarily verbal communicators. In a nutshell, humans talk and dogs observe. Dogs rely mainly on visual and olfactory cues for communication. Humans rely mainly on words; in fact, unless we're playing charades, we rarely keep our mouths shut when we're trying to convey a message. This natural difference in communication styles creates an extra challenge between dogs and humans. But it's a challenge we can overcome. We just need to learn how to "listen" to our dogs with our eyes.

Is That Really True?

What motivates a dog like Lady to be aggressive? Is she trying to dominate her owner? Does she feel threatened by Kate's approach? Does she feel bad after the incident?

There are two big myths that sabotage many human-canine relationships: the first is that dogs are trying to dominate us; the second is that they know when they've done something wrong and feel guilty about it.

The Dominance Myth
The dominance myth proposes that undesirable behavior occurs because a dog wants to be dominant or the pack leader. There are many

problems with this theory, but perhaps the biggest is that many dogs show body language that is clearly fearful, anxious, or submissive during their supposed attempts to take over. A "leader dog" is confident, calm, cool, and collected. In fact, the leader of a pack is usually the dog who shows the *least* amount of aggression, not the most.

What Does That Mean?

The terms behaviorists use to describe behaviors and emotional states have very specific meanings. These meanings may or may not be the same as what these words mean in common use. So, because we're discussing clear communication, let's be clear about what we mean when we say the following:

Dominance: In a relationship between two dogs, the dog who more often than not controls access to valuable resources is considered to have dominance over the other dog. Dominance does *not* equal aggression. Dominance can also depend on context; one dog may be the winner in one context but not in another.

Submissiveness: In a relationship between two dogs, the dog who more often than not relinquishes things of value or defers to the other dog is considered to be submissive. Again, this may not be the same in all contexts between the same two dogs.

Fear: The emotion of being scared or afraid of some situation or event.

Anxiety: An anticipation of danger or an undesirable outcome.

Threat: Something that an individual perceives as dangerous to him.

Snarl: A canine facial expression that involves pulling up the lips and exposing the teeth, usually associated with an aggressive threat.

Positive reinforcement: Something that is desirable and delivered in response to a behavior so that the behavior is more likely to be repeated in the future.

VETERINARY BEHAVIORISTS HAVE learned that most owner-directed aggression actually stems from anxiety, *not* a desire to dominate. This becomes clear by watching the dog's body language leading up to an aggressive encounter. Many dogs show signs that are consistent with fear, anxiety, and conflict right before the aggressive act. Lady became tense and was licking her lips — both signs of anxiety — just before she snapped at Kate.

Dolly is showing anxiety, as evidenced by partially closed eyes and ears turned back. *Jacqueline Neilson*

The dangerous consequence of the dominance myth is that owners try to physically dominate their dog in an attempt to change the dog's behavior. This "solution" is likely to cause the exact opposite of the result they want. A recent study by veterinary behaviorist Dr. Meghan Herron found that confrontational techniques are, in fact, more likely to escalate aggression, resulting in more dog bites to owners.

The Guilt Myth

The guilt myth says that the dog "looks guilty" in situations in which the owner is upset with him. This is often accompanied by the assertion "He knows he's done something wrong." Of course it's true a dog might look as if he knows he has committed a crime. Dogs do offer changes in their postures and eyes that look a lot like a kid caught with his hand in the cookie jar. In some dogs, these body postures are consistent with submissive signals or attempts to convey the message "I'm backing down, I'm no challenge; I'm no threat." But this isn't guilt; it's a response to you approaching angrily and demanding, "What have you done?" The dog sees you behaving aggressively and offers an appropriate submissive response. Other dogs would interpret this signal as a white flag of surrender and would stop any threatening behavior. But because we offer some of the same signals when we're feeling guilty, and because we've all been guilty of something, we assume the dog is feeling exactly what we would feel. So we keep scolding the dog: "Why did you do this when you knew it was wrong?"

This dog may look "guilty," but what his body language is really saying is that he's no threat.
Jacqueline Neilson

This puts the dog in a terrible situation: He's doing his very best to convey to the human that he is surrendering, but the human is getting a different message. The dog is showing canine body language that means "I surrender." But that same body language, among humans, means "I'm guilty." We're seeing it and jumping to the human conclusion. This breakdown in communication can ruin a relationship.

The Guilt Factor

Jeff and Diane were terribly frustrated with their dog, Archer, when they arrived for their appointment at the behavior clinic. Archer was urinating and defecating in the house once or twice a week when they were away at work. When they got home, Jeff and Diane always knew if the dog had an accident even before seeing the stain. That's because instead of coming to the door to greet them, Archer would be hiding under the coffee table, crouched down with wide eyes. If there was no accident, he would greet them at the door exuberantly.

They believed Archer knew that he had done something wrong. They felt he was defying them and being spiteful. And, since Archer clearly was exhibiting "guilt" by hiding under the coffee table, they believed he knew why they were angry. So they felt they had to punish him. They would find the urine or feces, drag him over to it, shove his nose near it, and tell him no in a stern voice. But this reprimand wasn't working; he still eliminated in the house.

The reprimand wasn't working, in part, because of the timing. To be effective, punishment has to occur *immediately* after the behavior in question — within one to two seconds. Archer was soiling the house while Jeff and Diane were at work, probably hours before they stuck his nose in it.

Archer's problem was a lapse in housetraining. The treatment plan for this included not using punishment at all if urine or feces was discovered, regardless of how "guilty" Archer looked. Jeff and Diane learned that Archer was actually showing submissive behaviors to defuse their tension and soften the impending punishment. Archer was smart: he'd figured out that if three factors occurred at the same time — owners present, urine or feces on the carpet, Archer present — he was likely to get punished. So he tried to avoid that punishment by taking on submissive body postures.

What he hadn't figured out was the connection between him soiling the house hours earlier and the anger of his owners. They had not clearly communicated to him that the action of soiling in the house was undesirable. It's easy for us to see the link because we explain it using words: "I'm angry at you because you defecated on the rug while I was away." But because we can't explain things that way to our dogs, our reactions to their behaviors must be immediate to be understood.

Jeff and Diane followed the instructions, but they were skeptical. As they worked on the re-housetraining, Archer stopped soiling in the house and everyone was happy. But the real understanding came two years later. They got a puppy, and the first time the puppy soiled in the house when they were at work, guess who was under the coffee table when they returned home? Archer. In his mind, the perfect storm had come again — owners present, feces on the carpet, Archer present. The size of the poop made it clear it was puppy poop, so Archer couldn't have committed the crime. Jeff and Diane finally understood that Archer wasn't showing guilt, he was trying to avoid punishment. It also taught them the critical lesson that punishment is very difficult to properly implement and that positive reinforcement for good behavior is much more successful.

How Do We Begin?

We can start with these six steps to better communication with our dogs:

- Learn their language.
- Listen with our eyes.
- Use cues that work for dogs.
- Avoid miscommunication traps.
- Teach a common language.
- Have realistic expectations.

Learn Their Language
The goal is not to learn our dogs' language so that we can "speak dog" back to them; that just won't work. Maybe we can wiggle our ears, but we certainly can't maneuver them the way a dog can. And we don't even *have* tails! But we can use a knowledge of canine language to better understand our dogs' emotional states and predict what they might do next.

Dogs communicate using body postures, facial expressions, and vocalizations. When you first start to build your observational skills, it can be helpful to look at each body part individually. But ultimately, you'll have to look at the entire dog and the situation to be able to accurately understand what is being communicated. For example, consider the growl. The growl can be a threatening warning behavior or it can be a vocalization between playing dogs. You have to know the context and look at the other parts of the body to interpret what that growl is truly saying. If the dog is stiff and tense, standing tall with shoulders high, hackles (the hair along the back) raised, staring intently at the approaching person, that growl is probably a warning threat. If the dog is at the park romping around, his body relaxed and his tail wagging, and if he growls as he starts wrestling with another dog, that growl is probably playful.

Table 1.1: Canine Body Language

Body Part	Position	What It Can Mean
Eyes	Unwavering, fixed stare	Challenge, threat, confident
	Casual gaze	Calm
	Averted gaze	Deference
	Pupils dilated (big, wide)	Fear
	Wide-eyed (whites of the eyes are visible)	Fear
	Quick, darting eyes	Fear
Ears	Relaxed, neutral position	Calm
	Forward, pricked	Alert, attentive, or aggressive
	Ears pinned back	Fear, defensive
Mouth	Panting	Hot, anxious, or excited
	Lip licking, tongue flicking	Anxious
	Yawn	Tired or anxious
	Snarl (lip curled, showing teeth)	Aggressive
	Growl	Aggressive, or playful
	Bark	Reactive, excited, playful, aggressive, or anxious
Tail	Up, still	Alert
	Up with fast wag	Excited
	Neutral, relaxed position	Calm
	Down, tucked	Fear, anxious, or submissive
	Stiff-wagging or still and high	Agitated, excited, and perhaps unfriendly
Body carriage	Soft, relaxed	Calm
	Tense, stiff	Alert or aggressive
	Hackles up	Alert or aggressive
	Rolling over	Submissive

Listen with Our Eyes

Michele Wan, PhD, and her colleagues recently showed videos of dogs to some human study participants. After each video, they gave the participants a little test, asking questions about the body postures and behaviors of the dogs they'd just viewed. Not too surprisingly, the participants scored best on recalling the dogs' vocalizations (growling and barking) but didn't score so well at recalling the dogs' body postures (tail position, ear carriage, and so on). This is probably because humans are primarily verbal communicators, so sounds are what we listen to and recall best.

When we are communicating with primarily nonverbal animals like dogs, we can miss a lot of important information if we don't learn to listen with our eyes. Make an effort to observe your dog; if you see signs of anxiety, distress, or threatening behavior, as described in the chart on the previous page, step back and consider how you can avoid further escalating the situation.

Use Cues That Work for Dogs

How can we best get our messages across to dogs? Since dogs are primarily nonverbal communicators, it makes sense that dogs respond better to visual cues than to verbal cues. In other words, dogs respond more readily to what we do and how we act rather than to what we say.

In one study, researchers taught dogs two new signals for two specific actions. Each action was taught with both a word and a hand signal, given simultaneously. When the dogs had learned the signals, the researchers tested them on their response rates when given just the word or just the hand signal. The dogs were more successful at responding to the hand signal than to the word. Then the researchers *really* tested the dogs: they gave the hand signal for one of the actions along with the verbal prompt for the other action. As you might have guessed, they responded to the hand signal.

Dogs can pick up the tone of our voices and they can certainly learn specific words. (Do you have to spell out t-r-e-a-t or w-a-l-k so your dog doesn't run to the treat jar or to the door?) But visual cues are easier to teach and can trump verbal cues. So when you are teaching your dog a new skill, remember that your body language may be your best tool for a successful lesson — or the reason for failure!

Avoid Miscommunication Traps

What would you do if you walked into an interview and the interviewer looked off to the side, quietly slid up next to you, and sniffed your back? You probably wouldn't take the job. What if a stranger in the park walked up to you and sniffed you all over? Not exactly politically correct. But if you were a dog, those greetings would be totally appropriate.

A normal human-to-human greeting involves direct eye contact, reaching physically toward each other for a handshake or a hug, and no sniffing. Not only are those human actions impolite in a dog greeting, they are downright threatening — especially when you add in the leaning and reaching over the head that most of us do to dogs because we're taller than they are. The respectful way to greet a dog is no direct eye contact and no reaching out or over the dog. Instead, give the dog a chance to sniff you before engaging in direct physical or visual contact.

It's also important to remember that a wagging tail does not always equal a friendly dog. A wagging tail indicates a willingness to interact; sometimes that may be in a friendly or happy way, but other times it can be in a defensive or aggressive way. The speed of the wag, how high the dog holds the tail, and how stiff the tail is all convey subtle differences in meaning.

When reading a dog, focusing merely on the tail can prove to be misleading because the message can be quite ambiguous. Consider two dogs, same breed, same yard, peering over a fence at the same neighbor. Both dogs' tails are wagging, but one has her tail raised, fairly stiff, and moving slowly side to side. The other has his tail mostly horizontal and wagging freely. Both tails are wagging. But are they saying the same thing?

Remember, a wagging tail only means "I want to interact with you." To get the answer about *how* each individual dog wants to interact, look at the opposite end of the dog. In the first dog you notice a fairly fixed, intent stare with ears perked up and forward. Her lips are very tightly closed, exposing only a small amount of the front teeth. The second dog holds his ears in a natural, relaxed position, and his mouth is wide open, tongue lazily protruding. The intent here is clearly different: The first dog is more likely to show an aggressive response than the second one, who is more likely to engage in a friendly interaction.

In the end, always believe the message being sent by the whole dog. While the information being projected from the front end of the dog can carry the most weight in deciphering his intention, remember that a dog's attitude at any given time is best understood by considering the sum of the body parts.

Teach a Common Language

Because of our physical limitations, people will never be able to "speak dog" and dogs will never be able to speak our verbal language. Therefore, we need to develop a language to help us communicate effectively with our dogs.

That language is called training. Various methods are used to train dogs, but evidence shows that the most effective way is to reward the behaviors we consider desirable. This concept is called "positive reinforcement." It's not only more humane than using punishment, it's also more effective.

Once this training language is established, you will be able to communicate and guide your dog and navigate the world together successfully.

Have Realistic Expectations

Let's face it: We're not all created equal. Consider the record-setting Olympic swimmer Michael Phelps. Certainly, hard work contributed to his success, but he also happens to have the perfect build for a swimmer, with a long torso and long arms. Sometimes our abilities are genetic, such as Phelps's body type, and sometimes they are a consequence of the opportunities we've had. If Michael Phelps had grown up without access to a swimming pool, he probably wouldn't have won eighteen gold medals.

The same is true for dogs — perhaps even more so because the various breeds were developed to have specific body types and to perform specific jobs. A team of English Bulldogs will never successfully pull a sled in the Iditarod. That is an unrealistic expectation, given their physical abilities and behavioral attributes. A team of Greyhounds would also fail, because although they can run fast, they don't have the physical build to pull a sled; they're built for sprinting, not stamina. And they don't have a warm double coat to withstand the cold. But several teams of Huskies complete this challenging race each year and seem to enjoy it. That's because they have the endurance and physical characteristics to handle the cold and distance and they are doing what they were bred to do.

When we think about our pet dogs, we aren't usually considering activities as extreme as running across a frozen tundra for hours on end. But we do need to keep in mind that some dogs won't be able to be successful in all situations. This may be due to inherited differences or differences in experiences. For example, consider the Shih Tzu Molly, whom eighty-year-old Margaret got for companionship. Molly had a nice, quiet lifestyle until the grandchildren came to visit for a week. Molly had never been around small children, because Margaret lived in a retirement community and the most activity Molly saw was a weekly game of bridge. Suddenly three kids invaded Molly's home and were in constant motion — yelling, running, jumping, playing. Molly tried to avoid the kids but found herself trapped on the sofa as the children started wrestling with one another. She felt threatened, so Molly lashed out and bit a child.

Is Molly at fault? Certainly there is no question that Molly inflicted the bite. But maybe Margaret had unrealistic expectations for Molly, who had never been around children before, let alone children who were unaware of how Molly might communicate. If she had been listening with her eyes, Margaret would have seen that Molly was nervous: She was showing active avoidance behaviors and trying to get away from the children. She was expressing anxiety with lots of lip licking and yawning. Molly had even growled at one of the children who had picked her up the day before. Margaret did not realize these were signs of anxiety.

Molly was doing her best to convey her anxiety, only resorting to the bite when she felt trapped and threatened. Realistic expectations would have helped Margaret realize that Molly needed some protection and time to acclimate to children. In this specific situation, Molly could have been removed from the room, or the children could have been asked to play elsewhere.

Interceding can not only prevent a bite but can also save the lives of dogs who are surrendered to shelters or euthanized because they are labeled as aggressive. Being a good owner involves accepting that dogs come with some limitations and respecting those limitations, so that we don't place dogs in situations where they are likely to fail.

Avoiding Pitfalls and Staying on Track

- Remember to look at the entire dog, not just one body part or a single vocalization, and to also look at the situation to get an accurate read of the dog's emotional state.
- Dogs understand some words, but they can't understand a full conversation. Gestures and body language are clearer ways to communicate with dogs. Clear communication takes attention and effort, but is well worth it!
- Not every dog can succeed in every situation. Watch your dog for signs of anxiety or aggression and change the circumstances so that the dog doesn't get overwhelmed.
- If something seems like it's about to happen, step in. Either remove the dog from the situation or change what's happening.

What Did We Say?

- Sometimes our dogs must feel the way you would if you were dropped into a place where you don't speak the language and no one speaks English.
- Dogs primarily use nonverbal communication. Learn to read dog body language. Listen with your eyes as well as your ears.

- Using visual cues and training techniques based on positive reinforcement will help you be more successful in communicating with your dog.
- Not every dog can do every task or succeed in every situation. Pay attention to your dog and make smart choices.

2

Choosing Your New Best Friend
How to Find the Best Match for You and Your Puppy

Meghan Elaine Herron, DVM, DACVB
Patrick Yves Melese, MA, DVM, DACVB

I just don't understand what I did wrong," sighed elderly Mrs. Burns as her one-year-old Australian Cattle Dog, Riggs, tugged and tore at her pants leg with a crazed grin and a playful growl. A few months ago Mrs. Burns had picked out an adorable little puppy from the local shelter, who quickly grew into a constantly active dog who seemed to destroy virtually everything he could get hold of that was not bolted down. Riggs also pulled hard on leash walks and lunged at every small animal in sight, making walks a holy terror for his owner. "He was such a cute, energetic little puppy, but now he is a complete monster!" she said.

Riggs was not a bad dog, nor was Mrs. Burns a bad owner. The two were simply a poor match.

Bringing a new dog into your home who will share your life for many years is a big decision. Choosing a dog who is well matched with your family and home will dramatically increase the chance that you will all live happily ever after and will minimize avoidable problems.

Although it is important when selecting a new dog to avoid serious hereditary physical conditions, such as hip dysplasia, heart disease, eye problems, and other ailments, if at all possible, our focus here is on choosing a *behaviorally* healthy dog. You have many important decisions to make when you get a new dog, including the breed, age, and gender of your new companion, where you might obtain her, and how to set her up for a successful life in your home. But whether you get your dog from a shelter, a pet store, a rescue group, an Internet or newspaper ad, or even a breeder, she will have certain behavioral characteristics based on her genetic makeup, prenatal environment, and life experiences. You must consider these characteristics carefully before bringing a new dog to your home.

Facts, Not Fiction

Thanks to decades of research on companion animals, we have quite a bit of information regarding breed dispositions, gender compatibility, and predictors of behavior in dogs. For example, we know that by selective breeding, certain breeds were designed to perform specific tasks. We also know that the basic temperament required to perform such tasks is directly related to certain behaviors that a breed may show in a home environment. Australian Shepherds, a herding breed, may nip at the heels of children. Terriers bred to be alert may be more apt to bark at passersby. This makes it vitally important to research the breeds that may be right for you.

We also know that the source and the background of a pet, particularly an adult dog, will have an effect on how that dog behaves in your home. The behavior and health of a dog's parents, as well as how she was handled during her early, formative weeks, are key to determining your dog's adult behavior. Fortunately, methodical behavior tests make it possible to evaluate and better predict adult dog behavior when information regarding a dog's parents and early environment are unavailable.

What Does That Mean?

Selective breeding: This is a process by which breeders select a set of characteristics (behavioral, physical, or both) that they find desirable and then choose to breed animals who have those characteristics, so that they will be more likely to pass them on to their offspring. Selective breeding has been going on for hundreds of years.

Highly invested breeder: This type of breeder strives to produce puppies who best represent the ideal health and behavior profile of a given dog breed. Reputable breeders should be able to provide information on the behavior of both parents, the conditions during pregnancy, and the behaviors of previous litters, as well as the standard physical health certifications known to be important for that particular breed.

Casual breeder: This is a general term used to describe people who are selling or giving away puppies who were born either from an unregistered mother or in a nonprofessional breeding setting. Often these are accidental breedings or families who want to experience having one or more litters from their family dog. These people tend to be less well informed and put less planning and care into the health and behavior of the puppies.

Temperament test: Also known as a behavior assessment or behavior evaluation, this process includes a series of standardized interactive tests, typically performed on shelter dogs, to assess the behavior and personality of the dogs. Most temperament tests assess dogs for social interest in people, compatibility with other dogs, physical handling issues, and potential for resource guarding and some other aggressive behaviors.

Rescue groups: These are typically nonprofit organizations that take in and rehome pets. Some rescue groups obtain their animals directly from families who wish to rehome their pet, while others pick up dogs from local municipal shelters who might otherwise be euthanized. Most of these pets then stay in temporary foster homes until they are matched with an adoptive family. There are breed-specific rescues for most dog breeds.

Puppy mills: These are high-volume breeding facilities. Usually, a broker purchases large numbers of puppies at once and sells or distributes them to local pet stores. The breeding animals are typically confined to cramped and solitary living spaces with limited to no social or physical stimulation and little or no regard for their physical and behavioral health.

How Do We Begin?

If you are thinking about getting a dog, first think very hard about the reality of having a dog join your life and your household. Although physical and behavioral characteristics vary widely between individual dogs and breeds, there are also many anatomical and behavioral traits that are shared by most breeds of dog, including mixed breeds. Domestic dogs, for instance, are highly social species and do best with regular companionship, adequate mental stimulation and training, and physical exercise.

For some people, bringing a young, very energetic puppy or a large, powerful, assertive canine into their home may create problems. Once you have decided to get a dog, it is important to choose a breed that best fits you and your family's current lifestyle.

ALTHOUGH WE MAY be drawn to a breed's physical appearance, keep in mind that appearances can be deceiving and that the personality, temperament, and behavior patterns of the new dog need to fit your life. Most all puppies are adorable, but it is important to get a good idea of what the adult dog will look and act like when she grows up. Unlike humans, puppies grow to young adults in a matter of months, and by one to two years of age, when human infants are barely toddling around, a dog is pretty much a physically fully formed adult. Selecting a new dog by focusing solely on the *puppy*'s appearance and behavior can set many new dog owners up for predictable trouble down the road.

Some people have fond memories of living with a certain breed they had as a child. All too often that memorable breed may simply not be suited to your current home and life. Furthermore, our memories of a childhood pet are often colored by the fact that we did most of the fun stuff with the dog while someone else had to deal with the training and the consequences of unwanted behaviors.

Much like in dating, during which you take into account the requirements for a long and happy relationship, consider what you are really looking for in a dog over the long term (remember, dogs live eight to twelve years on average) and also the capacity you and your family have to meet that dog's normal needs. Gauge how active you and your family currently are to determine the desired activity level of your new companion. A family that plays a lot of video games and enjoys watching movies, with little outdoor activity, should seek a dog who does not have a high need for physical stimulation and exercise. How much time do you have to devote to daily walks, basic training, or brushing out a long coat of hair to avoid matting? What is your interest in organized canine activities, such as agility, obedience, or other dog sports? Do you have small children in your family who might be overwhelmed by a large, powerful dog or who might not be old enough to trust with handling a delicate toy breed?

Purebred Versus Mixed-Breed Dogs

Mixed-Breed Dogs

Mixed-breed dogs make up the majority of the dogs found in shelters. Although not much can match the sense of gratification that comes with saving a dog, mixed-breed dogs can present a bit of mystery, and these unique dogs are rarely easily categorized. Unlike purebred dogs, a mixed breed's physical and behavioral characteristics are usually not easy to predict. Although conventional wisdom suggests that a mixed-breed dog may be more physically healthy (and even possibly have more desirable behavior) than a purebred, this is not reliably the case, since if either parent has a heritable problem, it is just as likely to be passed on to the mixed puppies as it is from purebred parents.

Getting a puppy from healthy and behaviorally sound parents is just as important for mixed-breed as for purebred dogs. Recent advances in DNA technology now enable owners of mixed-breed dogs to run laboratory tests to find out more about which breeds contributed to produce their canine family member. However, these DNA tests can only tell you about what breeds may be part of your pet's ancestry. These tests do not tell you about your dog's individual health, temperament, past experiences, or the health, temperament, and experiences of your dog's parents.

Purebred Dogs

Thousands of years of selective breeding by different human cultures have taken the wild canine ancestors of domestic dogs and developed hundreds of distinctive breeds. Over many generations humans have selectively bred dogs for certain characteristics, such as size, coat, color, and a myriad of other physical and behavioral traits. Highly invested breeders saw some set of characteristics they desired and selectively bred animals who had those features and would be more likely to pass them on to their offspring. Good breeders would not breed any offspring who did not have desirable traits, but rather sought out only the finest examples of the breed they were seeking to establish, so that they could produce puppies with a high chance of maintaining those desirable characteristics. For example, shepherds looking for a canine partner to keep watch over their flocks tended to select dogs with instincts to move the herd but not to hunt or harm them.

It is beyond our scope here to give individual information on dog breeds, but it is easy to find this information with the help of your veterinarian, at the library, in a bookstore, or on the Internet. There are many resources for researching breed characteristics. One book we suggest is *The Perfect Puppy* by Benjamin L. and Lynette A. Hart, which presents a statistically controlled summary of fifty-six breeds; it's the only book we know of based on a statistically validated study.

Where to Find Breed Information

- Visit an experienced veterinarian.
- Research breed registry organizations, such as the American Kennel Club (AKC) and the United Kennel Club (UKC), and breed organizations.
- Visit a dog show to see some of the adult individuals of a breed you may be considering. At a benched show (a dog show where you have access to the dogs and breeders or handlers), you can ask the handlers questions. Be aware that the more conventional "conformation" dog shows focus primarily on the physical attributes of the individual dogs (a bit like a beauty pageant), whereas a dog show that features competitions where the dogs must display innate and trained skills will focus on trainable qualities in the dogs.
- Books and Internet sites have a wealth of information on selecting and properly teaching a new dog how to live in your home. (See Recommended Resources at the end of this book.) Two available websites are www.purina.com/dogs/dog-breeds and www.akc

.org. Remember, books that specialize in a single breed are usually the author's favorite breed, and information is presented in such a favorable light that important problems and considerations may be overlooked. Be sure to learn the good, bad, and also the "ugly" about the breed so you know what to avoid and what to expect.

- Keep in mind that there can often be as much variation within a breed as there is across different breeds. This means that within every breed there will be good examples of the breed but also unsuitable dogs who do not meet the breed standard either physically or behaviorally.

An excellent investment of time is to research why a particular breed was created and what the function of that breed has been in society over the years. Let's look at the Border Collie. Over many generations Border Collies have been selected for their high energy and their propensity to be drawn to moving animals, herding them into groups. Herding is a hardwired behavior in most Border Collies, and if your home and lifestyle does not provide an outlet for this predisposition, the dog will likely create outlets of her own — compulsive chasing, destructive behaviors, or just herding all the children who may be trying to play in the yard. If you don't happen to have a herd of sheep handy

Jake, an Australian Shepherd, retrieves a Frisbee as part of his active lifestyle. *Jen Cooper*

for this very intelligent dog breed, your dog would best be served by pursuing a high-intensity dog sport, such as agility or flyball, along with lots of daily physical and mental exercise.

Picking a Breed

In general, you will find breed groups have common traits that may be helpful in making your decision. Retrievers want to retrieve (and will pick up nearly anything to hold in their mouth) and tend to need more active lifestyles as well as social companionship. Terriers tend to be on the more tenacious side, and their intelligent nature can lead them into trouble if they are not given outlets for mental stimulation and their natural propensity to hunt small prey.

Breed Groups

Traditional breed groupings, such as those used by the AKC, usually take into account the historical functions of dog breeds.

- **Sporting dogs:** These dogs were bred to hunt game birds both on land and in the water.
- **Hound dogs:** These dogs were bred for hunting other game by sight or scent.
- **Working dogs:** These dogs were bred to pull carts, guard property, and perform search-and-rescue services.
- **Terriers:** These dogs were generally bred to rid property of vermin such as rats.
- **Toy dogs:** These dogs were bred to be household companions.
- **Non-sporting dogs:** These dogs vary in size and function, and many are considered companion dogs.
- **Herding:** These dogs were bred to help shepherds and ranchers herd their livestock.

Keep in mind that big personalities may also come in small packages. A Jack Russell Terrier may be compact and fit easily into your carry-on luggage, but this breed packs a punch when it comes to intelligence and drive. This is a breed designed to hunt and chase small, burrowing animals and to enjoy one of the most active lifestyles of all the modern dog breeds. Unlike Eddie from the TV sitcom *Frasier*, most Jack Russell Terriers are not couch potatoes, so think again if you are looking for a calm, quiet lap dog for Grandpa.

For more information on selecting a dog, see the "Books on Choosing a Dog" section in the Recommended Resources at the end of this book.

Since different people are looking for different things in a dog, and their home environments differ widely, there is no "best breed" that will fit everyone. Be aware that although some dog breeds (typically smaller breeds) can live up to eighteen years, some of the very large breeds have a much shorter lifespan. An eight-year-old Bichon Frise may be just barely hitting middle age, but a Great Dane of the same age is likely to be at the very end of her life.

After narrowing the field down to one or two breeds, it helps to find at least two or three people who have adult members of that breed (and the gender you are looking for, if possible) and to visit the dogs in their home environment. Remember that your dog will be an adult for all but the first year of her life, so don't just judge based on puppies you meet.

Knowledgeable individuals, such as your veterinarian, reputable breeders, or members of a dog breed club, can also give you the benefit of their own experiences with individual breeds and particular bloodlines in your local area.

Variations Within Breeds

Some breeds can have wide variations in behavior and physical appearance. These differences can be so great behaviorally that two dogs of the same breed may act like very different dogs, and this finding is now supported by recent advances in analyzing DNA.

For example, in breeds like the Border Collie, show lines and working lines have such different behavior patterns that they are almost distinct breeds. Show lines are families of dogs who are selected for qualities that are most appropriate for conformation (how they look and move), while working lines are dogs who are selected and bred for

A Border Collie from working bloodlines in a typical herding position, moving the sheep as a group. *Janet Elliott*

strengths that relate to their working tasks. Border Collies from show lines may exhibit little of the typical behavior patterns so pronounced in the working lines (the tendency to herd, in this case). The same can apply to various hunting breeds, which have field lines (retrieving of birds, for example) and show lines — such breeds as Labrador Retrievers and Golden Retrievers, both very popular family companions.

Designer Dogs

Designer dogs are generally the result of selectively breeding two purebred dogs. The concept seems to have started in the late twentieth century, when Standard Poodles were selectively bred with other breeds, presumably to contribute their intelligence and nonshedding, less-allergenic coat. The results of breeding these full-size Poodles with Labrador Retrievers created hybrids named Labradoodles.

Puppies resulting from these purposeful mixes are called by portmanteau words, made up of syllables or sounds from the breed names of the two purebred parents, such as Schnoodle (Schnauzer and Poodle) and Puggle (Pug and Beagle). Now there are many more types of these designer dogs, as more and more breeders join the fad.

A breed is meant to represent a consistent type of offspring when two individuals from that breed are mated with each other — in other words, the offspring will have the same breed characteristics (coat, size, and so on) as their parents. This does not always happen with designer dogs. The offspring may have the characteristics of one or the other parent breed or a blend of both, and puppies within the litter may differ greatly from one another.

As the public takes to these designer dogs and demands more of them, a proliferation of puppy mills have started cashing in on the trend. Puppy mills are set up, all too often in squalid conditions, to produce puppies as fast as the mother dogs can give birth. The offspring, who may already be in poor health, are shipped long distances to pet shops or are sold through newspaper ads and the Internet. Transportation also puts a huge stress on the pups, and many sicken and die en route. Due to all these stress-inducing factors, there is a potential for these dogs to be psychologically abnormal in their development.

One Dog or Two?

In two separate studies, veterinary behaviorist Dr. Barbara L. Sherman and Kathryn Wrubel, PhD, found that based on owner reports, getting two puppies from the same litter resulted in the two siblings staying so closely bonded to each other that it was harder for them to bond as successfully with their people. In addition, they may be more likely to start fighting with each other when they approach social maturity, typically around one and a half to two years of age. And two puppies can be more than twice the work when it comes to housetraining, obedience training, and teaching simple household manners. Keep this in mind when you see a litter of puppies and think about getting two at the same time, and be sure you are ready for the additional work.

Where to Get Your New Dog

You can get a dog from a variety of sources, including breeders (both highly invested and casual), animal shelters, breed rescue organizations, private sellers, and pet stores. Animal shelters and breed rescues are often saving lives by finding homes for previously unwanted pets who were either surrendered by their owners or picked up as strays. Keep in mind that there may be behavioral reasons why these dogs lost their previous home, and the more information you can gather about their past, the more you can anticipate their behavior in your home.

Be wary of anyone who advertises puppies and then tells you they will bring the dog to you. Reputable breeders should be willing to meet with you, proudly show you their facilities, and not only discuss all concerns you might have but also ask you questions to be sure they are comfortable placing their puppies in your home.

A Shelter or Rescue Group

In general, there are two kinds of pet shelters, based on their admission policies. What dogs are available can differ between the two types of shelters.

- **Open admission:** These are often municipal shelters contracted with the city or county to take all stray, abandoned, and surrendered animals in the region. Although this kind of shelter varies greatly, depending on the municipality, funding, and staffing, open admission shelters may have less information about a dog's background. They may be limited in their ability to perform behavioral assessments due to budget limitations. Many of the dogs found at these shelters are strays and abandoned dogs. Owners can surrender their pets for any reason to these types of shelters.

- **Limited admission:** These are typically privately funded shelters with their own individual guidelines regarding the sources, types, and conditions of animals they admit. This kind of shelter can make admission rules, including requiring the previous owners to fill out information on the pet's history and provide reasons why they are surrendering the pet. A number of private shelters do a great job of assessing the physical and behavioral health of dogs they admit, and may have the staff and budget (this varies widely) to help dogs with problems so that they can become more adoptable. Because these shelters have limited space, once they are full they no longer accept additional dogs. If the accepted dogs do not find new homes promptly, they may remain in the shelter for months or even longer.

A fairly new trend over the past several years has been relocation, where animals in the shelter and rescue system are moved from certain cities, states, or countries (for example, from Mexico to the United States) to areas that are perceived to be better options for successful adoptions. Relocating dogs can also meet a shortage (sometimes the perception of a shortage) of certain types of dogs available for adoption in a particular area, where the demand for puppies and dogs may outstrip the local supply.

Dog relocation increased dramatically after Hurricane Katrina affected Mississippi and Louisiana in 2005 and left many more animals than could be properly cared for and adopted locally in the struggling region. Since then, relocation efforts have continued to spread widely throughout the country. This trend makes it harder and harder to know much of anything about a shelter dog's history, since whatever information was originally available is often lost as the pet is moved between shelters, and a family looking for a shelter dog may no longer even know what region the dog came from.

Most shelters and rescue groups require an application process. Be prepared to show proof that your previous pets have had proper veterinary care and, if you're a renter, that your landlord allows dogs in your home.

Be sure to ask about results of temperament or behavior testing and any prior history before adopting your dog, so that you have the best chance of knowing what to expect. Although behavioral testing at shelters is certainly not perfect, you may wish to look elsewhere if the shelter you are considering provides no prior history or temperament testing. (See the section called "Temperament Testing" later in this chapter.)

Pet Store Puppies

Pet stores offer a variety of purebred and even "designer dogs" (a specific mix of two breeds). There is typically no application process required. While this makes pet stores a potentially more convenient source for a variety of puppies, their puppies are not likely to be the most sound.

Pet store environments are typically bright and shiny, offering cute puppies in all shapes and sizes, but these puppies often come from environments that are not so bright and wholesome. Many commercial pet stores purchase puppies from large breeding facilities or brokers of these facilities, also known as puppy mills.

Smartest Breeds

Psychologist Stanley Coren, a widely published author from the University of British Columbia, studied data from 208 dog-obedience judges in the United States and Canada to determine which breeds are the smartest, based on how well they perform in formal obedience exercises. There are, in fact, many contexts in which dogs perform and get to show off their abilities, such as service dog work, drug detection, and agility competitions. Performance in obedience competitions is just one of those areas in which dogs get to show off a little, and breed results can vary depending upon the activity in question.

While assessing true intelligence is not a straightforward task, Coren's list can be a fun way to stimulate discussion with your friends while at the dog park. Also, be careful what you wish for. A highly intelligent dog can be very draining for the average family, because it is not always easy to stay one step ahead of her.

1. Border Collie
2. Poodle
3. German Shepherd
4. Golden Retriever
5. Doberman Pinscher
6. Shetland Sheepdog
7. Labrador Retriever
8. Papillon
9. Rottweiler
10. Australian Cattle Dog

Since buyers rarely get to meet the parents of their puppy, they have no assurance of quality breeding stock. In addition, the condition of the parents can be dire and the breeding mother is often subject to mental and physical distress. This stress is shared with the developing puppies during pregnancy, because the hormones released by the mother are shared with the babies via the fetal blood supply. As has been shown in studies of several species of mammals, such as those reported by animal physiologist Dr. Gary Moberg in *The Biology of Animal Stress,* prenatal exposure to elevated levels of stress hormones, such as cortisol and adrenaline, can set puppies up to develop abnormal brain chemistries, specifically, an abnormal regulation in the pathway between the hypothalamus in the brain and the adrenal glands (glands that produce stress-related hormones), called the hypothalamic-pituitary-adrenal (HPA) axis. HPA axis abnormalities can lead to anxiety, fear, and even aggression problems as adults. While you may be able to whisk away your new puppy before she spends much time in a pet store, unfortunately, much of the emotional damage was done before she was even born.

Most large, purebred breeding facilities offer AKC-registered breeds, and most will even have registration and pedigree papers describing a quality lineage. But if you are not able to observe the parents' behavior or living conditions during pregnancy, you have no way of knowing if pet store puppies are coming from reliable sources.

Getting a Puppy from a Highly Invested Breeder

If you get a healthy new purebred puppy from a reputable and ethical breeder, you can expect your young dog to grow into an adult who will reliably show the physical and temperamental traits of her forebears. Another potential advantage of getting a purebred dog from a reputable breeder is that the parents will be tested for serious health conditions that are known to be passed on to their offspring. Some of these include musculoskeletal problems such as hip dysplasia and elbow problems, which can be tested through not-for-profit veterinary health organizations, including the Orthopedic Foundation for Animals (OFA) or PennHIP, as well as eye problems, tested through the Canine Eye Registration Foundation (CERF), and other testing services.

A reputable breeder should be able to provide information on the behavior of both parents, the conditions during pregnancy, and the behaviors of previous litters, as well as standard physical health certifications known to be important for that particular breed. Seek recommendations from your veterinarian and local breed clubs for a reputable breeder in your area.

If you are looking for a puppy from a breeder, ask to meet one or, ideally, both parents and note how these dogs all interact with members of your family (including children), strangers, and other dogs or cats. If the breeder will not allow you to meet the parents, be suspicious that the dogs may have unwanted behavioral traits.

Be sure the puppy was raised in a loving, secure, and nontraumatic environment. Study the litter to find a balanced puppy who is neither withdrawn from people nor overly rambunctious or assertive. It may be helpful to make sure a puppy responds comfortably to gentle handling and restraint. However, as reported by Drs. Bob Wilson and Hal Sundgren in a 1998 article, and also by behaviorist Dr. James Serpell, most current formal puppy temperament tests have not been shown to be accurate predictors of future adult behavior.

In most cases, puppies should remain with their mother and littermates until they are approximately eight to ten weeks of age. This somewhat depends on the socialization practices of the breeder, the enrichment quality of the breeding environment (what opportunities the puppies have to engage in normal social, mental, and physical activities), as well as your own ability to provide a good learning environment after you get the puppy home.

Breed Fads

Breeds that used to be rarely seen and hard to obtain can become substantially more popular and, therefore, more easily available. For example, as recently as thirty years ago the Cavalier King Charles Spaniel (whose ancestry dates back hundreds of years but was only recognized by the AKC in 1995) could be found only listed in the AKC *Complete Dog Book* in the miscellaneous class and seldom, if ever, mentioned in most books about choosing a dog breed. As has happened so many times when a breed appears in the media, the Cavalier became popular when it was featured on *Sex and the City*.

The same overnight increase in popularity of a breed was also seen with Collies after *Lassie*, Dalmatians following the movie *101 Dalmatians*, and Jack Russell Terriers following *Frasier*.

As a breed becomes more and more popular, there is greater pressure on breeders to increase production due to demand. This process can lead to eventual temperament problems if breeders lose sight of the importance of selectively breeding only physically and behaviorally healthy representatives of the breed. The take-home message here is that if you are drawn to a breed of dog by popular exposure, always go the route of obtaining your puppy from a breeder, and take the time to carefully research your options to find a reputable one.

What About Private Adoptions?

Obtaining a puppy or adult dog from a private party or a backyard breeder often involves responding to an ad online or in a newspaper or seeing the proverbial box of puppies offered in a public marketplace. Private parties usually are offering either an adult dog being surrendered by the owner (using the newspaper rather than a shelter) or a litter of mixed-breed puppies who resulted from an accidental breeding.

If you do choose this route to pick a dog, be sure to find out as much as you can regarding the *real* reason an adult dog is being given up, since you may be taking on someone else's medical or, more commonly, behavioral problem. Of course, it may well be that this lovely adult dog just needs a new home due to unavoidable circumstances.

Adopting a puppy in this manner can either be brilliant — if you can actually meet the puppy's parents and determine that they are both medically and behaviorally healthy — or a complete shot in the dark if you know nothing more than that the puppies are cute.

Puppy or Adult: What Age of Dog Should You Adopt?

Although you can get puppies from all the sources we mentioned, there are some things to consider about the age at which a new dog will join your household. One advantage of choosing a puppy between eight and ten weeks of age is that the pup is still in the sensitive period of socialization. (See chapter 6 for more about socialization.) This means you still have substantial influence over the puppy's exposure to people, other dogs, and even other types of animals with which she is likely to share her life. You will also be in charge of her early learning, so you can protect the vulnerable puppy from overly traumatic experiences and help teach her how to be a welcome and well-behaved member of your community.

On the other hand, adopting a young puppy is not for everyone, since puppies usually go through chewing/teething phases and must learn housetraining, which can be a time-consuming process. Not every home is puppy proof enough to weather the newcomer's likely destructive behavior, and not every dog owner can put up with a puppy soiling the house as she learns where to properly eliminate.

Adopting an adult dog can be a better choice only if she is already well housetrained, well socialized, and has learned what she can and cannot chew. With an adult you will often inherit whatever the dog has learned as she grew up (good and bad) and have somewhat less influence on her behavior, since the primary socialization period is likely already past.

Male or Female: Which Is Likely to Make the Best Pet?

In general, personality differences between individual dogs overshadow any gender differences. This means there is enough variability between individual animals, regardless of their gender, to make a discussion of the behavior of male versus female less important. In addition, since most puppies will be neutered before they reach sexual maturity, the effect of sex hormones on behavior is reduced. Socialization through early exposure to many varied positive situations can have a much greater effect on the behavior of a maturing puppy than merely choosing based on gender.

Temperament Testing

Many modern shelters use a temperament test to try to predict if an adult dog is likely to be suitable for adoption and what kind of family the dog might be the best match for. Work is still in progress to demonstrate these tests' ability to predict the newly adopted dog's behavior in the new home. Tests used by shelters include Meet Your Match/ SAFER (Safety Assessment for Evaluating Rehoming), Match-Up II, and Assess-a-Pet.

Dr. Amy Marder of the Center for Shelter Dogs, part of the Animal Rescue League of Boston, evaluates its dogs with the Match-Up II personality test. This test is designed to incorporate information from a dog's behavioral history and behavior in the shelter to match the needs of each dog with a suitable home, leading to a successful adoption. You can find more information and videos demonstrating this program at www.centerforshelterdogs.org.

Although each temperament test is unique, most have common elements and goals, including assessing social behavior with people and dogs, trainability, handling ability, and propensity for aggression based on food or resource guarding. Studies, including one reported by veterinary behaviorist Dr. E'Lise Christensen in 2007, have shown that shelter temperament tests have difficulty predicting certain traits, such as separation anxiety, territorial behaviors, and aggression directed at familiar family members. Therefore, behavioral assessment testing is best supplemented with as complete a behavior history from prior owners as possible, along with observations of the experienced shelter staff, such as with the Match-Up II evaluation.

If you have young children or other pets living in your home, before completing the adoption be sure to observe how they interact with the dog you are considering. Dogs who are comfortable around children are usually less likely to show aggression toward them. These more-suitable family dogs will greet the children in an appropriate manner and seek just as much attention from the kids as they do from the adults in the family. A dog who shows no interest in your children or who actively avoids them is likely a bit fearful of children and may not be a good match for your family. (Chapter 8 discusses kids and dogs in more detail.)

If you have a cat in your home, ask if the dog has been "cat tested." Dogs with high prey drive may chase or even attack a resident cat, making this combination quite dangerous. If at all possible, you should also introduce your household dogs to any proposed new pet before adoption, to make sure there is mutual interest and comfort.

It may also be helpful to ask about dogs available for adoption who have been fostered in homes that have children or other pets. This can give you a much more accurate assessment than just a temperament test or brief observation. However, remember that pet personalities differ and that doing well at a foster home does not ensure the newcomer will do well with your own resident pets or in the environment that you provide.

Some dogs may not exhibit certain behavior problems for several weeks. This is the so-called postadoption honeymoon period, during which many dogs may behave differently than they will in several months' time, as they become more comfortable in their new environment. As a dog starts bonding closely with her new family and becoming familiar with her territory, aggression problems may develop, so pay attention as the new dog adapts to her surroundings.

Is That Really True?

If a dog suffers from separation anxiety, will getting a second dog cure her? Although some dogs with separation anxiety find comfort in the companionship of a second dog, many anxious dogs do not see another dog as a viable substitute for people and will continue to have anxiety when left home without humans. In addition, the distress of your current pet can affect the behavior of your new dog, which may lead to double trouble. Finally, if the two dogs are not compatible, fights can occur and even more stress is placed on both you and your current pet. (For more on separation anxiety, see chapter 11.)

Is it true that getting a dog of the opposite sex (for example, getting a male if you already have a female) will prevent any fighting between the two dogs? Although studies of many social animals in nature have shown that members of the opposite sex rarely fight, in our domesticated and typically neutered pets, we still regularly see cases where male and female dogs fight within a household (as reported by Dr. Kathryn Wrubel and her colleagues at Tufts College of Veterinary Medicine in 2011). Although in nature males and females may see each other as potential mates and also have fewer issues to fight over, in our homes even dogs of the opposite sex may fight, since they compete over coveted food, chew toys and bones, people, and many other desired resources. Our dogs are also usually neutered, so they are unlikely to see each other as potential mates the way their wild ancestors would have.

If a puppy comes with AKC-registered papers, does that mean she did not come from a puppy mill? Most puppies from puppy mills or commercial breeding facilities have a registered pedigree through the American Kennel Club or another registry. These high-volume breeding facilities keep pedigrees on their animals. The presence of a champion in the pedigree is also no assurance, since puppy mills can obtain puppies for breeding purposes from champion dogs or dogs bred to champions.

Avoiding Pitfalls and Staying on Track

Now that you have done your homework and picked out your new companion, it's time to start your new dog off on the right paw. Your work begins the moment you get the dog, as you make every effort to establish good habits and avoid problem behaviors.

The first few days are critical for every newly introduced dog, but especially for puppies. The sensitive socialization period, when a puppy needs to learn what is safe and acceptable in life (see chapter 6), winds down at around twelve to fourteen weeks of age. Avoid letting the puppy have unrestricted and unsupervised access to the entire house or relegating her to be alone in the backyard, since both of these will likely set your puppy up to learn unwanted behaviors.

Crate (or den) training is a beneficial start, because it provides a safe way to prevent soiling in the house, a place where the puppy can go to escape excessive handling by small children, and also a way to prevent destructive and potentially dangerous behaviors in the house when you are away. In addition, the crate can be used to teach independence by preparing the puppy to be calm when left alone. (For more information on training and socialization, see chapter 6; for help with housetraining, see chapter 4; and for crate training, see the appendix at the end of this book.)

What Did We Say?

- To select a dog who will be a welcome member of your family for her entire life, you must spend some time and effort to make the best selection. Carefully assess if a dog is right for you, and research which breed or mixed breed you feel would best match you and the environment you will provide.
- Avoid being led by TV or movies that portray certain carefully selected and highly trained individual dogs as representatives of their breeds. Likewise, do not fall prey to wistful memories of a childhood dog who was either exceptional or seemed so with selective memory, since your current situation may be very different and that breed may no longer fit your lifestyle.
- Once you have decided on some likely options, think hard about where you can find a new dog or puppy, and carefully consider the options of adopting from a shelter or purchasing from a reputable breeder.
- Select a dog who seems well-balanced and neither too rough nor too shy.
- Get ready to fall in love with your dog and guide her to be well-adjusted to her new home and live happily ever after with you.

3

Creating a Mensa Dog
What Learning Really Is, and How Dogs Learn

Katherine Albro Houpt, VMD, PhD, DACVB

You have just adopted Farley, a one-year-old mixed-breed dog, and you would like to be sure he fits well in your active household. You have received many suggestions for where you can go to get training for Farley, but they all seem to have different views on how to train a dog. How do you choose which is the best approach for Farley?

Most people would like to have the smartest dog on the block — a Mensa dog. Mensa is an association of people who have scored very high on intelligence tests. So would you like Farley to be a Mensa dog? Are you sure? Some of the most unhappy dog owners are those with very smart dogs who are underemployed. Do you really want a dog who can open any door, knows what taking out the suitcases means, buries the nail clipper, and remembers the weak spot in the fence?

For most people, the perfect dog comes when called, drops even the most delicious food when asked, never jumps up on anyone, stays when told, and does a few tricks to amuse your guests. And you know what? He doesn't need a PhD to learn these things, and you don't need one to teach him. In this chapter you'll learn how to teach your dog tasks that can make your life and his easier. And you'll come to see the difference between what you think you're teaching and what the dog thinks you're teaching.

Facts, Not Fiction

"You can't teach an old dog new tricks." That is definitely fiction. Snowy was a ten-year-old Westie who learned to sit at ten years of age.

Up until that time, for what his owners needed, he was the perfect dog. He never really had to be taught anything. He lived in the country and could roam in the yard that he never left. He jumped in greeting, but jumped in the air, not on people. He taught himself to sit up and beg. The only reason he needed to learn to sit at age ten is that this is when his life circumstances changed. And guess what? He did learn to sit when asked, demonstrating that, in fact, you *can* teach an old dog new tricks.

What is true is that dogs learn more slowly in old age, just as humans do. The decline in learning ability (and cognitive function) can be slowed to a great extent in dogs, as in humans, with the right diet and environmental enrichment, especially social enrichment — increased opportunities for interactions with other dogs and people. (See chapter 14 for more on aging in dogs.)

The Smartest Dogs

All dogs are smart enough to teach us to provide them with food, water, shelter, and, usually, exercise and veterinary care. Which dogs are the smartest? It depends on how you define smart. At the moment, the dog with the best memory for words is a Border Collie, who can retrieve more than four hundred different objects by name. This is a form of associative learning: the dog learns to associate words with objects. It is a prodigious feat. But what may be more impressive is *insightful* behavior. We all know that dogs can be sneaky, and recently this was proven in an experiment in which a dog could take a treat from either a dish that made noise when he touched it or from a silent container. If a person was not watching, the dog chose the silent container, thus not alerting the owner. He was being insightful.

Border Collies have a reputation for being brilliant. And, in fact, the breeds that are rated as the most trainable are Poodles and Border Collies. Those rated least trainable are Beagles and Basset Hounds. However, when a series of learning tests was given to five breeds, the differences within breed (individual dogs of the same breed) were greater than the variations between dogs of different breeds. In other words, a dog's breed is not the last word on his trainability.

It's important to remember that trainability is not necessarily intelligence, and that certain breeds have been genetically selected over time to be more easily trained for a specific task, such as to herd sheep, leap into the water after objects, run after rabbits, or attack other dogs or people. The features of each breed are not inherited as a package but rather as separate traits, probably on separate chromosomes. So if a Newfoundland is crossed with a Border Collie, some of the descendants will love water like a Newfoundland and stare at sheep like a Border Collie; others will show one or the other of those traits.

So what are the mental abilities of dogs? They can certainly learn to associate objects and also tasks with words. They can match to sample — a task in which the dog is shown one object and then must choose between that object and a novel one; choosing the familiar object is rewarded. For example, if you show a dog a red rubber squirrel and then show him a pile of toys, picking out the red rubber squirrel from the pile is matching to sample. Dogs do not do as well at matching toys with photographs of toys, though.

While it is unlikely that dogs understand geometry, they can make mental maps. If you walk a dog on a leash in an L-shaped path away from a goal (food), when released he will take a shortcut (the hypotenuse of the triangle) to make his way back to the food. These mental maps persist too. Hide a toy or treat, and he can remember where it was hidden for half an hour.

However, dogs are not so good at barrier problems. If they are inside of a V-shaped barrier, they can figure out how to run around the barrier to get a reward on the outside of the V. But if they are outside the V, they have trouble understanding that they must run around the barrier to get the reward inside the V.

What Is Learning?

Learning is defined as acquiring knowledge by instruction. At its most basic, it's a multistep physical process involving electrical impulses, release of chemicals, and formation of proteins.

Information is received by nerve cells that send an electrical impulse to the end of the nerve, where neurochemicals are released and stimulate the next nerve. When this process is repeated enough times, the nerve will form new proteins and eventually grow new pathways. In other words, your dog's brain actually changes as he learns. The more often a given combination of nerves is stimulated, the more likely the behavior will occur in response to that specific stimulus. The next time you say "sit" and your dog sits, think about all the processes that were involved in forming that memory.

In fact, your dog is learning all the time — when you specifically teach him and when you don't. Remember when, as a puppy, he stuck his nose in a candle flame? He learned to avoid fire with no assistance from you. Similarly, he learned on his own that there really wasn't another dog in the mirror. Every day, every walk you take your dog on, he is constantly learning. It doesn't matter how young or old he is.

The following are some ways in which dogs learn.

Classical Conditioning

Almost everyone knows about Pavlov's dogs. The principle Pavlov discovered still applies today, and we can make use of it. Ivan Pavlov was actually studying salivation and won his Nobel Prize not for psychology but for his study of how the intestinal tract works. In the process of collecting saliva from his dogs, however, he realized that the dogs were salivating *before* they tasted any meat.

Salivating when tasting meat is an unconditioned response, meaning it does not have to be learned. It happens automatically. Pavlov's dogs had learned a conditioned response: they associated the preparations for the experiment with the meat they were fed, and responded as if they had tasted the meat. Pavlov found that not only the sight of meat but also the sound of a bell would cause the dogs to salivate if the sound had regularly occurred just before the meat was presented to the dog. This kind of conditioning — where an unconditioned response (in Pavlov's experiment, salivating) can be elicited by pairing it with an unrelated stimulus (ringing a bell) — is *classical conditioning*.

This same sort of conditioned response is the basis for a training method called "clicker training." Clicker training is an increasingly popular way to train dogs. The clicker is a plastic toylike device with a metal strip that makes a quick, clear, consistent, and distinctive clicking sound when pressed, making it ideal for this type of training.

The principle behind clicker training is classical conditioning: associate a sound (in this case a click) with an unconditioned response (the taste of a delicious treat). It will take only a few minutes for your dog to form the association: click means treat. The process of creating that association is simple enough. Give a single click, then immediately give or toss a treat to your dog. Do that about twenty times, and he will have formed the association that a click means the treat is coming. The click now becomes a reward all by itself, because the sound lets the dog predict that a treat will soon appear.

Now you can use this technique to teach your dog almost anything, using another form of learning — *operant conditioning*. You simply click the instant your dog does the behavior you are trying to teach, and then follow up with the treat. The click means "What you just did is exactly what I wanted, and now your reward is on the way."

Operant Conditioning

Operant conditioning is just a fancy term for training. It's different from classical conditioning in that it does not rely on an unconditioned, or "automatic," response. You can classically condition a dog to salivate when he sees you open a can of dog food, because salivation is a natural response dogs have to food. However, while Pavlov was able to get a dog to salivate automatically by presenting meat, there is nothing he could have presented that would have automatically stimulated the dog to push a ball. Instead, the dog must learn to operate on his environment to get a reward.

With operant conditioning, the dog learns that *any* behavior he performs (that is, whenever he "operates" on his surroundings) may possibly result in some tangible reward (a treat, or a click followed by a treat, for example). This tangible reward for a behavior is called "positive reinforcement."

There are many dog toys that rely on operant conditioning, such as the Buster FoodCube, a plastic container that the dog must turn over to get a treat, and the Kong Wobbler, a plastic beehive-shaped toy that the dog must push around so treats or kibble tumble out. A similar sort of toy is the Tug-a-Jug, which contains a rope inside a plastic bottle. If the dog manipulates the rope in a certain way, treats are released.

Zorrow and the Skinner Box

In psychology, operant conditioning is often associated with a rat in a cage pushing a lever. The rat "operates" on the lever and food is delivered. This apparatus is called a Skinner box, after the psychologist B. F. Skinner, who invented it.

Zorrow was a beautiful one-year-old Doberman Pinscher who had sustained a bad fracture of his leg and had to be kept quiet for six weeks — which meant pretty strict confinement and not much fun! His owners devised a dog-size Skinner box to help Zorrow cope with inactivity. They taught him to push a switch panel for one piece of kibble. He could use his paw or his nose to push. Then later he had to push twice for a kibble. They slowly increased the number of times he had to press the panel, until he had to press ten times for each kibble. It took him a long time to obtain his daily meals that way. But since he now had some mental stimulation, he could tolerate his convalescence.

Zorrow demonstrated another concept, as well: learning to learn. Once he had mastered the Skinner box, he would work for a very long time on it to get food, but he would also work for a long time opening doors, containers, and bags to get to food. He had learned that food could be obtained if only he persisted.

Making a Learned Behavior "Stick"

Most dogs, especially Mensa dogs, learn quickly that "sit" means a treat is coming, and they will quickly stop complying if you don't have a treat. The technical term is that the response will be *extinguished*. To avoid this problem, you have to teach your dog to be a gambler, like someone feeding those Las Vegas slot machines over and over, hoping for the big win.

That is, you want your dog to keep offering the learned response, even if he doesn't get a treat every time, in hopes that eventually the reward will appear. To turn him into a gambler, you can give him a reward every other time he sits (only *after* he learns "sit" reliably and is getting a reward every time). But every other time is too easy to predict, so you'll have to start offering rewards randomly — every second time, every tenth, every fifth, and so on. He can't predict when the reward will come, so he'll keep offering the response in hopes that next time will get him the payoff.

This is called a "variable ratio of reinforcement," which means the frequency of the reward (the rate of reinforcement) varies. Animals can learn to repeat actions hundreds of times for a single reward using this technique. Nini, a Cairn Terrier, was taught to jump into the car on request for a treat. She lived to sixteen and would still jump in the car when asked, even though eventually she got a treat only about every fourteenth time she was asked her to jump in.

Nini is waiting and hoping for her reward for jumping in the car. She receives a reward only infrequently—enduring a high ratio of responses to reward. Note also that she is wearing a seat belt. *T. Richard Houpt, VMD, PhD*

Punishment: What It Is and What It's Not

Punishment is what you do when you want to reduce the likelihood of a behavior happening again. The problem, as discussed in chapter 1, is that if the punishment — say a swat to the rump or a harsh word — occurs more than a second after the dog did the behavior, he will not associate the punishment with his action, therefore, he won't learn what you intend to teach.

However, he will learn something — and it may not be at all what you intend. Here's an example. Dorothy was tired of her dog, Angel, pulling on the leash, so she yanked on Angel's collar as hard as she could whenever the dog pulled. Her little dog adored children, and usually when Dorothy yanked, Angel was pulling to say hi to groups of children near a school. The punishment worked, and Angel quickly got the message — but it was the wrong message. She associated the pain of being yanked with her efforts to say hi to the kids. That's what she thought she was being punished for. After only three repetitions, her attitude about little kids changed for the worse. Meanwhile, Angel continued to pull on the leash.

Positive Training, Positive Results

Numerous recent studies have shown that punishment-based training methods (also known as aversive training) can do more harm than good because they may cause reduced welfare and increased fear and anxiety. Techniques based on positive reinforcement can result in improved learning. Behaviorist and veterinarian Sophia Yin demonstrated in studies done in 2008 that nonaversive, reward-based training techniques were more successful in promoting desired behaviors. In addition, veterinary behaviorist Meghan Herron's research in 2009 showed a greater number of episodes of aggression directed toward a dog's owners when punishment-based techniques were used in training. And John Bradshaw's studies in 2004 revealed increased numbers of problematic behaviors in dogs trained using aversive techniques.

When we're talking about operant conditioning, punishment can be positive or negative. You may ask, "Isn't all punishment negative?" But behavior scientists use the words *positive* and *negative* differently.

Negative punishment means *removing* something to decrease the frequency of a behavior; of course, it's most effective if it's something the dog likes. If Spike, your cute little Rat Terrier, snaps at your guests, you might consider immediately walking away from him and leaving the room. You are removing something he likes (your company) in response to the problem behavior. If your timing is right, Spike will eventually learn that snapping at guests means he loses your attention.

Positive punishment means *adding* something to decrease the behavior. Of course, it's most effective if it's something the dog doesn't like, such as a swat, a yell, or a squirt with a water bottle. But, as we have already seen, positive punishment poses some serious timing issues.

Negative Reinforcement

It's easy to confuse negative reinforcement with punishment, but they're not the same. Punishment follows the behavior and will reduce the likelihood of the dog exhibiting that behavior again. Punishment is initiated by something the dog did; if he does not jump on the coffee table, you won't punish him. Reinforcement is also initiated by something the dog did, but you would like to see that behavior continue. For example, if he sits on a mat by the door he gets a reward — that's positive reinforcement.

Negative reinforcement is something you keep doing to the dog that is unpleasant, until he does what you want. For example, you pull on the leash until he moves toward you. His reward is that you stop pulling. You are then removing something unpleasant (that's the negative part) to increase the likelihood that the dog will move toward you again (that's the reinforcement part). Your pulling should increase the probability that he will approach you when he feels the tension on the leash increase.

The bottom line is that punishment is intended to *decrease* the frequency of a behavior, and reinforcement is meant to *increase* it. The positive means adding something to the situation, and the negative means taking something away.

Avoidance Learning

Dogs can learn to associate good things with an arbitrary stimulus, like a click or the refrigerator door opening. They can also learn to associate an arbitrary stimulus with something unpleasant. This is the basis of much of the older style of dog training, in which a dog may learn to heel to avoid a strong jerk on his neck with a choke collar. Avoidance learning is also the basis for electronic fences. These consist of a buried wire that will transmit a signal to a special dog collar that will sound a tone when the dog is within three feet of the boundary and then, if the dog moves closer, administer a shock. The dog learns to stay within the boundaries to avoid a shock.

Extinguishing a Behavior: How to Make It Stop

A behavior will naturally decrease if the reward is removed. This is what is meant by extinguishing a behavior. Ignoring behaviors may make the behavior stop, if the goal of the behavior is to get your attention (for example, jumping up on you when you come home). However, barking at passersby will probably not extinguish if you ignore the yapping, because the dog is rewarded when the people go away. He's thinking, "Look at what happens when I bark; the people go away. This works perfectly!" Also, for lots of dogs, barking is fun — which means it's self-rewarding. If you ignore it, this behavior won't stop.

What Does That Mean?

Classical conditioning: Learning in which the presence of one event becomes associated with another event that naturally elicits the desired response

Operant conditioning: Learning that occurs when a particular behavior produces consequences — either reinforcement or punishment

Avoidance learning: Learning that occurs when a stimulus becomes associated with something the dog would like to avoid

Reinforcement: Any change in an animal's surroundings that occurs after a behavior or response and increases the likelihood of that behavior occurring again. Reinforcement can be positive (something is added to the situation) or negative (something is taken away from the situation).

Punishment: Any change in an animal's surroundings that occurs after a behavior or response and reduces the likelihood of that behavior occurring again. Punishment can be positive (something is added to the situation) or negative (something is taken away from the situation).

Variable ratio of reinforcement: A reinforcement or reward schedule in which the number of correct responses necessary to get a reward varies

Extinguish: To make a learned response disappear when it is not rewarded or reinforced

Generalize: To learn that after a behavior is established in one particular environment, it should also occur in all other environments

Is That Really True?

We've heard a lot about the dominance theory of dog training. This idea states that what we need to do to train our dogs is to show them who is boss.

Is it true that if we are dominant, by using force-based training methods, our dogs will obey? The theory goes like this: Since dogs are essentially domesticated wolves, and wolves have a rigid dominance hierarchy within their pack, the same must be true for dogs. Simple, right? But that thinking turns out to be wrong.

Two recent findings have led us to abandon the dominance-hierarchy approach to dog training. First, wolves don't actually have rigid hierarchies, except in captivity. In the wild, packs are not ruled by a despot (an absolute ruler who wields power in an arbitrary or cruel manner). Second, dogs genetically separated from wolves much farther back (fifteen thousand to twenty thousand years ago) than was originally thought, and their behavior is now quite different. Recent studies have revealed that feral dogs (free-living dogs that are descended from domestic dogs) do not live in packs but rather alone or in small groups.

Are Wolves Smarter Than Dogs?

Another popular theory is that wolves are smarter than dogs. Is there any truth to that statement? Wolves can't be all that smart as a species or they wouldn't have become endangered over much of their range, while dogs are thriving, lounging inside our air-conditioned homes and relaxing in recliners. Nevertheless, there is some evidence that wolves are more intelligent than dogs.

Wolves have larger brains than dogs of the same weight. Brain size is not an entirely accurate measure of intelligence, because the smaller brains of women were once used to "prove" they were not as smart as men. A better IQ test is problem solving, and wolves are better at solving problems on their own than dogs are. Groundbreaking research by Brian Hare and Adam Miklosi found that dogs look for help from humans when they can't solve a problem (more on this in "Teaching 'Look'" later in this chapter). This trait seems to be innate in dogs because puppies do it, whereas even human-reared wolves are very slow to learn to look to a human for help.

The definition of dominance is priority access to resources. Therefore, walking beside the human or sitting down when told does not seem to have much to do with dominance, because it does not affect the dog's access to any resources. Furthermore, it is not clear that dogs perceive us as members of their social group.

They can certainly learn to fear us, but is that really the relationship you want with your best friend? You want a dog who *wants* to do what you ask. And for that to happen, what is important to the dog is consistency. So if you say "sit" and he sits, good things happen — consistently. When they do, he will be less anxious — and anxiety is the root of many canine misbehaviors, especially aggression.

How Do We Begin?

Let's try to teach Farley to sit. First, the environment should be conducive to learning. That means no distractions — no squirrels outside the window, no loud music or other dogs barking. You should not be distracted either — no watching TV out of the corner of your eye. For learning to take place, both you and your dog need a calm, focused environment.

To teach "sit," hold a piece of delicious food right in front of his nose, then pass your hand back between his ears. He should put his nose up, and when his nose goes up, his rump goes down. When his rump touches the floor, say "sit" and give him the food. Don't say "sit" until he starts to squat, because he has no idea what that word means until you have paired his action of sitting and the word at least a dozen times. Once he has learned to sit in that nice quiet environment, it is time to help him generalize by asking him to sit in other places and in more distracting situations. (Generalizing is when an animal learns that after a behavior is established in one particular environment or with one particular person, it should also occur in all other environments with everyone.) When you do that, you have a chance of controlling his behavior even when he is aroused or frightened.

Next let's teach Farley to lie down. There are ways to force a dog to lie down by pulling his front legs forward or to trick him into lying down by holding food on the floor. But the easiest way is to wait for him to lie down spontaneously and then reinforce that behavior.

If you're using a clicker, he already knows what the clicker means (he did exactly the right behavior, and now a treat is on the way!), so you can sit back and wait for him to lie down. Just as he does, mark the moment with a click. Then you have a few seconds to toss him a treat. You don't have to say anything — and in fact, you should wait until he is repeatedly lying down before pairing his action with words and a hand signal.

Why use both a word *and* a hand signal? Dogs are visual animals and communicate primarily by reading body posture. Research work done by veterinary behaviorist Daniel Mills suggests that dogs seem to respond better to hand signals than to words. Also, hand signals can enhance your elderly dog's quality of life. Hopefully, your dog will live well into his teens. If he does, he'll probably lose some of his hearing ability, at which time he will respond only to the request he perceives — a hand signal. Still, the spoken word can save your dog's life. What if he's running toward a squirrel that's on the other side of the street? He won't see your hand signal as he runs toward the squirrel, but he can hear you calling and will lie down rather than dart out into a busy street.

Timing Is Everything

For most appointments with a veterinary behaviorist, pet owners are asked to fill out a long history form before they arrive at the behavior clinic. One of the questions is about learning. One question might concern what percent of the time the dog complies with the following requests: "sit," "down," "stay," and "come." When Jerry, an extra-cute Pomeranian, was carried into the consultation room (he was nearly always carried), Jerry's owner was asked to demonstrate how he responds to the request to sit. Although Jerry's owner had said he complied 80 percent of the time, she said "sit" twenty times and he still did not sit. Was his owner lying? No. She meant that if there are no distractions and she has a particularly good treat, then maybe he will sit the tenth time she says the word.

Jerry's owner wasn't fibbing and Jerry wasn't stupid. In a very few minutes he sat for a bit of squeeze cheese. After a dozen rewarded sits, it was hard to get him to stop sitting long enough for the request to be given again. Was this super training? Not at all. It was just a great example of how effective it is for a reward to be given quickly after the correct behavior is performed.

Teaching "Look"

One of the quickest tricks for a dog to learn is "look." Hold a treat at arm's length, well above your dog's head. Just hold it there. He will look at the treat and maybe try to jump for it, but after ten seconds or so he'll look at you. Quickly pop the treat in his mouth. Repeat about ten times, and you'll find that he begins to look at you more quickly. Now you can pair saying "look" (or "watch me") with this action. If you only say "look," he won't know what you mean, so you must say it *just* as he is turning his eyes to yours. He will associate this action with the word.

It's surprisingly easy for people to teach this cue to their dogs. This is where understanding dogs meets practicality. It's easy to teach "look" or "watch me" because dogs innately look to humans to solve their problems. Try this: Ask a friend to place a treat out of reach of your dog while you are out of the room. When you return, your dog will stare at the treat and then at you and then back at the treat. Even puppies will do this. Dogs may not be as smart as wolves, but they know where to go for help.

Why is the "look" request so important? Because it can save your dog's life. Imagine you and your dog are walking along a country road and you see a car coming. There are all sorts of fascinating things on the other side of the road, and your dog is tempted to cross. If you say "look," he'll turn and look at you and not run in front of that car.

A Word About Words

Dogs can learn many words: "walkies," "ride in car," "dinner," "fetch." But they can become confused if we misuse words. In one clinic, the veterinary behaviorist always asks owners if the dog knows "down." Most say yes. When the dog jumps on them, they say "down." However, if they want the dog to lie down, they also say "down." How does the poor dog know the difference? In one case it means "get your paws off me" and in the other case it means "please lie with your chest and belly on the floor." You can see why the dog is confused. In other cases, Mrs. Owner says "sit" and Mr. Owner says "sit down." *Of course* their dog is confused.

Everyone working with the dog should use the same word every time for a given action. And one word is better than two. So skip "lay down" (every dog and grammar teacher knows it should be "lie down," anyway) and just say "down." And when you want your dog to get off of you, say "off."

It's Not What You Say but How You Say It

The tone of your voice is also important. If you want the dog to come or do anything active, like fetch, use short, rapidly repeated notes. If you want him to stop doing something immediately, use a sharp, single note. Slowing or soothing your dog is best done with a long, monotone note, like "Staaaaaaaay" or "Eaaaaaasy."

Patricia McConnell, PhD, CAAB, and author of *The Other End of the Leash*, recorded the signals from professional animal handlers from all over the world (from Quechua-speaking handlers of sheepdogs to Spanish-speaking jockeys for racehorses) and found that no matter the language, short, rapidly repeated notes were used to increase activity, and long, slow ones were used to slow an animal's action or calm it down. She confirmed this by training puppies to come and to stay. Some pups were taught to come to short, repeated, computer-generated whistles, and to sit/stay to long, flat or descending ones. The other pups were taught with the signals reversed. The dogs learned fastest when the short, repeated notes were linked with coming when called, just as you would do if you called your dog to come with hand claps or "Pup pup pup!"

Rewards That Are Rewarding

"Come" is one of the most difficult actions to teach, because dogs know when there is nothing restraining them, and they certainly know when a chipmunk is running by or the compost heap awaits. Teaching this skill, then, gives us some insight into the value of the right reward for getting a dog to perform the desired behavior.

There are many ways to teach "come." The way that worked for Denver was the banana method. Denver is a Cairn Terrier and absolutely loved bananas, even more than typical treats like chicken or cheese. He was initially trained to come by calling him when he was very close and rewarding him with a slice of banana.

Gradually, Denver was able to get farther away before being called. Soon he was almost perfect as long as he was called within ninety seconds of his departure. After ninety seconds, he was too far away either to hear or to care. But he always returned to the house within a few minutes, because when Denver returns to the house voluntarily he always gets a slice of banana. The morals of this story are that if the reward is good enough, the dog will work to earn that reward, and, second, what is one dog's most valued reward may not be another's.

What You Learned Is Not What I Meant to Teach

Denver is twenty pounds of unconditional love, but he usually has muddy paws. He used to invade the personal space of visitors to jump on and lick them. His problem was cured by teaching him "place" and "stay."

There are many ways to teach a dog not to jump on you. Most are physical — a knee in the chest or stepping on the dog's toes or holding the front paws and pushing the dog backward while shouting "Off!" The trouble with these methods is that although the dog may get off you at that moment, he will probably jump on you the next time you come home. Why?

Why do dogs do anything? They do things because they are rewarded with something: food, petting, the thrill of running, a romp with a friend, or attention. We should say they do it for our *attention!* — because dogs usually crave attention.

When Denver jumps up on you, he gets your attention. You may pet him, especially if he weighs twenty pounds and you are wearing old clothes. If he weighs eighty pounds, however, you might shout at him and push him off, especially if you are wearing your best white slacks. In either case, he gets attention.

Yelling at him or kneeing him is attention. Remember, it is punishment *only* if it reduces the probability of the action happening again. Unless you are pretty strong, your actions are probably not going to reduce the likelihood of him jumping again. So you will not be punishing him for jumping on you. Instead, you will be rewarding him.

Unfortunately, we inadvertently teach our dogs the wrong lesson more often than we would like.

So how do we teach the right lessons? Keeping in mind that jumping is usually an attempt to get attention, the solution to most jumping problems is to ignore the behavior. Do not speak to the dog or look at him or touch him. Turn your back. If he jumps on your back, leave the room. The behavior will eventually be extinguished.

The problem is that while this may work well for you, your dog may not generalize to everyone. Generalizing is not so easy for dogs.

This is where the "stay" command is useful. If a dog is staying ten feet from the door, he cannot be jumping on your guests. He may be highly motivated to jump, but if he has learned to inhibit this urge, he will be a much better pet. And to teach him to inhibit himself, you must make an alternate behavior — one that is incompatible with jumping — just as rewarding.

Teaching "Stay"

As soon as your dog knows "sit," he can begin to learn "stay." Stand right in front of the dog. Hold the palm of your hand in front of him like a traffic cop and say "stay." Count to three and then release him. The release word can be "okay," but be careful because we use "okay" in too many other contexts. You don't want to accidentally teach him the wrong thing.

You can use "come" as the release word; this will help him be eager to come to you. Or you can use "free dog." Gradually increase the length of time you require the dog to stay. A minute is a long time for a dog.

"Stay" is the one request you should repeat. You should use a low, soothing tone with a dropping inflection: Denver's owners used "stay, Denver, stay, stay," as sort of a mantra.

Combining "Place" and "Stay"

Chose a spot ten feet or so from the door. The perfect spot varies with the architecture of your house. For example, if the stairs in your house end close to the front door, you may have to teach your dog to go to the sixth stair.

Your first step would be to call him to the spot you chose and say "place" as he arrives, at which time he gets a treat. After a few repetitions you would then say "place" and pat the area, and when he comes give him his treat. Finally, you would go to the door and say "place" and have your dog go to his spot for his treat.

Your final step would be to add "stay," so that your guests could get all the way in the house and then greet your dog. The added benefit is that your dog is unlikely to run out the door and down the street if he is staying in his spot away from the door.

"Come," or Off-Leash Recall

There are many ways to teach "come," and you can use all of them. A fun way to teach a family dog is to have all the members of the family sit in a circle with the dog — a kind of Doggy in the Middle game. Have a leash attached to the dog's collar and a light weight of some sort at the end of the leash.

Toss the weighted end to Dad, who says "Shep, come." If Shep doesn't come, Dad pulls him gently to him and, when the dog arrives, pets him or gives him a treat. Dad tosses the end of the leash to a child, who calls "Shep, come" and rewards him for coming. Notice we are using negative reinforcement here with the release of leash pressure, and positive reinforcement with the giving of a treat to encourage and then reward the correct response: coming. Then the child tosses the leash to a sibling and the game proceeds. Shep can't predict who will call him next, so he has to pay attention to which person is calling him. Two people can play the game, but Shep will simply learn to run back and forth from one to the other; at least three people is best.

You can also teach "come" if you are by yourself. Just walk around the house and call the dog from different rooms, rewarding him each time he comes, so he gets lots of experience seeking you out even when he can't see you.

Another way to teach "come" is to use the word as the release from the stay position. Instead of saying "okay," say "come," and the dog will be very happy to bound over to you because "come" will signal the end of staying, which is hard work for a dog. First practice this in the house off leash, and then on walks, on leash in the beginning.

To be extra careful, keep your dog on a leash while practicing "come." When he's reliable on a regular leash, then you can use a long line, and finally a fishing line so light that he won't realize it's there. When you feel confident, release the dog in an enclosed area, such as a tennis court, and call him. Set up some distractions, such as his favorite toys or additional people in the area. He can't escape, but it's a good test, and you will be able to determine whether he is actually proficient at off-leash recall.

Finally, when your dog is dependably coming when called, take him off the leash, but always assess the location for dangers to your dog before you release him.

Avoiding Pitfalls and Staying on Track

Getting Angry

Farley is not too good at the recall, and today he heads for the neighbor's house when you are in a hurry to leave. You call and call and he ignores you. Finally, you follow him and call again. He comes to you, and as soon as he gets to you, you begin to berate him. "Bad dog, bad Farley."

Poor Farley is very confused; he came, but you scolded him when he did. You may even have jerked his collar. He thought he knew what "come" meant, but now it means "come and be scolded by a really angry person." The next time you call him, he may not come, or he might come with head and tail down.

It is very hard to keep your temper when a dog does not do what you ask. But you must remain calm and relaxed if you want a well-trained dog. This is true of all the behaviors you teach your dog, but especially "come."

Food-Reward Pitfalls

Often when dog owners are asked during a behavioral consultation to demonstrate their dog's response to "sit" and "down," many say, "Oh, he'll only do that if I have food." But your dog should comply with a request every time you ask, whether you have food or not. What's wrong?

You have to reward the dog if you expect him to do something for you. He is no more likely to work for no salary than you are. But once he has made the association between a word and an action, you do not have to reward him every single time. In fact, you shouldn't. Never knowing when the reward will come will keep your dog "gambling" in hopes of the big payoff. Remember our discussion of variable reinforcement (rewarding a well-learned behavior intermittently instead of continuously after each repetition of the behavior).

Failure to Generalize
What if your dog does very well at obedience school and in your living room, but he doesn't seem to understand your requests when you visit other people or while you're walking? This is likely a failure to generalize his learning from one environment to another. Practice in a variety of situations — and with various distractions — to help him generalize his skills.

What Did We Say?

- Your dog is always learning; his brain is always developing.
- Take advantage of your dog's ability to learn! Train him to do the simple tasks that give his life consistency and your life joy.
- Dogs need incentives, just like all animals, including people, do. They will offer a response many times for a reward but eventually will stop responding if there is no reward.
- Dogs can be classically conditioned to find a click rewarding. Clicker training can be very useful in training a variety of behaviors. Your choice of words and tone of voice when training are equally important.
- Dogs are not wolves in Poodles' clothing. It is not necessary to be dominant over your dog in order to teach him to be the perfect dog. You can easily teach him to look at you, to sit, to stay, and to come using positive reinforcement. Your dog will enjoy receiving rewards, and he will learn to trust rather than fear you. The relationship from the perspectives of both ends of the leash will be stronger.

4

Housetraining 101
Do It Here, Do It Now

Leslie Larson Cooper, DVM, DACVB

I can't understand it." Chloe's owner, Marge, was perplexed and hurt. "We have a comfortable home with a big backyard and a dog door, so Chloe can go outside to 'do her business' anytime she wants, yet she still pees and poops in the house!" Chloe, a tiny Maltese, smiled a very happy dog smile at both of us; clearly, all was right with her world. Further discussion revealed that Chloe, now an adult, had been eliminating in the house ever since she'd come to Marge's home as a puppy. We all agreed: Chloe had never really been housetrained.

Housetraining is important wherever dogs live in close proximity with people. In fact, the close relationship between dogs and humans that developed during the process of domestication is partly due to their ability to be housetrained. Dogs, as a species, are naturally inclined to keep their sleeping areas (dens) clean of feces and urine, thus minimizing the dogs' chances of being reinfested with parasites. They may also choose the edges of their territory when eliminating in order to communicate to other dogs through marking behaviors that this is their space. The predictability of canine elimination patterns was a strong behavioral reason why dogs would have been seen as good candidates for domestication.

Yet, even with these predisposing factors, housetraining can sometimes be a problem. In fact, recent studies have shown that the primary reason animals are relinquished to shelters is urinating and/or defecating in the house. Those dogs with housetraining problems who do stay in the home often end up banished to the outdoors with minimal human contact. Clearly, learning to eliminate in the right place at the right time can save a dog's life and prevent euthanasia.

So there's a lot at stake here — for humans and dogs. The good news is that we have the tools and the know-how to make housetraining happen.

Facts, Not Fiction

A newborn puppy has no control over her own elimination. In fact, urination and defecation are stimulated by the mother licking the puppy's belly and genital areas. This triggers a reflex, called the "anogenital reflex," that causes the puppy to eliminate right away. This ensures that Mom will be there to keep urine and feces from soiling the nest and attracting predators or insects to the area. Puppies lose this reflex early on and are urinating and defecating on their own by sixteen to eighteen days old.

Beginning at about three weeks of age, puppies are able to walk away from their immediate area to eliminate somewhere nearby. By around nine weeks they begin to concentrate on a specific toileting area, often the same area used by their mother. Substrate (that's the type of surface the puppy eliminates on) and location preferences (where to eliminate) are also learned at this time. The good news is that often when puppies are going to new homes, they are primed to learn housetraining.

Housetraining depends on directing these natural tendencies to urinate and defecate away from the place where the dog rests and to a specific toileting area, defined by a surface and location, that is acceptable to us. In other words, dogs are preprogrammed to do this, and we're just stacking the deck in our favor through housetraining, to ensure that the places they use to eliminate are okay with us.

In general, we do this by preventing elimination indoors and encouraging elimination at an appropriate toileting spot, generally outdoors. To be more specific, we prevent indoor accidents by predicting when the puppy is likely to eliminate and taking her to the appropriate toilet spot to do her business. At all other times, the puppy is either supervised or kept somewhere that she is unlikely to eliminate. We encourage her to use appropriate toileting spots by teaching the puppy location and surface preferences (routinely taking her to the same place) and through intrinsic rewards (the relief of emptying a full bladder or bowel) and external reinforcement for using the designated location (food treats and praise).

What Does That Mean?

Housetraining: The process by which a dog learns to urinate and defecate when and where you designate. While there may be some leeway with the when and the where, in general we mean not in the house but at a designated toileting area.

Elimination: Urination and defecation

Toileting area: An approved area for elimination; potty area

Accidents: Eliminating in what we consider to be the wrong spot

Tie-down: Attaching a leash to something secure, such as a heavy piece of furniture or an eyebolt screwed into a wall, to limit where the dog can go in the house. This should *only* be done when someone is home to supervise and is nearby.

Is That Really True?

My dog poops and pees in the house because she is mad at me. While cartoons have used this as a basis for some very funny jokes, in reality, attributing that kind of reasoning to a dog is pretty far-fetched. Unlike some humans, when dogs are mad at us they are quite open about it, and we know it because they growl or glare at us. While a lapse in housetraining may play into our feelings of guilt ("I feel bad about leaving my dog alone for so long, so she must be mad at me"), it's more likely that the confinement or alone time was simply too long for your dog to wait to eliminate. The result was, as they say, "When you've got to go, you've got to go."

I know my dog knows she's done something wrong when I find an

accident, because she looks guilty. Let's look at Dakota, a six-month-old Jack Russell Terrier.

Dakota's owner, Terry, was having a very hard time stopping her from pooping in the house. He tried everything, including rubbing Dakota's nose in the poop and swatting her on the hind end if he found a mess in the house when he came home. Now, not only was he finding poop, but Dakota was cowering and had her tail tucked and her ears down when Terry entered the house. Terry was sure this meant Dakota realized she had done wrong, since she looked so guilty. What Terry did not understand is that Dakota didn't know why Terry was so angry with her and was acting submissive to avoid being punished. Because Terry's punishment was so much later than Dakota's elimination, Dakota had no way of associating the punishment with the act. If this approach continued, there was a good chance Dakota might develop an aggressive response toward Terry to prevent being punished.

A human might think, "My dog avoids me or looks sheepish because she knows that pooping in the house is unacceptable and she should not do it. Furthermore, she could have *chosen* not to do it, but did it anyway." Humans will then try to figure out why the dog *consciously chose* to go against what she knew was "the right thing to do." They may conclude that the dog is willful, spiteful, or just plain stupid, or that she "doesn't want to do what I want her to do, and is being stubborn."

When accidents continue, humans tend to get their feelings hurt. We think the next time the dog feels the urge to eliminate indoors, she should remember how angry we were about this and choose not to do it again. But that's not how dog behavior works.

Dogs do not repeat a behavior that caused an unpleasant outcome because they *want* to be punished. And they don't feel guilty about it later. Yes, the dog makes an association between her owner's anger and a pile of poop, but *not* the same one the human does. Dogs do not understand that the act of defecating on the floor is the behavior that makes the humans angry. What they *do* seem to associate with the owners' reaction is: "Poop being on the floor [not the *act* of putting poop on the floor] will make my owner angry." Being a dog, the canine response to anger is to attempt to either avoid the owner's angry response, usually by hiding, or to show submissive behavior that is designed to deflect aggression.

Unfortunately for the dog, this does not work. The owner is still angry about finding a pile of poop on the floor. And now the dog is looking sheepish, an attempt at appeasement. The owner thinks, "You knew from my previous response that this is wrong. Looking 'guilty' proves it. Yet you chose to do it again!" And the dog thinks, "I've shown the right behavior for the circumstances, so why are you still so angry?" No wonder both parties walk away upset and confused and nothing changes.

What Is Marking?

Some dogs, most commonly males, use urine to communicate territoriality. They may be responding to aggression or anxiety issues with other dogs or to activities in the household, or they may simply be spreading scent in the home. Marking is characterized by the following:

- Urine being deposited in small amounts
- Urine being deposited on personal or novel items in the home
- Normal urination and defecation outdoors
- A posture during urination that is commonly known as "leg-lifting"

Treatment usually involves the typical suggestions for housetraining (while especially stressing close supervision), occasional use of antianxiety medication, and, as a last resort, belly bands. Belly bands are wraps that inhibit male dogs from urinating, since they absorb urine and make urinating uncomfortable for the dog.

If my dog has an accident, rubbing her nose in the poop or pee will help prevent future accidents. In one study, owners giving their dogs up at shelters were asked for a response to the statement "It is helpful to rub the dog's nose in her mess when she soils in the house." Almost one-third (31.8 percent) said they believed that was true, and another 11.4 percent said they were "not sure." The authors of the study noted that there was "room for improvement" in educating dog owners about appropriate housetraining methods.

Of all the housetraining myths floating around, this one has the most potential to be harmful. Practically speaking, most accidents are discovered several minutes to several hours after they have occurred. We know from experiments on how learning takes place that punishment must be closely associated (within seconds) with the action being punished for there to be any possibility that the punishment will actually decrease or stop the behavior from occurring in the future. Punishment several hours *after* elimination is not going to be linked to the *act* of eliminating, making it ineffective for teaching what we really want the dog to learn — to eliminate only at the correct time and place.

Unfortunately, the "rub their nose in it" approach has persisted for quite some time. Here are some of the reasons why some people mistakenly think it is a useful response:

- The dog learns to avoid the area where the accident took place. We can wonder how many dogs avoid being in that room when their owners are around after this kind of experience. Of course, the dog doesn't learn to avoid the action; instead, she may learn to defecate in a less-conspicuous place next time.

- The circumstances that led up to the accident are not repeated, making the owner think rubbing the dog's nose in it worked. For example, the dog isn't left alone for long periods of time until her bladder control is better or the weather gets better, so she empties her bladder fully each time she is at the proper elimination location. For feces accidents, the owner locks the trash away so there are no more "dietary indiscretions" that cause diarrhea. Because everything appears to go well after the incident, the owner concludes that the problem was solved by the punishment. But in fact, it was better management that solved the problem.

- The owner can employ more active management changes, so the problem does not reoccur. For example, the weather gets better, so the dog spends more time outside where it doesn't matter how often she has to eliminate. Or the owners decide to gate the dog away from the soiled area, reducing the dog's living area to coincide with the dog's idea of a den. Or they employ someone to come over and take the dog out when they must be gone for long periods of time.

- We humans sometimes put more weight on action than avoidance, so in our minds the action (nose rubbing) seems to explain why the dog is no longer having accidents.

Of greater concern than being largely ineffective, rubbing a dog's nose in her own excrement has another undesirable effect: because the dog does not understand what humans want, we become unreliable partners in social communication, potentially damaging our relationship with our best friend. The dog does not understand why she is being punished and chooses to avoid us or continues to show submissive behaviors. She comes away having no clue why we are so angry, never mind having no idea what we *do* want. Because the dog does not understand what we want her to do, she can't make us happy. Ever had a boss or a family member like that? It's not comfortable for anyone.

Many dog owners report the "guilt effect," and some even confess to rubbing their dog's nose in her feces. They are upset that their dog avoids them or appears uncomfortable around them, and frustrated because it has not worked the way they thought it would, since the dog still soils in the house. The first step in repairing the social bond and changing the dog's behavior is to stop engaging in human behaviors that don't work.

How Do We Begin?

"An ounce of prevention . . ." If circumstances permit, do some pre-planning about where the toilet area will be and how you will set up indoor confinement and a potty schedule *before* the puppy comes to your home. Ideally, the toilet area should be somewhere with a surface that is not like those encountered indoors (grass, if it's available, or pavement or what is readily available to you), in a place that can be sheltered a bit during inclement weather.

Indoor confinement should be in an area large enough that the puppy can lie down and turn comfortably, yet small enough that her natural desire to keep the location clean is not compromised. If the area is too big, the puppy can soil it and still get away from the mess. This could be a crate, a pen, a gated area, a leash attached to a tie-down (only when someone is home and supervising) or to a person, or all of the above, depending on the circumstances. But remember, if the puppy needs to eliminate and no one is available to take the dog to her elimination location, regardless of how small the area is, the puppy is likely to eliminate. (For more on crates, see the section "To Crate or Not to Crate, That Is the Question" later in this chapter.)

The Importance of Schedules

Often you can anticipate when a puppy is likely to eliminate, so you can have her at the toilet spot in time for her to do the right thing. Scheduling meals means you can pretty much predict when the puppy will need to eliminate. A puppy is likely to eliminate at the following times:

- When she first wakes up, both first thing in the morning and after a nap
- After eating and drinking, and again twenty to thirty minutes later
- After play time or excitement
- After she exits or before she enters her confinement location (such as a crate)

Scheduling involves not only keeping track of feeding and access to water, but also activities such as playing and sleeping.

Most feeding schedules for young puppies (eight to sixteen weeks, depending on their size) plan for three to four meals a day. So with meals, activity times (play and walks), and naps, plan on at least eight to ten potty breaks per day, and perhaps one at midnight for very young puppies (eight to twelve weeks of age). If house soiling is ongoing, it is possible in some cases to restrict water intake at night from before the last potty break until the next morning, but this varies with the dog's age and health and your local climate. Always discuss this step with your veterinarian before restricting your dog's water intake.

A housetraining log will be helpful, because it will enable you to record and evaluate whether accidents are becoming less frequent. If you don't keep a log, all you will remember and have to judge by is the last accident; you may not realize it has been weeks since the last one — and there could be more progress than you thought! Your log should include the schedule, what was done and when (urination and defecation), and note any accidents (time and location). It's pretty easy to set up a notebook or spreadsheet, or for those who are technically savvy, there's an app for that, available for smartphones. These applications can help keep track of housetraining facts and figures in your home. Examples include Android "Dog and Puppy Housetraining" by Growling Software, and for iPhone users, "Puppy Coach 101."

X Marks the Spot

At first, don't expect that you will pick up on your puppy's pre-elimination body language — the movements that say "I've got to go." You'll need to depend on the schedule and just take her out when the schedule indicates. Eventually, you will get to know her particular body language cues and know when she has to go. Watch for sniffing the floor, whining, pacing, panting, or losing focus on interactions and wandering away. These are all signals that your puppy needs to eliminate.

In some homes, getting your dog to the spot you've chosen as the elimination location can be a long trip and may involve stairs or elevators. Eventually, your puppy will need to negotiate these barriers, but while she is learning where to eliminate, you may have to carry her to avoid an accident en route.

Teaching the Puppy to Signal

There are many ways to teach your puppy to let you know that she needs to eliminate. You might consider training her to go to the door and sit before each trip to the toilet area. This approach has the benefit of having the dog focus on something other than urinating while you gather your keys. Now, she's also trained to go to the door to signal a need for elimination.

Another method of teaching this behavior is to hang a bell on the door you go out from for elimination purposes. Then, when you are about to take your puppy out that door, ring the bell using the puppy's paw, then immediately go outside for elimination. It is important to use this exit only for elimination and not for play, so the puppy does not use the ringing of the bell to signal a desire to play as well as the need to eliminate.

When You Get There, Make It Positive

Ever have too many beers at the ball game, then bolt out of your seat, only to find a long line at the toilet? When you finally have your chance, it feels good. Just being able to let go and eliminate is self-rewarding. External rewards (usually food) are also important for dogs, and you can add in a verbal phrase, such as "go potty," so the dog will associate a specific word or phrase with the action of elimination.

To be understood, the reward must be immediately linked to the action. Therefore, as you are working to establish a reliable outdoor elimination pattern, it is essential for someone to go outside with the puppy to give the reward immediately after the puppy eliminates. If you remain comfortably indoors while your puppy (or dog, if you are retraining) eliminates, you are missing the chance to reward outdoor elimination. Instead, you are really rewarding the dog for coming back inside. This could result in a dog or puppy coming back inside for the reward before she has emptied her bladder — then urinating on the kitchen floor ten minutes later.

How to Respond to Accidents

When accidents happen, just clean them up with an enzyme-based cleaner and tighten up your system. If you happen to catch your puppy squatting to urinate, you can clap your hands or say "Hey!" to try to interrupt the urination, then immediately and swiftly move the puppy to the toilet spot and reward her when she finishes — although this may not always work and may even frighten your puppy. You will have to gauge her reaction. Defecation is hard to interrupt, so it's best to wait without comment until the puppy finishes, then clean and supervise better in the future.

Yes, you read that right. *Wait without comment.* That means no scolding or correction, even though you've caught her in the act. Scolding could result in the puppy developing a fear of you. Or she may learn to simply eliminate in secret to avoid punishment.

Over time, as bladder control improves, as you learn your puppy's behavioral and physical rhythms, and as your puppy learns the potty routine, you can gradually increase her living area and decrease the strict supervision.

Housetraining isn't rocket science. However, it's important to understand that we are all different, and so are our puppies and their previous experiences. Some breeders might have offered a housetraining head start, for example. So please don't be discouraged when you see books that guarantee that a dog can be housetrained "in seven days" or less. That's just not reasonable, especially not for a puppy. More reasonable expectations range from six to eight months of age up to two to three years for some individuals.

So how do you know when your puppy is fully housetrained? A good rule of thumb is when she can comfortably stay in the house, unrestricted, without eliminating for up to eight hours.

Things to Work on While You're Waiting

Pottying on request can and should be a priority. Sometimes it's incredibly handy to be able to say "go potty" and have your dog comply as instantly as she responds to "sit." Imagine you're in a thunderstorm or in the midst of a winter blizzard. You don't want to be standing outside waiting for your dog to go. Or maybe you're about to go for a long drive and you want your dog to empty her bladder before you get in the car. Wouldn't it be nice to simply open the door, have the dog run into the yard, and go potty because you ask her to? This is well within your reach!

First, pick a phrase you won't mind saying in public: "do your business," "hurry up," or "get busy" are suggestions for those who shy away from the P word. Pick just one cue and stick to it, so your dog will learn what you mean. Then, every time she eliminates, say the phrase once in a calm voice (repeating it over and over can be distracting). Then reward her right after she eliminates. Repeat. It may take a bit of time for her to get what you mean, but it's invaluable when she gets it, especially when you travel to a new area and want her to go in an acceptable spot she's never seen before.

If you take her to her usual toilet spot and keep her on leash as you practice your potty cue, then you are automatically practicing "potty on leash" and "potty in my presence," both of which are helpful if your dog takes vacations with you. You can use the cue to get your dog accustomed to doing her business in a variety of areas and on different surfaces so that she won't have a problem while traveling. In urban areas, you can position your puppy's rear end over the curb, say your cue, and reward what ensues; this is known as "curbing" your dog. Pick a very quiet street to begin this kind of training; your dog doesn't need any distractions!

Be prepared for your dog to spend some time sniffing this spot . . .

Photos by Leslie Larson Cooper, DVM, DACVB

. . . and even that spot . . .

. . . before finding just the right spot to pee.

And while we're on the subject, don't get caught without a way to pick up and dispose of feces. Some leashes have bag holders attached to them, or you can just tie a bag on the leash or stick one in your pocket whenever you go for a walk. You can be green and purchase environmentally friendly bags, or simply save plastic bags you'd otherwise toss, like the bag the daily newspaper is delivered in.

Feces on sidewalks or in public parks are unsanitary and can spread intestinal parasites. It's also impolite not to clean up after your dog in a public area. It makes people who don't have dogs unhappy and perhaps unsympathetic to pet owners. Even other dog owners don't enjoy stepping in it. So do us all a favor and clean up after your dog.

To Crate or Not to Crate, That Is the Question

Crates are great! With a little training, a crate or travel carrier can become

- a home away from home while traveling and a safe place for a puppy to be in transit (in the car, plane, or carried by hand into the veterinary office);
- a comfortable place to stay during the day when there's a lot of activity and a puppy underfoot could get hurt;
- a nice bed at night, so everyone knows where the puppy is;
- an essential piece of equipment in emergencies, when you all have to assemble and get out right away;
- a place where a puppy is likely to hold it when she is not under direct supervision during housetraining.

Have you ever heard the saying "Start out the way you mean to go on"? This is certainly true for crate training a puppy. Start out with the crate as the puppy's nighttime sleeping place. Set up the crate with soft bedding and place a food puzzle toy, such as a Kong or a Tug-a-Jug, inside with part of her dinner, to encourage the puppy to go in and settle down for a rest and a chew.

To be useful for housetraining, the crate needs to be just big enough

A crate can be a safe home during housetraining. Notice that Pepper does not have enough space to move away from his bed to eliminate.
Debbie Maus

for the puppy to lie down and turn around comfortably, but not so big as to allow the puppy to create a potty spot within. For puppies who will grow to be large dogs, you may need to make some adjustments. Crate dividers enable you to shrink and enlarge a crate as your puppy grows. Or you may need to buy several crates of different sizes to meet the puppy's growth needs in the first year.

Give her a few pats and a treat before closing the door to the crate. It's best to not push your luck, so make the first few times inside with the door closed short and sweet, just five to fifteen minutes. As time goes on and your puppy readily goes into the crate by herself, start pairing the phrase "go to the crate" with that action, and reward her with a tossed treat.

How Long Can You Crate a Puppy?

As the puppy grows, the hours she can spend in a crate without needing to eliminate can be extended to match her age. The general rule for this is one hour per month of the puppy's age, plus one hour. So, at two months of age it would be three hours, at three months of age it would be four hours, and so on. The maximum is four to five hours *a day* in the crate for a puppy.

This basic rule applies *if* she is sleeping through the night. This means that with some puppies of this age, you will likely need to get up during the night for a potty break to prevent accidents. Be prepared to be flexible; every puppy is different.

An Indoor Toilet

Because of their relatively small urinary bladder and the inability of their kidneys to concentrate urine to the same degree as adult dogs, puppies can't hold urine for more than four or five hours. This should be the upper limit of confinement; any longer and you're just asking for accidents. If a pup is pushed to eliminate frequently within the safe spot of a crate or pen, that will pretty much erase its effectiveness as a housetraining tool. So if you must leave your pup for longer, she needs an acceptable spot indoors to eliminate.

Fortunately, we are no longer limited to paper training. In fact, newer indoor potty systems are made of more durable material, usually a potty pad or an artificial grass mat with a waterproof tray to go underneath. Or you can put together your own system using an artificial grass mat and a tray from a large cat litter box or a plastic clothes-storage box. Some commercial systems also include an attractant, though you can use a tiny bit of your own dog's urine as an attractant.

Indoor toilet systems, whether commercial or homemade, are handy when you live in a city apartment, where inclement weather sometimes makes outdoor toileting difficult, or if you travel frequently with your dog or your lifestyle requires that your dog stay indoors on her own for long periods of time. For obvious reasons, smaller dogs (with less to clean up) are better prospects for indoor housetraining.

With any system, or indeed with newspaper, if you want to shift to some other toilet surface later on, expect some delays. You may need to take whatever surface you have been using to the new toilet area for a while so your dog can learn the new system.

The primary problem owners face when crate training a puppy is whining and fussing when the door is closed and the rest of the family is beyond the puppy's reach. *Do not* let the puppy out when she is whining or barking, or you will give her the wrong idea: "Hey, when I whine, I get out!" Instead, let the puppy out when she is not whining. Toss a treat into the crate during a calm period (of even a few seconds) as a reward for being quiet; it may also keep the puppy occupied and quiet for a few extra seconds so that you can open the door! A short petting session with the door open will also reinforce quiet behavior.

Don't place the puppy in the crate when you are scolding her or as a punishment. Let's keep things positive so the puppy remains comfortable in the crate.

Crate-Training Tips

In most cases, it is easier to crate train a young puppy than an older dog, so work on this early. The breeder may have begun the process, assuming the puppy has to travel to her new home in a crate. If you want to use a crate as part of housetraining an adult dog (more on that in "Housetraining or Retraining an Adult Dog"), first see how the dog tolerates close confinement while you are home, using the same training routine as described for puppies, before leaving the dog crated for extended periods of time. (For more tips on crate training, see the appendix.)

Some dogs (and indeed, a few puppies) do not do well in small, en-

Adult dogs may respond better to confinement in a larger area behind a baby gate.
Rachel Berkley, DVM

closed spaces for any length of time. Alternative confinement options, such as gating off a small room or using an open-top exercise pen, are more successful and comfortable for these dogs.

One final note on crate training: if, after several weeks of vigorously working on the routine described, your puppy is still violently objecting to the crate (barking, whining, chewing up things in the crate, eliminating in the crate, drooling, or injuring herself trying to get out), consider the possibility that your puppy is experiencing separation anxiety (which is discussed in detail in chapter 11). This is a serious though very treatable behavioral condition and requires the assistance of a veterinarian or a veterinary behaviorist to manage successfully.

Housetraining or Retraining an Adult Dog

Adult dogs may come with baggage, including less-than-perfect housetraining habits. Unless you have been given the dog's history, you don't know if your new dog is already housetrained. Even dogs who were housetrained in the past can begin to have accidents due to health problems, changes in environment, or scheduling changes.

Luckily, you can use the same protocol for puppy housetraining outlined here to re-housetrain an adult dog. Encourage the dog to use an appropriate toilet area and avoid elimination indoors through scheduling, supervision, and confinement. Start off right and you have a better chance of success than by playing catch-up after repeated accidents.

Avoiding Pitfalls and Staying on Track

Be assured, there *will* be *accidents*. Usually these happen when we are not paying attention or when the puppy is unable to hold it for the length of time we require. If you forget to follow the program, expect an accident. Remember that accidents are common, a part of the learning process (for owners even more than puppies), and they are most certainly not the end of the world. To help you navigate the trouble spots, here are some common situations that can pose problems, with suggested solutions.

Our puppy has to be confined for more than four to five hours at a time. Don't play housetraining Russian roulette, hoping your puppy will exceed your expectations and not have an accident. Not only is this possibly setting your puppy up to fail, but it may result in a puppy who learns to eliminate indoors because she can never get to the outdoor elimination spot when needed.

If you suspect you are going to be away longer than your puppy can hold it, set up an approved toilet surface (pee pad, artificial grass — something that's not bedding) in a pen large enough so that the toilet area and the bed can be separated. It's a plus (but not essential) if the toileting surface in the pen is similar to the outdoor toilet area.

It's a long way from the confinement area to the toilet area. Increase your chances of getting there without an accident by walking briskly with the puppy (on leash, if need be) to the toilet area. Longer trips may necessitate carrying the pup at first, but as your puppy's bladder control improves, switch to walking. For long elevator rides (where the wait can encourage the puppy to squat and pee there), you may need to hold her or carry her outside in a small carrier.

Our puppy won't potty outside, but comes right back in and pees on the floor. The first few minutes of outdoor time at a toilet area should be focused on getting down to business, not playing. If your puppy doesn't eliminate on that outing, go back inside, put the puppy in her crate for ten or fifteen minutes, then go back out to the toilet area. Repeat until she eliminates.

An alternative to the crate in this situation is to attach a leash to your puppy when you bring her inside, and tie the other end to your waist or belt loop. In this way you will make sure the puppy stays within your view until you take her back outside for another try.

We're having problems moving from the strict confinement of the crate to giving the puppy the run of the whole house. Some clarification can be useful here. The den concept only goes so far: the whole house will never be viewed as a den. What your dog will do is divide up the living space into a core area (where the family lives and sleeps) and a noncore area (where elimination might be okay). Many homes are not set up for housetraining; they're too open and too big for a small puppy to readily see a particular core area. Or there are too many noncore areas where no one ever goes, and these appear to the puppy as appropriate "away from my den" locations for elimination. In some cases, sitting with the dog in these noncore areas from time to time while reading a book may help the dog learn that these areas are lived in and are part of the core area.

Here's where leashes and tie-downs (attaching a leash to something secure, such as a heavy piece of furniture or an eyebolt screwed into a wall) can help out. Remember, always supervise your dog while she is in a tie-down, to avoid injury, and never leave the house with your dog in a tie-down. There are commercially available leash-belt systems (a leash that ties around your waist at one end and attaches to the puppy's collar at the other end) that enable you to keep the puppy close to you as you move through the house.

When using a tie-down or a leash-belt system, attach the leash to a sturdy object near you, with a comfortable bed for the puppy and something to keep her occupied (chew toy, food-enhanced toy) while you work nearby. Now you have created confinement, supervision, and socialization all in one package.

It's cold outside and our puppy doesn't want to do her business. And we don't want to wait out there either! Puppies born in cold months have a rougher time housetraining, especially in areas where it gets really cold. If you must go outside, try to find a sheltered area for a toilet spot. Set your own coat and boots near the door so you can grab them and go quickly (and avoid an in-transit accident).

Salt spread on icy streets can be hard on tender paws, so dog boots can be helpful. Dog coats, especially for small dogs, are needed to help the dog feel comfortable enough to stay out and completely eliminate. If it is just way too cold, you may want to consider using an indoor system until the weather gets better, and then transition to an outdoor toilet area.

I never know when she needs to go outside because she does not signal her needs. This is a supervision issue, but it also might be that you are not recognizing the signals that the puppy has a full bladder or bowel. Keep your puppy close by and look for signs of discomfort (whining, sniffing, circling, or going by the door that you typically use to take her outside).

You might also be able to develop a phrase that can trigger a puppy to want to go outside to eliminate. If you use a phrase such as "Do you need to go potty?" at a time when you know she has to eliminate, the puppy will likely begin to recognize the phrase, then move toward the door to be quickly whisked outside. Over time, your puppy will learn that if she's near you and signals in a certain way (such as pacing) or shows some discomfort and you say that phrase, outdoor access will be provided.

When Things Just Aren't Working Out

How important is housetraining from the dog's point of view? Keeping their resting places clean (removing intestinal parasites from the den) was a life-or-death matter for our dogs' ancestors, and those who did so were more likely to survive and pass on their "clean" genes. With the advent of antiparasite medications, cleanliness and those genes are of less importance. Today, many dogs thrive without them. Without this challenge, Genetics 101 tells us that genetic-selection pressure eases and genetic variation increases. So we end up with some dogs who are naturally very good at keeping a large area free of urine and feces, and others who are not so good at this.

Sometimes early learning is the culprit. Puppies kept in environments where they don't have a chance to get away from their own urine and feces are not able to implement the den concept they were born with. We depend on puppies to keep at least a small area clean, but if they're forced to eliminate in that small area because they have been left longer than they can hold their eliminations, they may ignore their innate tendency to keep their area clean. (But remember, some of these dogs may suffer from separation anxiety, and if the elimination occurs primarily when you are gone, videotaping your dog may help determine if separation anxiety, not a lack of housetraining, is the culprit.)

You may need to redefine your rules of confinement to enable these dogs to learn to keep clean again. There was a Miniature Poodle who would urinate and defecate on her bedding when confined to a medium-size crate, but when that space was cut in half (still large enough for her to turn around in but not much more), she would not soil her bedding. Her owner reported that she had come from a dubious pet store as a puppy, and he suspected her living area had not been kept as clean as it should have been, nor were the puppies taken out for elimination very often. Along with proper scheduling of food, water, and toileting opportunities, owners can minimize the availability of soft, absorbent bedding in the crate for a time, so that if accidents do occur, they are harder for the puppy to ignore.

Can most dogs be housetrained? Yes, but some may take more time, effort, and attention to detail if their internal guidelines are a bit lax.

Sometimes We're Missing Something

When we've done our best at scheduling, confining, and providing proper toileting opportunities, and accidents still happen, it's time for some in-depth thinking. Causes for ongoing problems may include the following:

- **Physical or medical issues.** It's hard to avoid accidents when your pet can't control when and where she urinates or defecates. Diseases or medications that cause diarrhea or increased urine production, and physical dysfunctions with associated incontinence, can result in incomplete housetraining. Make sure to consult with your veterinarian if you have an ongoing housetraining problem. And always consult your veterinarian if you have a dog (regardless of age) who you firmly believe is housetrained but begins to inexplicably have accidents.

- **Excitement and separation anxiety.** Does the puppy pee on the floor when she is excited or showing submissive behavior? Do you find urine and feces in the house only when you are gone, and you know your dog gets really unhappy when she's left alone? Separation anxiety (see chapter 11) may be to blame. Your focus may need to shift from housetraining to dealing with these other behavioral issues.

- **Just can't hold it that long.** Do you have realistic expectations of how long your puppy or dog can wait to eliminate? When we have what we think are realistic expectations for how long we can leave dogs, and accidents routinely happen anyway, we may need to revise our expectations.

Figuring out the causes of incomplete housetraining can take some sleuthing. Start with a complete medical workup by your veterinarian to help rule out diseases or physical abnormalities. If your dog gets a clean bill of health, then a visit to a veterinary behaviorist may be in order. Your behaviorist will look for clues that point to behavioral patterns, so the dog's motivations can be identified and dealt with more effectively.

Finding a Compromise

Many of the cases behaviorists see are truly incomplete housetraining, in the sense that some parts of housetraining are working while others are not. Chloe's case, from the beginning of the chapter, is a prime example. Because her owner had a large home with an open floor plan, it was hard to achieve the "gradually increasing confinement" portion of housetraining.

Are Smaller Dogs More Difficult to Housetrain?

Housetraining issues can show up in any breed or mix of breeds, but many sources say that smaller breed dogs are generally more difficult to housetrain. The truth of this is unclear.

In their research for *The Perfect Puppy*, Drs. Ben and Lynette Hart looked at whether a dog's breed can predict certain behavioral traits, including ease of housetraining. Although size was not directly addressed, small-breed dogs were scattered throughout all dogs studied, at every level, from those who were very easy to housetrain to those who were very difficult. The study's authors noted that breed was not a good predictor of housetraining ease.

However, if we think about it, there are several common-sense reasons for why a small dog may very well be harder to housetrain.

- Smaller bladder size might limit how long small dogs can hold it, even as adults.
- In their eyes, the house may be too big for a den.
- Smaller dogs may be more sensitive to inclement weather and thus more likely to dislike eliminating outdoors when it's cold and wet.
- Owners initially are not as concerned with accidents in small dogs, since the mess is not that large, and they may not use good supervision and confinement to refine housetraining skills.

Chloe lived in a large two-story home. Somewhere along the line, Chloe had made the decision that part of the house was "not den," and had eliminated there often enough that it became a habit. She never had accidents in the upstairs rooms, but the rest of the house was apparently okay as a toilet area. In a smaller, more easily compartmentalized home, she might have learned something different, but Chloe and her owner were not going to be moving in the near future. They had to compromise.

When Chloe was alone, she was kept upstairs or outside (no accidents upstairs; okay to go outside). When Marge, her owner, was home,

Chloe was at first leashed to her or on a tie-down in an area with a comfortable bed, while Marge worked nearby on the computer or watched TV.

The breakthrough came when Marge decided to try creating an indoor toilet area and improvised a piece of sod (grass was Chloe's normal outdoor toilet surface) in a low-sided pan in the living room. She called it Chloe Park, and she noted that as long as the grass was green, Chloe would seek out that place to eliminate indoors, even when Marge's supervision was a little lax.

Were Marge and Chloe happy with the compromise? Yes — at least according to Marge. While she was not initially too excited about an indoor dog toilet, she said it was much better than the alternatives — cleaning up after her dog daily or giving her up to a shelter. Was Chloe completely housetrained? As long as the grass was green, that was good enough for her.

What Did We Say?

- A dog's natural inclination to keep sleeping or den areas clean, and adhere to the substrate and location preferences learned early in life, help make housetraining a dog possible.
- Until a puppy or dog is reliably housetrained, she should either be in an area where elimination is acceptable, under your direct supervision, or confined to an area where she is not likely to eliminate.
- Set routines for meals and exercise, and frequently scheduled potty breaks, to avoid indoor accidents.
- Appropriate toilet areas are usually outdoors, although indoor potty systems can be helpful for special circumstances, such as long hours, unsupervised smaller dogs, urban living, or travel.
- Housetraining accidents will happen. When they do, just calmly clean up and resolve to tighten up your scheduling and supervision.

5

Tools of the Trade
Humane and Safe Training Tools

Lori Gaskins, DVM, DACVB

John adopted Butch, a five-month-old male Labrador Retriever, as a companion and was eager to take him for a walk around the neighborhood to show him off. John's idea of a perfect walk was for Butch to stay beside him, in heeling position, at all times and to never veer off on explorations. Someone had suggested to John that dog owners have to be in control at all times on walks so that the dog knows who is boss.

Butch's idea of the perfect walk was to see the world, to stop and sniff as many things as possible, and to meet and greet other dogs and people. John and Butch's expectations and goals were not the same.

John started Butch out on a buckle collar, as most puppy owners do. When Butch inevitably pulled on the leash in his excitement to see the world, John yanked on the collar to get Butch back into position beside him. This didn't decrease Butch's desire to veer off, so John decided he needed help and took Butch to an obedience training class. John thought surely they could help him teach Butch to walk nicely on a leash. This particular class recommended a choke collar, and John was told to yank on it to punish Butch for not walking beside him. John tried this, but that didn't stop the pulling either. A prong collar was recommended next. John had some reservations about using this collar because it looked scary, but other people were using it on their dogs, so he tried it. But again, this collar did not have the desired effect.

By this point, John dreaded going on walks because it was a constant battle between him and Butch. After all John's efforts, Butch still pulled on the leash. Because of this, the two went out on walks less often. Finally, John decided something had to be done; he had gotten Butch as a companion and he wanted to be able to take his dog out on leisurely leash walks.

In a desperate last attempt to teach Butch to heel on walks, John bought an electronic shock collar, thinking that if the punishment for sniffing, greeting, and exploring was harsh enough, Butch would stop doing those things. They were barely out the front door when Butch got a whiff of the neighbor's cat and headed in that direction. John thought, "This is the perfect opportunity to teach Butch not to stray from my side," and he shocked his dog. Butch yelped, pulled the leash from John's hand, and ran back up the house steps, trembling and frantically trying to get into the house.

After that episode, Butch decided he couldn't go out in the front yard again because there was something extremely scary out there. John felt horribly guilty for putting Butch through this and was at his wits' end as to what to do next. All he had wanted was for Butch to heel at his side during walks, and he ended up with a dog who didn't want to leave the house through the front yard. From that day forward, the only way to get Butch out of the house was to leave through the back door that led into the side yard. Even then, Butch looked warily toward the front yard as they passed by.

As compassionate people, we must always use the most welfare-friendly tools with our best friends. Wanting a dog to walk nicely or even heel while on leash is not an uncommon goal for dog owners. And it is an achievable goal if we use the appropriate tools to teach dogs what is expected of them. There are many options available to prevent and help treat behavior problems in dogs without causing distress for owner or dog.

Facts, Not Fiction

There are many tools to help teach dogs how to live in harmony with their owners. Some of these tools are very effective. Some may not work; at worst, some may be cruel and have undesirable side effects, as in Butch's case. When you are trying to sort through all the tools available for training, it helps to think, "Would I want this to be used on me?" or, "Would I use this on a child?" If the answer to either question is no, then don't use it on your dog.

Dogs can wear buckle collars all the time, and the collars can hold identification tags, but they are not the easiest way to teach a dog to walk on a leash. If John had started with a correctly fitted head collar, Butch would have easily understood what John was trying to teach him and the whole progression to harsher and harsher tools would have been avoided. Head collars encircle the neck and muzzle and are used to control movement, because a dog's body must follow where his head goes (a more complete description occurs later in this chapter).

Research shows that dogs are no more bothered by head collars than by regular buckle collars. A 2003 study by veterinary behaviorist Dr. Margaret Duxbury demonstrated that puppies adopted from a shelter who wore head collars were more likely to stay in their home, compared to dogs who wore other types of collars. Their owners may have been less frustrated with their dogs' behavior and therefore less likely to relinquish them, because they used appropriate tools in training.

The inappropriate use of choke collars is still advocated in many training situations, even on young puppies, as with Butch. These collars are meant to be aversive (something that results in the dog avoiding a situation or activity), and therefore can be scary and painful, even when used correctly.

Studies by Dr. Matthijs Schilder in 2004 and Dr. Esther Schalke in 2010 show that shock and prong collars cause pain and stress in dogs. Schilder also determined that shock collars may cause fear of the owner and fear of the area where the dog is trained. Using a shock collar is actually illegal in some areas of the world. Most dog owners are not skilled enough in using them, and the risk of side effects is too great to recommend their use in pet dogs. Obviously, John wished he had not tried the shock collar on Butch.

What Does That Mean?

Veterinary behaviorists recommend using tools that are gentle and welfare-friendly, such as head collars and clickers, and discourage the use of tools that cause pain and discomfort, such as prong and shock collars. Which of these tools do you think fit the bill as humane tools for managing your dog's behavior?

Collars
Collars are used to hold a dog's identification tag or are used with a leash for walking. Neck collars encircle only the neck. There are many types of neck collars.

Buckle collars are placed around the neck and are buckled or snapped. They are commonly used by dog owners. They provide minimal control of the dog when on leash, so if a behavior problem requires control of the dog, veterinary behaviorists are more likely to recommend a head collar or a front-attachment harness.

A buckle collar with an identification tag
Lori Gaskins

Martingale or limited-slip collars get smaller when pulled but cannot tighten completely around the neck. Owners of dog breeds whose neck is thicker than their head (such as Greyhounds) are likely to use these. Owners of all dog breeds may use them as alternatives to choke or slip collars, or they may be used on dogs who can back out of regular buckle collars. While these do offer some limited control, they are not helpful for dogs with behavior problems or excessive pulling.

Choke or slip collars tighten around the neck when pulled, and if used improperly, can cut off the dog's air supply. Owners commonly use these for training, but they are not recommended by veterinary behaviorists.

Prong or pinch collars are metal or plastic collars with prongs point-

(Left) A Martingale or limited-slip collar cannot tighten all the way. *(Right)* A choke or slip collar can tighten completely around a dog's neck. *Lori Gaskins*

ing toward the dog's neck. When the collar tightens, the prongs cause pain. Dog owners may use these to discourage pulling on leash. Veterinary behaviorists are more likely to recommend a head collar or a front-attachment harness for this problem.

A prong or pinch collar can cause pain when tightened. *Lori Gaskins*

Shock collars produce a painful shock or a warning tone followed by a painful shock. They are outlawed in some countries and are not recommended by veterinary behaviorists for treating behavior problems or for training.

Head collars are similar to halters used on horses. Like a halter on a horse, head collars work because pressure on the back of the neck and over the nose is created when the dog pulls forward, and is released when the dog walks calmly by your side and the leash is loose. If we can control a twelve-hundred-pound horse with this type of device, it certainly will work for a dog. It helps decrease pulling when the dog is on a leash, and may be used by veterinary behaviorists while treating other behavior problems, such as aggression and compulsive behaviors.

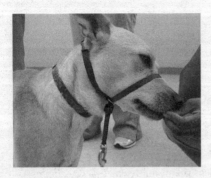

A Gentle Leader head collar can decrease pulling on leash.
Lori Gaskins

Leashes

Leashes are usually made of nylon, leather, or metal and attach to a neck collar, head collar, or harness. These tools give us some control over the movements of the dog because owners can control forward progress and redirect the dog while on leash. Leashes may also be used as an added safety device to tether dogs (under supervision) while treating some behavior problems.

Retractable leashes provide variable lengths in a single leash and give the dog room to roam. But these leashes provide little real control over the dog's movements and are unlikely to be recommended by veterinary behaviorists. In emergency situations it is difficult to retract the leash, and injuries (abrasions, cuts, and severe lacerations) have occurred when dog owners grabbed or got tangled in the thin portion of the leash in an attempt to pull their dog back to them.

Regular, nonretractable leashes come in a variety of lengths and can be used in a variety of situations — walks, training, and tethering when supervised. Veterinary behaviorists prefer these types of leashes for walking and training because owners have more control over the dog's movement. These leashes are the best type to use with a head collar, because they let you control the tension. You can easily release tension to teach the dog to walk on a loose leash. By releasing the tension on the leash when the dog walks the way you want him to, you are using negative reinforcement — removing something negative (the tension on the leash) — in response to the dog performing the desired behavior, making it more likely that this behavior will occur more often, the reinforcement part. (See chapter 3 for more on learning and negative reinforcement.) Retractable leashes, in contrast, create constant pressure to certain parts of the head collar, which the dog may find uncomfortable. If the dog is walking with a head collar with constant pressure from the retractable leash, over time the dog habituates to (gets used to) the pressure and it ceases being an effective tool to limit pulling. That's because the dog gets to go forward anyway at his own speed and thus is rewarded for pulling.

Body Harnesses

Body harnesses wrap around the upper body of the dog and may be used instead of buckle collars for walking dogs. They are also useful for dogs with neck injuries or for dogs with health conditions that make it inadvisable to put any pressure on their neck.

Anti-pull harnesses typically have a leash attachment in front of the dog to decrease pulling when on leash, but harnesses also allow the owner to redirect the dog's body and stop forward movement. These are commonly recommended by veterinary behaviorists for dogs who pull when on leash.

Regular harnesses have leash attachments at the dog's back. Often, leash pulling is encouraged when the dog is wearing this type of harness. It is rarely recommended by veterinary behaviorists, especially if the dog is pulling on leash or if you need better control of the dog.

Muzzles

Muzzles fit over the dog's mouth and buckle behind his neck. They prevent the dog from biting. Muzzles may be used for added safety while treating aggressive behaviors or as part of treating a disorder called pica (eating non-food items).

An Easy Walk harness discourages pulling while on a leash.
Lori Gaskins

A basket muzzle can be used as an added safety device.

Lori Gaskins

Nylon muzzles encircle the dog's muzzle to keep his mouth from opening. These types of muzzles may make panting and eating treats difficult. They are often used by veterinarians for short-term applications, such as when performing medical tasks, injections, and examinations.

Basket muzzles may be made of wire, leather, or plastic. These allow the dog to open his mouth to pant and take treats, and some dogs learn to drink with a basket muzzle on by submerging their mouth in a water bowl. These are commonly used by veterinary behaviorists when treating behavior problems, as they can be more comfortable than nylon muzzles for long-term use, such as when you have guests in your home.

Crates and Containment

Crates are enclosed containers for confining dogs and are usually made of molded plastic or wire. Travel crates for small dogs may be made of fabric. If the dog tolerates it, a crate can be a safe place to keep him when visitors or workers come to the house or you need him not to be underfoot. Veterinary behaviorists commonly recommend crates to facilitate housetraining (see chapter 4) and while treating other behavior problems, such as destructive behaviors, chewing, or aggression. (For crate-training tips, see the appendix.)

Other tools that can be used for containment include baby gates in doorways, closed doors, and open-topped wire pens.

Reinforcement Devices

Reward or reinforcement devices add something pleasant in response to a behavior performed by a dog, and so they increase the likelihood

A dog crate can be a comfortable and safe place for dogs. This one has food, water, some bedding, and a Kong toy.
Lori Gaskins

that the dog will repeat that behavior. (See chapter 3 for more about positive reinforcement.) Veterinary behaviorists commonly use these tools to enrich a dog's life, to teach new behaviors, or as part of the treatment plan for some behavior problems.

Clickers are noisemakers used to mark desired behaviors and increase their frequency (see photo, overleaf). Once the dog makes the association between the sound of the click and a treat, the marker (the click sound) tells the dog that the behavior he just performed is correct and the reward is on the way. Clicker training can be used to train almost any behavior you want a dog to perform, including teaching a previously aggressive dog to be calm around other dogs.

The MannersMinder is a remotely activated treat-dispensing tool. Veterinary behaviorists may use this tool when treating behavior problems such as jumping up on visitors, separation anxiety, fear of noises, fear of strangers at the door that occurs without biting, and territorial aggression at windows. (*Text continues on page 93.*)

MannersMinder

The MannersMinder is a remote-controlled reward system that uses positive reinforcement to train a dog. By rewarding or reinforcing desired behaviors, the system can be used to teach new behaviors such as sit, down, come, and stay. For example, if you want your dog to sit quietly by the door when visitors enter your home, the MannersMinder can help.

One way to use it is to teach the dog to sit on a mat by putting the MannersMinder close to the mat, then pushing the handheld remote control; the device then dispenses a treat. The dog may become excited about the new treat dispenser and stand up, but you will only dispense a treat when the dog is sitting calmly on his mat. You teach the dog to do this and practice when there is no one at the door. Then, when someone comes to visit, you ask the dog to go to his mat, you greet your visitor, and remotely dispense treats as long as the dog is sitting by the MannersMinder. Now you have a dog who no longer jumps on or barks at visitors.

When treating behavior problems such as separation anxiety or fears and phobias, the system can be helpful, but a veterinarian should be involved in setting up these treatments. The MannersMinder system was developed by Dr. Sophia Yin, a veterinarian and applied animal behaviorist.

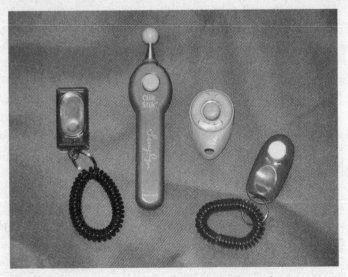

The sound of a clicker can be used as a marker to reinforce good behavior. *Lori Gaskins*

Food puzzle toys require the dog to manipulate them to get the reward inside. Veterinary behaviorists find these toys useful for entertaining dogs who must be left alone or confined for long periods of time, or in treating separation anxiety. You can buy many different types made by a variety of companies, including the Kong, Buster FoodCube, and Tug-a-Jug. You can also make food puzzle toys yourself from screw-top plastic containers; just cut holes in the sides so the food can drop out as the dog rolls it around.

Behavioral Deterrents

Deterrents add something aversive in response to a dog's behavior, and so they decrease the likelihood the dog will repeat that behavior or frequent an area again. (See chapter 3 for more about punishment.) Remote deterrents allow the dog to make a choice, and when used properly they may diminish the possibility of a fearful or aggressive response.

Deterrents can be used to keep dogs out of certain areas of the house or yard, or off furniture. Avoid those products that cause pain, as they can induce anxiety or fear of the particular location in which they are used.

Double-sided tape placed on the floor will stick to the dog's feet. Most dogs don't like this. Placing the tape on the floor in front of a potted plant can be one way to keep your dog from doing a little "indoor gardening." Carpet runners or car mats, when placed upside down with the plastic spikes facing up, are uncomfortable for a dog to step on, and can also keep a dog away from a specific spot without electric shock. Motion-activated devices that produce loud noises when triggered may keep dogs out of certain rooms but may cause distress for others.

Motion-activated sprinklers can be used to keep your dog out of parts of the yard — assuming he does not like water spraying at him! When connected to a garden hose, these sprinklers will spray water when your dog activates the motion sensor, helping to keep your dog out of certain sections of the yard, such as a flower garden.

Anti-bark collars attempt to deter barking. Two types are available:

a collar that either releases a spray of compressed air or citronella or one that provides an electronic shock. Veterinary behaviorists do not recommend electric shock bark collars. Research in 1996 by veterinary behaviorists Dr. Soraya V. Juarbe-Diaz and Dr. Katherine Albro Houpt concluded that citronella anti-bark collars are better received by dog owners and more effective for controlling barking than are electronic shock collars. Keep in mind that barking can be multifactor and often anxiety based, and in those situations bark collars are inappropriate. If bark collars are going to be useful, they will work quickly and are likely to only work when *on* the dog. If the dog continues to bark, the collar is not the appropriate treatment.

Electronic underground fencing is quite common and is used to keep dogs in the yard but is not without risks. A wire emitting an electrical signal is buried around the area in which the dog is to be confined. The dog is outfitted with a receiving collar. At first this wire perimeter is marked by flags to give the dog (and its owner) a visual representation of the buried fence. When the dog nears the boundary, an audio signal is transmitted to the collar, warning the dog. If the dog advances closer to the boundary or attempts to cross it, a punishment, or shock, is transmitted through the collar. Once the dog picks up the audio warning signals as a sign not to advance any farther, the flags are gradually removed.

Some dogs learn quickly to avoid the boundary. But any dog exposed to this type of training may become fearful of the yard, and dogs with strong territorial issues may run through the boundary in spite of the shock. Fences are generally installed around the complete perimeter of the property, often placing the dog too close to the stimulus and increasing frustration and aggressive displays. This type of fencing is not without hazard and risk to the dog and others. Whenever possible, other fencing choices should be utilized. Dogs restrained behind these types of fences should not be left outdoors unsupervised or when no one is home. Owners should be aware of the dangers of using these types of fences and always monitor the responses of their dog for fear, anxiety, and aggression.

Antianxiety Devices

Antianxiety devices are tools that help decrease arousal, fear, and anxiety in dogs and are commonly recommended by veterinary behaviorists and used in addition to other treatments. If you think your dog has a fear, phobia, or anxiety disorder, check with your veterinarian for appropriate treatment or for a referral to a veterinary behaviorist.

Calming Caps decrease visual stimulation, which can be helpful for dogs who become highly aroused or anxious in certain situations. Consider these for dogs who become aggressive or aroused at the sight of other animals or people or for any other situation that causes undue excitement.

Mutt Muffs, earplugs, and cotton balls may decrease sound levels for dogs in noisy environments (such as shelters, airplanes, and busy roads) and can treat dogs who have a fear of noises. In addition, background noise such as a TV, radio, or even an iPod strapped to the dog's harness, with the earbuds secured to the dog's collar (not in his ears!), can provide calming music to help drown out other scary noises.

Body wraps may provide calming effects by applying constant pressure to the body. These may provide some benefit while treating dogs with generalized anxiety, noise, or thunderstorm phobias. Two commercial brands are Anxiety Wrap and Thundershirt.

Pheromones (see the "Dog-Appeasing Pheromones" section) are natural chemicals released by dogs to affect the behavior of other dogs. Synthetic pheromones can be used as a calming agent in dogs with anxiety or a fear or phobia. They are supplied commercially as wall plug-in diffusers you can use at home and as sprays and wipes you can use at home or in crates and travel cages. Pheromone collars have the calming agent manufactured into the collar, so pheromones are activated and released over time, allowing dogs to take the calming pheromones with them. These may be helpful in obedience classes, for car travel, to help young puppies adjust, or at the veterinarian's office.

Dog-Appeasing Pheromones

Pheromones are chemicals released by many members of the animal kingdom, from ants to people to dogs. The first pheromone was identified in silkworm moths in 1956 by a team of German researchers. Pheromones are species-specific, and so moth pheromones, which are sexual attractants, affect only other moths. Likewise, dog pheromones only affect other dogs.

A specific appeasing pheromone of dogs was first identified in 1999 by Dr. Patrick Pageat, a French veterinarian. Within three to five days of giving birth, the female dog produces pheromones from the tissues between her mammary glands, which give her puppies a sense of well-being and reassurance. These pheromones have since been synthesized to provide dogs with a calming effect. They are now available in many forms and have been used for dogs of all ages with anxiety, fears, and phobias.

Is That Really True?

Some people believe that using aversive or painful devices will make a bigger impression on the dog and therefore cause him to learn better or quicker. In fact, using a positive reinforcement method, such as clicker training, produces faster and better learning than aversive devices and has the added benefit of making learning fun. In 2010, Dr. Emily Blackwell found that the use of punishment-based training methods is actually associated with the development of problem behaviors, including fear and aggression. In contrast, positive reinforcement–based approaches resulted in fewer undesirable behaviors.

If positive reinforcement training is the best, then is all punishment bad? Not necessarily. Removing something a dog wants, with the goal of decreasing an unwanted behavior, is a form of punishment routinely used by veterinary behaviorists. For example, if the unwanted behavior is jumping up during greetings, walking away from the dog when he jumps (removing your attention) is a form of punishment. The jumping should decrease as a result. (See chapter 3 on learning.)

Punishment can also involve using aversives (things the dog doesn't want or things the dog wants to avoid). Aversive physical punishments delivered directly by people (such as hitting, choking, scruffing, or rolling the dog) are not recommended. As veterinary behaviorist Dr. Meghan Herron found in her 2009 study of dog owners, these confrontational methods are more likely to provoke aggression in pet dogs than are nonconfrontational methods. Veterinary behaviorists also do not recommend aversive tools (such as shock devices or even harsh physical reprimands), because these can cause mistrust, fear, or aggression in the dog. Veterinary behaviorists recommend using remote deterrents to reduce the likelihood of the dog engaging in the problem behavior when not supervised and to prevent the dog from associating the owner with the device. It is important to also give the dog the option to choose to do a desired behavior once deterred from engaging in the problem behavior, and to reinforce the right choice with a reward.

Deterrents and Rewards

Here's an example of using a behavioral deterrent appropriately. Butch currently gets up on all the furniture in the living room, but John wants Butch to stay off his favorite chair. He has tried yelling at Butch when he catches him in the chair, which results in Butch staying off the chair when John is home. But there is dog hair on the chair, so Butch obviously gets on it when John is away.

John cuts a piece of carpet runner to the size of the chair cushion, and places it, spiky side up, on the chair. He also leaves Butch's favorite toys on the couch, with extra treats hidden inside them, whenever he is not home. Now when John is away, the carpet runner serves to deter Butch from getting up on the chair, and if Butch decides to get on the couch, he is remotely rewarded for that decision. Butch can easily avoid the deterrent and get rewarded for making the right decision.

Butch isn't stupid, so he chooses to do what earns him rewards. John has successfully set it up so that Butch makes the decision John wants him to make. When John comes home, he simply removes the carpet runner and sits in his dog-hair-free chair.

How Do We Begin?

Use a fun and gentle method to teach your dog to change his behavior. Learning will be scary with tools that cause fear or pain. We cannot say it enough: learning should be fun for all involved — you and your dog.

Preventing Behavior Problems
To prevent many behavior problems in dogs, use these training tools as soon as you get your dog:

- Use a head collar or front-attaching harness to teach your dog to walk nicely on leash.
- Use a comfortable crate to give your dog a safe place to retire, to keep him out of trouble, and to help with housetraining. (For more on crates, see chapter 4 and the appendix.)
- Ask your dog to perform a desired behavior (such as "sit" or "watch me") before he gets anything he wants or anything you want to give him. Examples include petting, food, play, walks, car rides, and so on. This approach involves you requesting a behavior, the dog responding appropriately, and then you giving him a reward (request-response-reward). This technique will help you be consistent in the way you interact with your dog and will encourage calm, relaxed behavior in all situations. While this technique is not a physical tool you can put your hands on, it can create clear communication between you and your dog so you can build a good relationship.

Request-Response-Reward

Here's an example of the request-response-reward technique in action. John wants to feed Butch his breakfast. He wants Butch to have good manners, be calm, and comply with his requests, and he knows that this technique will provide the clear communication needed to teach these lessons. Butch already knows how to sit, so now John asks him to sit (the request) before putting Butch's food bowl on the floor. Butch is so excited that he dances around and does not sit (incorrect response). John does not put the bowl on the floor, because he doesn't want to *reward* Butch for dancing around. He wants Butch to sit after just one request. So John doesn't ask Butch to sit again. He just puts the bowl on the counter and walks away. Butch's inappropriate response just made him lose his opportunity for breakfast! Wow! That's negative punishment (taking away something pleasurable — the food) for not sitting when requested to do so.

A few minutes later, John repeats the request to sit. Butch responds appropriately this time (correct response), so John puts the food bowl on the floor (reward). Now Butch knows how to calmly wait for his meals, and he knows that John means business when he makes a request.

If Butch offers an incorrect response, he doesn't get whatever reward he was working toward. The reward in this example was breakfast, but the reward could also be petting, getting on the couch, going for a car ride, or playing tug with John. Anything John wants to give him, or anything Butch wants, can be the reward. Now John and Butch have a clear and calm way to communicate with each other.

Additional examples of the use of positive reinforcement involve helping your dog adapt to wearing a head collar or going into his crate. To make sure that the first time your dog sees the head collar and crate he thinks they are the greatest things ever, offer him frequent, small treats when putting the collar on and taking it off, as well as when going into the crate. This will create a positive association with these tools. If you have already tried some of these tools and your dog didn't like them or was afraid of them, then consider using desensitization (gradually exposing him to the thing that is frightening him) and counterconditioning (teaching a more desirable and relaxing behavior, such as sitting) to help him learn to better accept these tools. (See chapters 11 and 12 for more information on desensitization and counterconditioning.)

Using Tools to Change Behavior Problems

In 2008, Dr. Elsie Shore, a professor of human psychology, surveyed dog owners and found that they are most concerned with five behaviors: aggression toward people or animals; house soiling; chewing and destructive behavior; barking; and fear of people, storms, or noises. Let's look at how using the right tools can enhance and improve behavior and complement a treatment plan designed by your veterinarian or a veterinary behaviorist. But remember: try to avoid situations that predictably cause the problem behavior, until you can get a complete treatment plan from a veterinary behaviorist.

Aggression to People or Animals

- If aggression is triggered when your dog is inside and sees people or animals outside the home, block or decrease the dog's vision with curtains or decorative window films, or use the Calming Cap.
- Putting the dog in a crate, behind a closed door or baby gate, or tethering him to sturdy furniture with a harness and leash (only when you can supervise, never when you are gone) can keep everyone in the house safe. Adding pheromones may help a fearfully aggressive dog be more relaxed and therefore less likely to react in stressful situations.
- Head collars can be used for added control of the biting end of the dog during treatment. Redirecting the dog or focusing the dog's attention away from the target of aggression is easier with a head collar because it can give you better control of the dog's head.
- Veterinary behaviorists may recommend using a muzzle for added safety while treating aggression, so make sure your aggressive dog is happy to wear one.

(See chapter 10 for more on aggression.)

An Extra Measure of Safety

Think of a muzzle as like an airbag in your car. An airbag is in the car for added safety, and you hope you never need it. It doesn't give you permission to run into a tree. In the same way, a muzzle is worn for added safety, but having the dog wear one doesn't give you permission to put him in a situation that predictably causes him aggression.

House Soiling
- If a dog soils because he has not yet been adequately trained, consider using a crate or other small confinement area to facilitate training. When not crated, tether the dog to you with a leash so you can better supervise him and prevent house-soiling accidents.
- For small dogs in apartments, consider using an indoor dog potty or doggy litter box.
- If house soiling is part of a separation anxiety issue, get a full medical checkup and treatment plan for the dog. The treatment plan may include using pheromones and food puzzle toys provided just before leaving home to change the dog's emotions during departures. (See chapter 11 for more information on separation anxiety.)

(See chapter 4 for more on house soiling.)

Chewing and Destructive Behavior
- If your dog chews a lot or is destructive when you are away from home, it could be related to separation anxiety (see chapter 11). Get a full medical checkup and treatment plan for your dog. See the previous section on house soiling for ideas.
- If your dog chews a lot or is destructive when you are home, be proactive. For example, remove the items your dog typically chews, confine or tether the dog away from items he predictably chews (but *never* use tethers when you are gone), and give him a food puzzle toy he can chew to keep his mouth occupied.

(See chapter 7 for more on destructive behavior.)

Barking
- Try to pinpoint the trigger and avoid that situation as much as possible. If barking occurs when strangers enter the house, change the situation. Confine the dog to a crate in a back room of the house with a food puzzle toy and turn on a radio so that he does not know someone is coming in.
- If the barking is due to the dog asking for attention or begging for food, teach the dog to be quiet on request, then reward his quiet behavior with attention or food. Head collars that have an adjust-

able nose loop can facilitate this training because you can gently close the dog's mouth by tugging on the leash while giving a verbal cue. If you use an anti-bark collar, choose a remote bark-activated citronella collar, so when the dog barks, he'll be sprayed with an annoying but harmless shot of citronella, which is more welfare-friendly. If fear and anxiety are the cause for barking, see your veterinarian or a veterinary behaviorist. If barking is a new behavior and is occurring in an older dog, it may be related to canine dementia. (See chapter 14 for more information.)

(See chapter 7 for more on problem barking.)

Fear of People, Storms, Noises

- These dogs need a complete medical checkup and treatment plan. Any of the antianxiety devices listed, such as the Thundershirt, Mutt Muffs, and Anxiety Wrap, may be used to facilitate treatment.

(See chapters 10 and 12 for more on fears and phobias.)

Avoiding Pitfalls and Staying on Track

Head Collars

Some people have tried head collars and given up because their dog seems fearful or uncertain about putting one on. Never force the head collar on your dog. Start by asking the dog to put it on himself. Do this

He'll have to stick his nose through to get the treat.

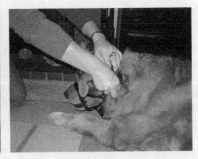

And now it's on.

Emily Elizabeth Jefferson

by holding a favorite treat or peanut butter on a spoon in front of the collar so that the only way he can get the treat is to put his head through the collar. When he is happy to put his head through the collar for a treat, drop additional treats on the floor, or use a long-lasting treat such as rawhide or a food bowl with canned food smashed in it to keep him occupied while you buckle the collar around his neck.

Many dogs will paw at their face when wearing a head collar, just as you might readjust your clothing. If your dog does this, check the fit, because a head collar that fits improperly may not be comfortable. If it is fitted correctly and the pawing continues, simply redirect your dog's attention to all the wonderful things available to sniff or see on the walk, or offer treats to redirect his attention and get him walking nicely. Take off the head collar only when he is calm and not pawing at it.

Body Harnesses

Harnesses are usually not very scary for most dogs. Even so, use treats the first time you ask your dog to step into the harness. Remember, pairing good things with anything new helps him create a pleasant association. If he seems concerned about the harness, redirect his attention with treats or by attaching the leash and going for a walk. Anything that will make him happy can be used to redirect his attention away from the harness. Make sure he is relaxed before you remove the harness.

Muzzles

Dogs who think of muzzles as treat dispensers will love to wear them. Use a technique similar to the one you used to teach your dog to put his head into a head collar. Never force the muzzle onto your dog. Giving him the control to put his nose in it on his own decreases his concern over the muzzle. If every time he chooses to put his nose in the muzzle there is something great to eat in there, he will put his nose in more often.

When he sees the muzzle and comes running as if to say, "May I please stick my nose in there?" and tries to put it on, you are ready to start buckling the neck strap. Smear a treat such as spray cheese or peanut butter into the end of the basket muzzle to keep him occupied as you fasten the neck strap. Take the muzzle off before he finishes the treat. Repeat, and if he is still happily wearing the muzzle when the smeared treats are gone, offer a few more through the muzzle to increase the amount of time he'll happily wear it.

Next time, offer treats at less frequent intervals, but always fast enough that he does not try to paw off the muzzle. If that happens, get his attention in some way (kissy noises, walk to the treat jar), give him some treats, and take off the muzzle only when he is calm.

Be cautious about how long your dog wears the muzzle. While basket muzzles allow some panting, in very hot climates a dog may only be able to wear one for short periods of time.

Reinforce the Right Things

When teaching dogs to accept new things, such as head collars, crates, and muzzles, always use positive reinforcements (treats, praise, or petting) to ensure the dog is having fun and is not afraid of the new item.

If the dog gets worried or starts trying to get a head collar or muzzle off, do not reinforce this behavior by taking off the collar or muzzle. Remember, you get the behavior you reinforce, and you do not want the dog to think that if he paws at these tools it will result in them being removed. Instead, try to redirect the dog's attention (walk away or make a noise) and then change his emotion with treats so you can remove the head collar or muzzle when he is happy and is not pawing at it. Now you are reinforcing or rewarding the behavior of being happy to wear the muzzle, and that is what you want.

Getting Help When You Need It

If you have trouble obtaining the results you want using a particular tool, you may need help. First check with your dog's regular veterinarian to make sure there isn't a medical reason for the unexpected results or failure. If your dog checks out fine, you may need help from a veterinary behaviorist.

Certainly, contact a veterinary behaviorist if your dog exhibits an abnormal behavior such as separation anxiety, aggression, or fears or phobias. If your dog has a training issue (normal but unwanted behaviors, such as not coming when called or barking too much), a veterinary behaviorist can help, or you can find a certified behavior consultant or a dog trainer. Your dog's regular veterinarian should be able to recommend someone for you. If you use a certified dog behavior consultant or a trainer, make sure to choose your dog's trainer as carefully as you would chose a babysitter. (See "Dog Trainer Dos and Don'ts," below.)

Dog Trainer Dos and Don'ts

DO choose a certified dog behavior consultant or a trainer who

- uses treats and toys to reward dogs when they do something right;
- uses and encourages head collars or body harnesses;
- adapts the training method to each individual dog;
- requires proof of vaccination from all dogs;
- allows you to observe a session without participating; watch the dogs during training and see if they are having fun.

DON'T choose a trainer who

- uses punishment-based techniques (yelling, jerking the collar, hitting, etc.);
- uses and encourages choke, prong, or shock collars;
- does not allow treats during training;
- makes you uncomfortable or scares your dog.

If John had done all the things discussed during this chapter, he would have started out with Butch on a head collar and offered lots of treats during walks to reward him for staying in the heel position. John would have provided clear instructions to Butch on what was expected of him and prevented all the anxiety and fear that the punishment-based tools caused. It's up to you to choose wisely for you and your dog.

What Did We Say?

- You can use tools to help prevent and treat some common behavior problems.
- The tools you choose should be gentle, fun, and humane.
- All dogs should be on the request-response-reward plan to ensure clear communication.
- Dogs should wear a head collar or front-attaching harness and have a safe and secure place of their own (which could be their crate).
- If you think punishment tools are needed to stop a behavior, review chapter 3 to see if there is an alternative behavior you can reinforce instead. Reinforcements are more fun and effective than punishments.
- If in doubt, don't use a tool on your dog if you would not use it on yourself or on a small child.
- If your results using a tool are unsatisfactory, discuss this with your veterinarian.
- If you take your dog to a trainer, choose the trainer carefully.

6

School Days
Practical Advice on Getting from a Puppy to a Dog

Gerrard Flannigan, MS, DVM, DACVB
Ellen M. Lindell, VMD, DACVB

Puppies come in all shapes and sizes, but they need the best start possible to become the best dog they can be. The journey from puppy to adult can take many different turns, depending on the personality and early background of each individual. Take Justice and Steve, for example.

Justice was a ten-week-old male Golden Retriever puppy. He was an outgoing puppy who interacted well with his littermates before he was adopted. Both his father and mother were well-adjusted, friendly dogs. When an unfamiliar person approached the litter, all the puppies ran over, eager for the possibility of attention. When Justice left his littermates to join his new household, he occasionally showed mild apprehension in new situations, but he remained eager to approach unfamiliar dogs and people. Over the next few weeks, Justice was at times mildly timid with unfamiliar adult dogs, but he quickly relaxed once a dog showed friendly behavior.

Steve was a ten-week-old male Terrier mix of unknown background. His owners did not meet either one of Steve's parents. When Steve was adopted, he showed mild fearful behavior with unfamiliar people: he was tentative when approached. Once he began to interact, he was actually quite excited, even overly so. And yet his owners noted that when an unfamiliar person picked up Steve, especially outside their home, he would become very sedate. When they described this very cute trait to Steve's astute veterinarian, she saw this as a red flag. She explained that Steve may not be as comfortable as the owners believed.

In fact, profound sedation can actually be a sign of anxiety! In addition, the owners noted that although Steve interacted well with small dogs and puppies, he cowered if approached by a large adult dog. In his first puppy class at eleven weeks of age, Steve played comfortably with the other puppies, but when the trainer's friendly adult Australian Shepherd approached, Steve growled.

Facts, Not Fiction

We often will hear dog owners say they are dismayed that their last dog was not more like their current dog — or vice versa. We've also heard some trainers say you can address all behaviors of all puppies in the same way. The fact is that not all puppies are created equal. Ultimately, behavior is affected by both genetic and environmental factors — nature and nurture. Puppies in the uterus are subject to the same stresses as their mother. Early illness and inadequate nutrition may increase a puppy's risk of developing behavioral disorders. As for the genetic contribution to behavior, even littermates do not share all the same genes and will not develop in the same way.

Although you are not exactly starting with a clean slate, you can have tremendous influence on the way your puppy develops. Though we cannot alter the puppy's genetic makeup (an adult Great Dane will *not* fit under your airplane seat!), we can provide a rich environment to help each puppy develop to the best of her potential. The ideal approach is to expose a young puppy to a wide variety of social experiences and an assortment of sights, sounds, and scents, all of which will provide a strong foundation for the development of a behaviorally healthy dog.

We have heard a lot of misconceptions about what socialization can and cannot accomplish.

Do dogs need to be adopted between six and eight weeks of age to bond with their new owners? No, even after eight weeks of age, puppies will form strong bonds with their new family, as long as their early interactions with people are positive.

Will allowing your dog to jump up on people and to pull while on a leash walk cause aggression? Not really. In fact, jumping up to get attention or in greeting is a normal dog behavior. So is pulling on a leash when your dog is eager to explore the world around her. Jumping up and pulling can be inconvenient, but it is up to you to decide which of these normal behaviors you will permit or not permit as you raise your puppy. Just remember that when large dogs jump up and pull, they can accidentally cause injuries and be annoying to other people.

Does allowing your puppy to rest on furniture cause aggression? Sleeping on furniture can exacerbate existing aggression if the dog finds being moved intolerable. However, it is unclear whether it can actually cause aggression. If it is your preference, you may invite your puppy to rest on furniture. However, if your dog has begun to *also* exhibit aggressive behavior while resting in these areas, then sharing furniture can pose safety concerns. Consult your veterinarian or veterinary behaviorist for guidance.

What Does That Mean?

Socialization: A learning process during which an individual dog learns to accept close proximity to various other species or to individuals of her own species.

Puppy socialization: Pleasant, safe, arranged introductions of puppies to people and dogs, as well as to other types of animals and places.

Puppy socialization classes: Classes specifically designed to facilitate socialization. Although some basic skills may be taught, obedience is not the focus.

Habituation: The reduced response to a stimulus that occurs with repeated exposure.

Sensitization: An *increased* response to a stimulus after repeated exposure. This is usually an undesirable response that occurs when, instead of habituating, a puppy becomes more and more frightened with each exposure.

Systematic desensitization: A process by which the exposure to a stimulus is done very gradually so that habituation can occur. If you try to introduce your puppy to something or someone new and she begins to tremble or tries to get away, take a break. She needs a slow, systematic approach.

Is That Really True?

Of course, everyone can tell the difference between a Yorkshire Terrier and a Mastiff. But in some ways they're more alike than different. Although different breeds of dogs look and act differently, they actually have very similar needs. The tendency to offer certain behaviors may vary from breed to breed, but most behavioral repertoires are shared. Dogs of all breeds and sizes may bark at unfamiliar people, lick food remnants from accessible dishes, and steal naps on vacant sofas. And absolutely all dogs begin their lives as puppies. Thus, we can establish some general puppy-raising guidelines that are helpful for all puppies and puppy owners. But first, let's separate some facts from fiction.

Socialization

Whether you expect your puppy to grow up to be gigantic or petite, she will benefit from appropriate socialization. Pioneering research by biologists John Paul Scott and John L. Fuller, reported in their 1965 book *Genetics and the Social Behavior of the Dog*, suggests that in the course of development, there is a period during which puppies are most accepting of new stimuli. This period is called the "socialization" period.

In dogs, the socialization period begins at three weeks of age and continues to roughly three months of age. Between three and five weeks of age, puppies undergo a primary socialization, in which experiences within the litter have a great effect on future emotional behavior (see chapter 2).

Socialization then continues from six through twelve weeks of age, as puppies make additional social contacts and form bonds with other species. In their new household, puppies grow comfortable with adults,

This puppy is learning to politely greet a new person. She is receiving a treat for sitting calmly instead of jumping up. Unless your toy dog will spend a lifetime in your arms, she should be socialized on the ground. *Linda J. Lew*

children, dogs, cats, and other pets. That is why Scott and Fuller call the six-to-twelve-week period the *critical* period for socialization. Many behaviorists prefer the term *sensitive* period, suggesting that the period does not end abruptly.

It is true that beyond twelve to fourteen weeks of age, a dog may meet new experiences with more suspicion. However, just because your puppy is beyond the *ideal* socialization age, you should not simply abandon socializing her altogether. In fact, as long as you see no signs that your puppy is distressed, exposure to many different places, people, and things should continue at least until your puppy is officially a dog.

Depending on their size (small dogs mature more quickly), dogs reach social maturity somewhere between one and three years of age. The intensity of developing behavior problems often increases when dogs are socially mature. A young puppy who is afraid of men with hats might back away and bark meekly. As the puppy matures, she may step forward and bark more fiercely, eventually leading to the more familiar signs of aggression, such as lunging and biting. While the display of the behavior changes as the dog develops, the same underlying fear or anxiety is what drives the dog's behavior. It is much more difficult to achieve a change in the adult dog's response through social interactions alone, since the ideal socialization period has ended. So if you notice a similar progression of behavior, you should seek the advice of a veterinary behaviorist.

To better understand how socialization works, we need to understand three important behavior concepts. The first is *habituation*, which simply means getting used to something. For example, when you first move next door to a railroad track, you might lose some sleep, alert to the *whoosh* and squeal of every train (the stimulus in this case). With time, you habituate (get used to it) and sleep soundly.

The second is *sensitization*. This happens when, instead of habituating, a puppy becomes more and more frightened with each exposure to something. So you end up with an *increased* response to a stimulus after repeated exposure. This is usually an undesirable response. For example, suppose you like to pop corn for your evening snack. The first time your puppy hears the popper, she runs out of the room. You would expect that next time she might come out to investigate, especially since the machine generates food and it truly did her no harm. Instead, your puppy runs away even before you switch the popper on. Your puppy is sensitized: she expects the machine is going to frighten her and takes off ahead of time.

The third concept is *systematic desensitization*, which is the way you gradually expose a puppy to a stimulus so that you can be sure she habituates rather than becomes sensitized to it. Let's go back to the example of the puppy who is afraid of the popcorn popper. She needs to be desensitized. The stimulus (the popper) needs to be presented in a manner that does not lead the puppy to run off. You might take the machine out and feed your puppy some popcorn that is already made — no noise, and the machine provides snacks. Now the machine is not so bad. Next, turn the machine on with the puppy on the other side of the room. Toss some treats and turn off the machine. Little by little, your puppy should discover that even though the machine is noisy, it is not scary after all. If you try to introduce your puppy to something or someone new and she begins to tremble or tries to get away, take a break. She needs a slow, systematic approach. As you can see, the intensity of the stimulus is everything — so you must manipulate either how close it is, how noisy it is, how novel it might be, or some combination of these variables to help your puppy learn not to be afraid.

Developing a Socialization Program for Your Puppy

1. Identify situations your puppy will probably encounter as an adult and make sure these situations are part of her socialization. For instance, if you hope to travel with your puppy when she grows up, begin to take her on car rides to places other than the veterinary clinic.

2. Expose your puppy to new situations in a nonconfrontational and calm manner. Do not force her if she shows signs of fear or anxiety, often exhibited by hesitation and cowering. If she balks when you try to walk her past a fire hydrant, for example, sit nearby for a while. Pet her, let her relax, then move a little closer. As she relaxes, she may choose to venture closer and give the hydrant a little sniff.

3. Recognize that a small amount of hesitation in new situations is a normal and healthy part of learning. Reward her confidence with verbal praise and a small food treat. If your pup is only showing normal reluctance to a new situation, she should gradually show greater relaxation and interest after a few exposures to the stimulus.

4. Address any concerns early; they won't just disappear! If your pup is growing more concerned or anxious in everyday situations, you might try setting up a slower progression of exposure (systematic desensitization) for specific problem areas. If in doubt, discuss your concern with a veterinary behaviorist, your veterinarian, or a qualified trainer.

But My Puppy Is Young and Vulnerable!

Your veterinarian may tell you that your puppy should not go out in public areas until she has completed her vaccination series. This has been a source of controversy among puppy owners and veterinarians. Veterinarians worry that puppies will contract serious illnesses, such as parvovirus, if they interact with other dogs, or even if they simply walk in the street.

It is important to remember that by the time your puppy has completed her full vaccination series, she will have passed the sensitive period for socialization. We can't say that there is zero risk to taking your puppy out of her sheltered home environment to see the world. But the fact is, the risk that a puppy will grow up to develop a serious behavior problem is far greater than the risk that she will succumb to a serious illness. Plus, with a little care, you can anticipate and reduce certain risks.

To keep socialization safe, follow these rules:

- Don't bring your puppy to areas frequented by unvaccinated or stray dogs.
- Do avoid contact with dogs who are known to be infectious.
- Do prevent your puppy from sniffing or ingesting the feces of other animals, including other dogs.
- Do make certain any puppy class your pup is enrolled in has easily cleaned surfaces to help prevent the spread of infection.
- Do vaccinate your puppy, based on your veterinarian's advice.

Myths About Manners

Since part of your puppy's early education involves learning social skills — manners, if you will — it is important to think carefully about what we might call socially unacceptable behaviors.

Consider the following:

1. Why do dogs favor couches for resting?
2. Why do dogs rush ahead of their people on walks?
3. Why do dogs jump up on people to greet them?

Some might say that these behaviors reflect a dog's desire to control the household, to dominate you. You might fear that by allowing your dog to engage in these behaviors, you put your puppy at risk of developing aggressive behavior. Let us assure you, this is not the case at all. Accurate information about dominance theory and puppies can be found in chapters 1, 3, and 10. Suffice it to say that most socially unacceptable behaviors — what we call misbehaviors — are simply *normal canine behaviors.* In other words, puppies are dogs. And when dogs, large or small, find a behavior to be rewarding, they will repeat that behavior again and again.

Let's revisit those questions:

1. Perhaps dogs favor couches for resting because couches are soft and smell like the dogs' favorite people and because everyone else in the house sits on them.
2. Perhaps dogs rush ahead of their people on walks because they are eager to explore the exciting world, and people are too darned slow.
3. Perhaps dogs jump up on people to greet them because proximity to the face allows more effective communication or simply because exuberant greetings are just more fun.

Does My Dog Need to Share?

You may have heard that dogs should be expected to share, or even to relinquish food and other valuable items on demand. What should you do while your dog eats? Suggestions run the gamut from letting the puppy eat in peace, to petting and hugging her while she dines, to routinely taking her food dish away to promote sharing.

The fact of the matter is that some puppies don't mind sharing and others do. Just how many puppies are sharers versus guarders is not known. Many factors influence a puppy's response to having her supper removed. The food may be very valuable, since it is only provided once or twice a day. The puppy may be very hungry. Perhaps the puppy learned to fight for her food because her littermates were bullies — or because the people in her home kept taking her food away! How would you respond if you were at a restaurant with your second mouthful of chocolate mousse on the spoon and the server gave you a big hug and then proceeded to snatch away your dessert, including that spoonful already in your hand?

There is no clear answer as to whether any single intervention can or should be applied to encourage sharing or whether intervention can prevent future guarding behaviors. Your puppy may grow up with no concern whatsoever about the proximity of humans during her dinner. She may not like to have people around at all. In either case, it's always a safe bet to simply go about your business, leaving your puppy to eat in peace.

We find that certain interventions, specifically those that involve repeatedly taking food away, can actually make worse any underlying tendency to display aggression while eating. Remember the concept of sensitization, where repeated exposure to a stimulus results in an *increased* reaction rather than a reduced reaction.

Take Murphy, a three-month-old Cocker Spaniel puppy, for instance. He was just about to settle in for a delicious dinner. He was hungry. He has tiny teeth, and it takes him a while to chew his crunchy kibble. As Murphy contemplated his task, Jean, his owner, snatched up his plate. Until then, it had not occurred to Murphy that a human would want some of his dog food. The next day, he was more alert as he ate. He began to eat faster. Jean told her veterinarian that Murphy ate as if he were starving.

Within a few days, Murphy began to glare and stiffen slightly when Jean tried to reach for his dish. To another dog that message would be clear: "Mine!" But Jean was not familiar with Murphy's language. Jean ignored Murphy's message.

Murphy grew confused and frustrated. His signals were not effective with this alien species. What to do? Murphy had no choice but to use more powerful signals. He began to snarl and growl whenever he spied Jean approaching his dish. He wanted his dinner!

Murphy learned that the approach of a human while he was eating could have an unpleasant outcome. At the end of the day, taking a puppy's dish away time after time can actually encourage a pattern of aggressive responses.

Ultimately, it might be best to just leave your puppy alone while she eats. However, particularly in households with young children, someone may approach accidentally (even though children should never be unsupervised near a dog, particularly when the dog is eating!). In "Advice for Food Handling," you will find some safe exercises that encourage your puppy to enjoy company while she eats.

Advice for Food Handling

You can choose to just let your puppy eat in peace. But accidents do happen. Maybe a visitor or a child will see a dropped piece of kibble and feel obliged to put it into the dog food dish. There may then be a reason to teach the concept of sharing.

1. Put your puppy's dish on the floor and let her eat for a minute or two.
2. Stand beside her with a teaspoon of cottage cheese on a spoon.
3. As your puppy is eating, cheerfully say "bonus" and lower the loaded spoon into the dish.
4. Practice daily until your puppy eagerly looks up when she hears "bonus." Then surprise her. Wait a few feet away and let her eat for a bit. Then walk toward her with the delicious addition. As you get close, say "bonus" and deposit the treat in her dish. At this point, your puppy should be more accepting of humans who approach.

Please note: If your puppy stiffens, snarls, or growls, discontinue this exercise and seek behavior advice from your veterinarian or a veterinary behaviorist.

How Do We Begin?

Justice, our Golden Retriever from the beginning of the chapter, appeared to be a well-adjusted puppy. His owners followed a basic socialization protocol. Justice attended puppy socialization classes. He was introduced only to friendly dogs. Nevertheless, sometimes even friendly adult dogs curled their lips at Justice in response to his pushy puppy behavior. He backed off. He was learning a healthy respect for adult dog communication and that there are limits to tolerance. If Justice had ignored these gentle warnings, his owner would have intervened by quietly removing him from the situation.

Justice visited all sorts of dog-friendly places. He went along on trips to the bank and strolls through the farmers' market. Since his owners did not have children, they deliberately visited areas where Justice could meet many active children. Justice experienced baseball, soccer, and skateboarding. Regardless of the destination, Justice pranced ahead to meet the day, eagerly hopping into the car for his next adventure.

Justice's owners hoped to exhibit Justice in breed conformation shows, obedience competitions, and field trials. To increase his ability to perform and ignore distractions, they were advised to take him to environments that were crowded and noisy. Anticipating his need to perform at field trials, Justice's owners brought him to these events when possible, initially keeping him a comfortable distance from the loudest areas.

The owners of Steve, the Terrier mix, had different concerns, since Steve showed signs of fear. His owners had to learn to recognize these signs as they proceeded with his socialization. Steve's exposures to novel situations were done gradually so that they did not trigger fear. Whenever possible, Steve's owners arranged daily interactions with unfamiliar people. The goal was for Steve to meet five new people at each outing. His owners were instructed to bring treats along on all outings. Every unfamiliar person could hand Steve a tasty treat to help him learn that strangers bear pleasant gifts.

Steve's introduction to large dogs was also approached carefully. Only extremely patient, tolerant dogs were permitted to interact with Steve. If Steve was fearful (shaking, panting, or growling), his owners distracted him with a treat or a toy. They were not shy about asking the owner of the approaching dog to step aside so that Steve could relax. After a few minutes, they would try again, gently offering Steve the opportunity to approach the other dog. Frightening interactions with unfamiliar dogs were avoided; a single bad incident can carry over into adulthood.

Steve's owners did not plan to compete with him in dog events.

They wanted him to be a good companion. They needed to build his confidence, but their expectations were reasonable. They didn't rush him. Once Steve gained confidence, his owners began socialization in busier environments and allowed him to meet more active people and dogs.

Think about your goals for your puppy. When you envision yourself with your grown-up dog one year from now, what does the picture look like? Do you envision your dog coming to work with you, fraternizing with co-workers and their dogs during breaks? Do you plan to have children or adopt a cat? Do you hope to leave the city and retire to a cattle ranch, or leave the suburbs for the metropolis?

If your puppy spends her early weeks home alone, just growing, she may be unpleasantly surprised when thrust into the office. The onrush of people and possibly other dogs may be overwhelming. If the office is dog-friendly, then bring your puppy to work from the start. If you are too busy for necessary potty breaks, ask a pet-sitter or a friend to come to the office to help you out. If children are going to be in your future, bring your puppy to visit as many families with children as you can, or families with cats if felines are in your future.

Of course, no one has a crystal ball. Thankfully, dogs as a species are quite flexible. Our beloved dogs typically follow along as we go from noisy college apartments to solo homes and then again to lives with significant others and even children. But instead of leaving things to chance, do yourself and your dog a huge favor and expose young puppies to the types of situations that might be in your future together.

Exposure to Children

Whether your household includes children or not, it's a good idea to introduce your puppy to the world of children. If you don't have children, enlist the help of a friend's family so that as your dog grows, you can accompany their children to soccer games or on shopping trips. Have your puppy sit quietly to watch children laughing, crying, shouting, and running about. You can even allow clumsy toddlers to pat your puppy. Just be sure to stand very close in case you need to gently block a hand that is too rough or prevent a scratch from your puppy's sharp teeth.

Tips for Introducing Your Dog to Children

- Always closely supervise your dog with children.
- Don't allow young children to pick up your puppy; he's fragile at this age.
- Do have a puppy biscuit handy in case your puppy tries to mouth or jump up on a child who reaches out to pet her. Avoid problems by asking your puppy to sit for the treat.

Exposure to Adults

People come in many shapes and sizes, not just child and adult, so you need to introduce your puppy to a range of adults as well as children. Your puppy should meet tall and short, dark- and fair-skinned people. She should meet men and women, young and old. She should meet people with canes, in wheelchairs, on bicycles, and so on.

You will not have to worry when people pet your puppy if your puppy learns that she should sit rather than jump up to receive any pets or treats. That is, instead of trying to correct this unwanted but normal behavior, teach your puppy the greeting posture that you would like her to demonstrate. By practicing the "sit" for petting at home, you can help your puppy make a seamless transition to sitting for her petting when she's away from home. Hint: Whether your puppy is a little boisterous or a little shy, if the person has a treat in hand, it will make for a smoother greeting.

To help her during the early stages of socialization, have people pet her one or two times, then stop and hand her a tiny treat. Setting your puppy up for success means working within her comfort zone and being aware of her ability to remain calm. You want her to be interested, even eager, but not so excited that she cannot sit still.

If your puppy jumps, it is very important that you don't scold her. She will not be able to imagine what she did wrong. Your reprimand can create a fear of greeting new people. You don't want to create fear of people, or even of jumping, especially if you want to teach jumping on cue in another context, such as for tricks or a canine sport.

Exposure to Other Dogs

Your dog is likely to encounter other dogs in her environment. There will be dogs at the veterinarian's office. There may be other dogs walking in your neighborhood. Your puppy's social skills with other dogs will have a great impact on the type of activities you will be able to enjoy with her as she matures.

Your puppy should learn that not every dog is there for a playdate. Rather, she must accept that some dogs will be indifferent and some might be downright unfriendly. Your job is to help your puppy remain calm and quiet, to patiently watch those dogs who are not eager to interact. It is neither safe nor appropriate to allow your puppy to randomly greet unfamiliar dogs.

Sometimes this is easier said than done. Your puppy might find you to be boring. She might pull or bark to try to get a chance to play with a fellow canine. Don't be dull; have some amazing treats handy. Give your puppy a treat for sitting and paying attention to you. Keep a rope or braided fleecy toy in your pocket and pull it out for a *mild* tug game while the other dog passes by.

A tug toy can make you more interesting than a passing canine. *Linda J. Lew*

An important part of socialization with other dogs is learning to play appropriately. Give your young puppy the opportunity to greet and play with friendly dogs. During her sensitive period, just as she should meet a variety of people, she should meet dogs of assorted colors, ages, genders, and sizes. Be very sure that the dog to be introduced is patient and calm and will not snap or bite if your puppy makes a small canine social mistake. Puppies can be annoying, and an intolerant adult dog can frighten or injure your puppy. This is one reason why leash walks are not good times for puppies (or any age dog) to meet random and unfamiliar dogs. Being on a leash can inhibit normal canine greeting behaviors and make a dog feel more at risk of aggression from another dog. Your goal on leash walks should be to have a calm, relaxed pup who is content to walk confidently past another dog.

Puppy Socialization Classes

The purpose of a puppy socialization class, sometimes called "puppy kindergarten," is to offer puppies the opportunity to meet other puppies and their families. Puppy socialization classes provide a wonderful opportunity to socialize your puppy in controlled situations. The trainers and veterinarians who offer these classes are able to arrange for exposures to an assortment of people, dogs, and other companion animals, all within the classroom. Although most classes do help you teach your puppy some simple behaviors, such as "sit," an ideal class will emphasize teaching social skills. Ask your veterinarian if there are classes in your area.

Considering your dog's developmental timeline, you should enroll your puppy in a socialization class during her sensitive period for socialization. Remember, the sensitive period ends at twelve weeks. Many training facilities will allow you to register even before you adopt your puppy. Call ahead, as classes fill quickly. Most classes accept puppies at ten weeks of age, some even earlier. Your puppy will have just begun her vaccination series and may not be fully immune to all potential diseases, so be sure your class leader has asked for proof of immunization for every puppy who attends.

Skills your puppy will learn in puppy kindergarten include

- how to sit quietly — even while other puppies are playing;
- how to meet and greet people without jumping up;
- how to meet and greet other puppies (and maybe even adult dogs and cats);
- how to play politely with other puppies;
- how to sit, lie down, come when called, and walk nicely on a leash.

If classes are not available in your area, don't worry. You can do a fine job socializing your puppy on your own.

What to Look for in a Puppy Kindergarten

- The environment should be reasonably quiet so you and your puppy can hear the teacher.
- All family members should be encouraged to participate — especially children.
- A gentle approach is essential. The emphasis should be on guiding your puppy to behave appropriately using rewards such as food, toys, and praise.
- Smiling faces and wagging tails: this is meant to be fun!
- Puppies should be of similar age (preferably between eight and fourteen weeks of age when beginning class), and therefore at similar maturity levels.
- There should be opportunities to segregate puppies by size, to avoid large puppies overwhelming smaller puppies.

What to Avoid

- The teacher should not ask you to use a prong or choke collar correction.
- Puppies should not be held up by their scruff.
- Puppies should not be rolled over and pinned on their back.
- The teacher should not ask you to yell at, bite, bark at, or growl at your puppy.
- Essentially, harsh corrections should never be tolerated!

Looking Ahead at Home

With nurturing and proper socialization, your puppy will grow into a dog who is comfortable out in the big world. Hopefully, with early exposures under her harness, she will be able to calmly and confidently handle all sorts of future experiences.

All the while, though, she will be spending most of her days and nights with you, her human family. It is important for your puppy to be calm and confident in her home. Home is where you and your puppy will learn the most about communicating with each other.

Now is the time to sit down and write out some guidelines. You will need to teach your puppy about your personal expectations. What do you consider to be acceptable behavior in your home? We already discussed thinking about the dog your puppy will become when she grows up. Think about that now. Will you enjoy your puppy in bed when she is large and furry and maybe muddy? If yes, then the rule could be "Puppy may be in bed." Do you enjoy watching your dog walk in front of you so that you can see what she attempts to ingest? Then the rule is "Puppy may walk ahead."

There really is no right or wrong, unless a pet or person is in danger. You do need to be consistent, though, so that your puppy is not confused. So write down the rules and then stick to them.

Avoiding Pitfalls and Staying on Track

Everyone has heard the expression about too many cooks. Now with the advent of the Internet, we cannot even begin to count the number of cooks. It is estimated that forty-eight hours of YouTube videos are uploaded every minute, translating to about eight years of content every day, and many of those are about dogs!

One of the biggest pitfalls in raising your puppy is listening to a little advice from a multitude of sources and then attempting to apply bits and pieces of various theories and recommendations. You just don't need that many cooks. Above all, keep it sane, simple, and sensible.

First, create your vision of your ideal dog. Make a list of the rules you would like her to follow as an adult. Then, guide your puppy so that exhibiting the behaviors you have selected is as natural as can be. Apply careful management techniques to prevent behaviors you prefer not to see. Reward the behaviors you like.

Second, provide your puppy with a multitude of rich experiences. Watch your puppy's responses during all interactions. Take a photo of her when she is happy. Refer to that to be sure she is not exhibiting signs of fear or distress in new situations. Some puppies need more gentle exposures, while others relish walking on the wild side.

Finally, be realistic. Your puppy's individual temperament and personality, as well as her breed, will affect her tendency to exhibit certain behaviors. A shy or reserved puppy needs a different style of socialization than a gregarious puppy does. Most dogs thrive on learning and performing. Plan to offer your dog a lifetime of mental stimulation. In fact, for all dogs, it is safe to say that training is forever.

Justice and Steve, Revisited

Justice, now eight years of age, is a normal adult dog with good social skills in the company of both people and dogs. Although Justice didn't get his conformation championship, he had a good show career and appeared to enjoy the experience. Justice loves to work and has achieved a Junior Hunter working title. He continues to make new friends and is always welcomed at picnics and parties.

Steve is just over eighteen months of age and loves meeting all new people. He tolerates most adult large-breed dogs, and he can join his owners on hikes and other outings. However, he might nervously growl and attempt to back away (a sign of fear) if dogs approach him a little too closely. It takes Steve a while to warm up to large dogs, but his owners remain patient; Steve even has several large doggy friends.

What Did We Say?

- Behavior is affected by both genetics and environment (nature and nurture). Each puppy is an individual but comes with certain preset behaviors that are affected by her early experiences.

- To reach your puppy's highest potential, she should be exposed to a wide variety of social experiences. This is the time to begin shaping your future adult dog.
- Socialization is defined as a special learning process during which individuals learn to accept future social situations. Although exposure to social situations should continue until your puppy becomes an adult, it is very important that you begin when a puppy is most sensitive to new stimuli (the sensitive socialization period — six to twelve weeks of age).
- If your puppy has particular fears, be patient, distract her, and reward any confident progress with much-loved treats. But remember, if your puppy still shows fear and anxiety, consult with your veterinarian or a veterinary behaviorist for more help.
- Puppy socialization classes are an excellent and safe opportunity to socialize your puppy in a protected setting. In addition, you should take every opportunity outside of these classes to expand socialization.
- Beginning an obedience training program at this young age is crucial.
- Above all, this should be a fun process for both you and your new puppy!

You might think the suggestions in this chapter for training and socialization are overwhelming. The fact is, you only need to spend a few minutes each day actively training; your puppy will learn important lessons as you go through your normal daily routine and begin your lives together.

7

I Know They're Normal Behaviors, but How Do I Fix Them?

Common Problems That Can Drive Any Dog Owner to Howl

Jeannine Berger, DVM, DACVB
Lore I. Haug, MS, DVM, DACVB

Every night it's the same: Anna comes home after eight grueling hours at the office, and Rowdy, her happy-go-lucky Labrador Retriever mix, jumps on her. Scratch that: he barrels into her. At sixty pounds and with all the exuberance of his two years, Rowdy has almost toppled his petite owner on several occasions. Anna has lost some of her best outfits this way and often ends up with paw scratches on her stomach. She doesn't mind the jumping so much on weekends when she's in jeans and a T-shirt and the two of them wrestle on the lawn. But on a weekday in the evening, she's exhausted and wearing heels. No matter how many times she shouts "No!" and pushes him off, Rowdy still treats her like a trampoline every night. She has even tried spraying water in his face — to no avail.

Anna is certain Rowdy acts this way to dominate her. After all, he spends more time at home than she does. He also steals stuff from the kitchen counter if she leaves anything out, and he spreads the trash all over the floor if he can get to it. Clearly, he thinks he owns the place. The dog walker, who comes every day at noon and takes Rowdy for a two-hour walk, doesn't have any problems with him. She doesn't live in the house, so he feels no need to assert himself over her, Anna reasons.

So many of our dogs' behaviors are normal and have evolved because of their close relationship to humans. Nonetheless, some of these behaviors can annoy us to the point of damaging our relationship with our dogs. It is sometimes difficult to see how to change course and get back on track to a loving bond with our dogs if they steal our favorite shoes or tear into the expensive new couch. Even administering needed medications to our dogs can be challenging. What do you do when your veterinarian tells you to put medication in your dog's ears or eyes four times a day but your dog will not sit still for those treatments, or worse, hides and growls at you?

Anna is at her wits' end, and who wouldn't be? Nuisance behaviors — jumping, stealing things, trash diving, charging through the door, begging, and all the other things dogs do that drive us crazy — are deeply frustrating and can eat into the enjoyment of sharing your life with a dog. The good news is that nuisance behaviors are also totally preventable and correctable. Once we move out of the realm of myths, such as dominance, and understand what truly motivates the dog to behave the way he does, we can use his motivation to train an alternate behavior we prefer.

Let's explore how to address some common nuisance behaviors, such as jumping, stealing, and pulling on leash, as well as some typical tasks, such as brushing teeth, trimming nails, and administering medication. We emphasize improving your communication and training skills so you can implement suggested plans to improve your dog's behavior, leading to a tighter bond and a longer-lasting relationship with your canine buddy.

Facts, Not Fiction

Let's stay with jumping. Biologists tell us dogs have evolved a greeting ritual specifically to interact with humans. Jumping and grinning are innate to dogs, but dogs developed a greeting style just for us probably because we are missing some of the physical attributes they rely on for social interactions with other dogs: ears that move, tails, and certain glands that send olfactory signals. They use ritualized "I'm meeting a person" greetings to communicate varying degrees of recognition and attachment. Hence the difference between a modest tail wag when a dog meets a stranger and the dance of joy he breaks into when he greets his owner.

Jumping up, therefore, is not a bid for dominance but a normal canine greeting behavior. Rowdy has no idea how Anna would prefer to be greeted. Not only that, but Anna has inadvertently strengthened the jumping by reinforcing it some of the time — which is called "intermittent reinforcement" — when she welcomes Rowdy's jumping up on weekends. The pushing and scolding don't change Rowdy's behavior because that's attention, and attention is precisely what Rowdy craves after many hours without his best friend.

Don't forget, dogs are intensely social creatures. They therefore do many things to get and hold our attention. They may signal to us to take them outside to eliminate, they may be hungry and ask for food, and they may just want to play or have social interaction. In some cases, they may be insecure or anxious and may simply be asking us what they are supposed to do — interact or rest quietly. Our response often determines how persistent they might be and what they do next. They might jump on us, hump our legs, or steal the remote control — obviously a high-value object, given how much people clutch it. Dogs who hunger for our attention are "people dogs," that is, they're highly motivated by interactions with us. It then is up to us to give that attention only when they perform the behavior we are looking for (sitting, lying relaxed, or dropping the ball). A highly attention-motivated dog will often work for praise, and a pat on the head might trump food.

Rowdy gets a good amount of exercise, which is great and an absolute must for a young and energetic dog, but he still spends at least eight hours alone with no company and nothing to do except trash diving and counter surfing. This is also a behavior that's annoying to us — pointing out that we forgot again to clean up the countertops from last night's dinner — but that in a dog's world makes perfect sense; trash diving or counter surfing represents going for a "hunt" around the house. With nothing else to do, Rowdy goes on "hunting" trips, and his well-developed nose tells him exactly where last night's spaghetti plate was left on the counter. This is fun entertainment for many dogs because, again, the intermittent reinforcement — sometimes finding something — is very rewarding.

Intermittent reinforcement is a powerfully motivating force to all animals, including humans. Think of it as the Las Vegas effect: the anticipation of a periodic jackpot keeps us dropping coins into a slot machine, even though we only occasionally win. Dogs are no different. Sometimes there is a loaf of bread left on the counter, so it makes it worthwhile to keep looking. Intermittent reinforcement is an important aspect of training, because it helps solidify new behaviors once they are learned using continuous reinforcement (rewarding *every* time the desired behavior occurs). But reinforcement can also haunt you if you inadvertently reward your dog intermittently by periodically giving attention for jumping up, by sometimes leaving food out on counters, or by occasionally feeding him from the dinner table. (See chapter 3 for more information on learning.)

Chewing is another example of a normal canine behavior. For thousands of years, dogs had to grind down marrow and split bones to survive. To tone their jaw muscles for this challenging work, they begin chewing in the first tender weeks of puppyhood and never stop. Food may be served up in a bowl now, but the chewing urge is still there, hardwired into our dogs. In some dogs, chewing is what life is all about; others can take it or leave it. Either way, it is a deeply ingrained canine behavior, and that's the crucial thing to remember. Fido isn't chewing on your boyfriend's shoes because he is jealous; he simply finds calfskin leather irresistible.

What Does That Mean?

Intermittent reinforcement: Rewarding a behavior only sometimes instead of every time it occurs.

Reinforcers: Anything dogs want and will work for: food, treats, attention, praise, a belly rub, balls thrown, doors opened, the leash snapped on for a walk or taken off at the park, coming along for a car ride, etc.

Dominance: The ability to get and defend an important resource, such as food, resting places, territory, or mates, in competition with another individual with whom a social relationship exists.

Attention seeking: Behaviors dogs use to get a response from us, whether it is to be fed, petted, or played with.

Mental stimulation: Actions that we incorporate into a dog's life to cause increased activity and learning in the brain: interactive toys, games, and other outlets for canine energy that allow dogs to engage their natural skills and urges, such as chewing, scavenging for food, solving problems, and so on. Examples are hide-and-seek toys, chew toys, plush toys with squeakers, and food puzzle toys, like a stuffed Kong and treat balls.

Physical stimulation: Actions that we incorporate into a dog's life to cause increased physical activity. Regular play and exercise are essential to any dog's health and happiness.

Extinction burst: A sudden display of a behavior that was diminishing after it was no longer rewarded.

Is That Really True?

We tend to assign human motivations to dog behavior — and particularly nuisance behaviors, such as pulling on leash walks. Not only is that unfair to dogs, but it also sets up a power struggle. If we believe the dog is acting out of spite or is trying to dominate us, we start looking for ways to put him in his place without considering other explanations for his behavior. From this springs such unfortunate strategies as stepping on a dog's toes or kneeing him in the chest to stop him from jumping, which amounts to punishing the dog for being happy to see you.

A much better approach is to focus on helping our dogs learn what we would like them *to do instead;* for example, greet us politely by sitting in front of us or barking on cue when asked to "speak."

How Do We Begin?

Nuisance behaviors can be changed to polite manners or managed to a point where they don't bother us, depending on our preference. Here are four strategies:

- Management techniques
- Training consistent interactions
- Training solutions
- Physical and mental stimulation

Management Techniques

Many annoying behaviors can be prevented or managed to a point where they no longer present a problem. Keep in mind that management isn't training. The dog isn't learning how we would prefer him to behave; he is simply prevented from behaving in an unwanted way in a situation because we control the options and outcomes. But management is a great short-term measure for getting relief, especially for young animals with nuisance behaviors, and it often works well enough to satisfy many people in the long term too. Management also keeps the dog from practicing the problem behavior and thus learning bad habits by repeating the same behaviors over and over again. For example, keeping your dog out of the kitchen prevents him from jumping on the counter and being rewarded by finding leftover food. If he isn't allowed in the kitchen, he never learns that jumping on the counter yields rewards. Remember, for a behavior to be ongoing, it must be reinforcing for the dog; that is why he repeats it.

Management techniques might include setting up barriers such as baby gates and exercise pens, using humane anti-pull devices such as head halters or harnesses, and simply dog-proofing the house, stowing away food, and placing desirable things out of reach.

(*Text continues on page 134.*)

Table 7.1: Behavior Management Techniques

To Prevent This	Do This
Jumping on visitors to the home	Put the dog in another room when the doorbell rings
Jumping on you when you come home	Throw treats on the ground or a ball to retrieve
Barking at passersby outside	Draw the curtains or restrict the dog's access to the windows
Pulling on the leash	Use an anti-pull head halter or harness
Attacking the water hose	Put the dog inside while you are watering
Chewing on the furniture	Don't allow access; use a baby gate or crate

(Left) Here, he jumps up for a greeting, and treats and praise are withheld. *(Right)* He sits and is rewarded with treats and praise.

Robert J. Schroeder Photography

Substitute sitting for jumping on you by rewarding your puppy only when he is sitting. No punishment is needed, because he learns very quickly that when he sits, he gets what he wants. This allows him to explore different behaviors and make the correct decision.

The puppy will very likely offer this sitting behavior again. If you are consistent in your reactions, soon he will default into a sit position for greetings.

Training Consistent Interactions

This means using everyday situations to train and continually strengthen good manners — without spending a lot of time on dedicated dog training sessions. It boils down to this: Whatever the dog wants, don't give it away for free. Don't open the door just because the dog paws at it; don't throw the ball just because he barks at you. For those and countless other privileges, ask the dog to say "please" first by doing something like sitting quietly.

The benefits of this approach are many. For one thing, good manners become part of everyday routines rather than something the dog is asked to do only in special training situations. Your dog also learns a degree of impulse control. He realizes that not immediately acting on impulse, but rather stopping to consider alternative options, can be rewarding. Training also becomes linked in the dog's mind to all his favorite activities: he will sit for having his leash put on for a walk, he will comply with a request before being invited onto the couch, he will have to look at you before getting his breakfast or a chew toy, and he will release the ball before tossing it again and playing fetch with you. When all good things must be preceded by responding to a cue that you give, your dog quickly learns to behave politely.

The goal isn't to seek the perfect obedient response to "sit" or "stay"; it simply teaches your dog to say "please." If the dog puts his bottom to the floor, the item or attention will be provided. Soon it becomes second nature, and your dog might default into a "sit" behavior instead of jumping or pawing at you. You can then decide whether to ask for an additional behavior, such as "down" or "look." This is also a safety precaution: if your dog defaults into a sit position every time you get ready to open the car door, he will not bolt out and possibly get hurt. If he sits to have his leash put on, he will not run around and you will not have to chase him. This makes taking the dog out a pleasure instead of a struggle.

Use a "please" action before

- throwing a ball, Frisbee, etc.;
- handing over a toy;
- putting the food bowl down;
- giving a treat or chew toy;
- opening a door;
- clipping on a leash to go for a walk;
- taking off a leash at the park or beach;
- delivering a belly rub or a good ear scratch;
- allowing the dog into or out of the car.

Training Solutions

The trick with all nuisance behaviors is to train and reward an opposite or competing behavior. For example, Rowdy can't jump on Anna if he's sitting to greet her. He can't bark at visitors if he has a toy in his mouth, or beg at the dinner table if he is in a down-stay on his bed, or pull on his leash if he's by Anna's side making eye contact every five seconds. Whatever bothersome behavior the dog is engaging in, think of something that would preclude it, and train that behavior consistently.

Table 7.2: Training Alternate Behaviors

To Replace	Train to
Door dashing	Sit or down before opening the door
Eating trash off the ground	Carry a toy or keep eye contact with you
Barking at the doorbell	Get a toy
Digging up the roses	Fetch or hide-and-seek with dog toys
Pawing at you	Put pawing on a cue—so he uses his paw for a "high five" or "wave" when asked

When training any new behavior, especially to replace a well-established nuisance behavior, patience and consistency are key. It can take a while for the dog to give up strategies that have worked for him consistently, but if he is no longer rewarded for them and is instead consistently reinforced for an alternative behavior, he will soon choose that new response every time. Stick with it. Because the unwanted behavior worked in the past, your dog will most likely try it again, but harder, before he will give it up. This is called an "extinction burst." It's a sudden display of a behavior that was diminishing after you stopped rewarding it. It's sort of like your dog saying, "Was she *really* serious about that?" Don't give up; stick with your plan and you will be rewarded.

Can't Wait to Get There . . .

Will and Kristi had only one complaint about their Shepherd-Collie mix, Bo. Bo was well behaved, friendly to people and dogs, and easy around the house, but he was an inveterate puller. As soon as they snapped on the leash and opened the front door to head for the park, the sled-dog impersonation would begin. Kristi and their two kids, twelve and fifteen, walked Bo on a flexible (extendable/retractable) leash. Will, intent on more control, walked Bo on a regular fixed-length leash. Desperate to give their aching shoulders a break, they switched to a choke collar, but that didn't discourage Bo's pulling; he simply wheezed louder and kept going. Thankfully, after an hour's play at the park fetching Frisbees and playing chase with other dogs, Bo would pull considerably less on the way home.

Why didn't Bo ever figure out that pulling was unwanted? Was he dominant? Would "showing him who's boss" have fixed the problem? No! Bo was pulling for one simple reason: He was excited about going to the park, and the faster he moved, the sooner he'd get there. Bo likely pulled as a puppy and young dog, but Will and Kristi did not consider it a problem to worry about or to train another response to at that time. Consequently, Bo was reinforced for pulling on his leash from the outset: it got him where he wanted to go, three times a day. A flexible leash did not allow the family much control or ability to keep

Bo from pulling, and it actually may have encouraged him to forge ahead because the leash extends freely for a while when he pulled. The choke collar may have been uncomfortable, but not enough to cancel out Bo's excitement about the park and the end result: arriving at the park — the ultimate reward!

How to Solve Leash Pulling

1. Use a head collar or front buckle harness with a regular leash, not a flexible leash (see chapter 5).
2. Teach the dog loose-leash walking.
3. Whenever the dog pulls (the leash goes taut), immediately stop walking or turn and walk in the opposite direction. Lesson to the dog: When you pull, you're not going anywhere, or worse, we are going back.
4. When the leash is slack, start walking again.
5. Frequently reward the dog with treats and praise when he walks without pulling, and especially for being right by your side.
6. Walk fast enough for the dog not to get bored and start sniffing and peeing every few minutes.
7. When you allow your dog to sniff and go potty, deliberately stop and let your dog do his business, perhaps signaling with a phrase like "Go sniff" or "Go potty." When you're ready to walk again, say, "Let's go!" That way, the dog knows when it's okay to sniff and when he should begin walking again.
8. Don't vary leash length by stretching out your arm.
9. Be consistent. Everyone in the family should use the same rules, cues, and equipment. Don't ever let the dog pull.

Physical and Mental Stimulation

For dogs and humans alike, physical exercise is fundamental to good health. We all know the couch-potato lifestyle comes with a host of health problems. But in dogs, a lack of activity can also prompt nuisance behaviors. The majority of dogs were bred with a working purpose in mind — and that's not just the herding and hunting breeds. For example, the seemingly dainty Yorkshire Terrier was originally meant for rat hunting. Providing dogs with vigorous, daily exercise has profound effects on their behavior. Tired dogs chew less, bark less, sleep more, and are more likely to relax when home alone.

A good daily workout and, if the dog is social, regular play sessions with other dogs are great ways to exercise a dog. So is time spent interacting with his owners, whether that's playing hide-and-seek in the yard or coming along to the office.

If, like Anna's Rowdy, a dog gets hours of exercise every day and still tears through the trash or disembowels the bedroom pillows, it's safe to assume he lacks mental stimulation. Much as people turn to crossword puzzles, books, chess games, and other brain-vitalizing activities for the fun of mental gymnastics, dogs need to solve doggie problems.

For one thing, dogs are meant to work for their food. When they were in the wild, nobody just handed them a bowl of kibble. Dogs are natural hunters and problem solvers, so the more closely we can mimic this process, in many cases the less troublesome the dog will be to live with. Serving all the dog's meals in a stuffed Kong or treat ball, in food-dispensing devices, or through a game such as hide-and-seek or in food puzzle toys can relieve many nuisance behaviors.

Interesting dog toys are another great way to engage a dog's brain. Dogs have distinct preferences when it comes to toys, so it's worth doing a bit of sleuthing to figure out what hooks a particular dog. Some are never happier than when they get to dissect a stuffed toy; others can spend hours entertaining themselves with a rope toy. Get an assortment and switch them out each day so the dog doesn't have time to get bored. Of course, you want to make sure you use safe toys so your dog does not ingest parts and pieces of his toys. There are especially tough toys available, including a variety of Kong toys, Jolly Balls, Buster Food-Cubes, and the Tug-a-Jug.

My Dog Fights Me Every Time I Try to Clip His Nails

Mark and Jenni have given up on trying to cut Max's nails. As soon as Max sees the nail clippers, he runs and hides under the bed. If

Mark tries to pull him out, Max tries to bite. Jenni can sometimes trick Max into coming out from under the bed by getting his leash and pretending to take him for a walk. Once they have Max restrained, Mark has to sit on him and hold his mouth shut while Jenni tries to clip his nails. All the while Max is yelping, growling, and trying to bite them or the nail clippers. Max has become so difficult that even the groomer and the veterinarian do not want to try to trim his nails.

This is a common scenario in dog-owning households across the nation. Like nail trimming, many grooming and body-care procedures — ear cleaning, toothbrushing, pulling out burrs — can be painfully difficult for dogs and their owners. Dogs' resistance to handling and maintenance is not an attempt at domination, any more than your toddler's resistance to the dentist is. Resistance to these procedures stems from fear, pain, and distrust of the procedure or the person administering it.

Dogs respond to potential threats by either moving away (fleeing) or trying to drive the threat away (fighting). These are natural, biologically hardwired reactions to danger. If you poke a hornet's nest, you understand that the insects will swarm out in defense and try to sting you to drive you away. Similarly, if your dog feels that you are a threat to his safety, he may react aggressively. If your dog first tries to run away and you prevent this by grabbing or holding him, he may turn and try to bite you so you will let go.

Why would the dog you love and who loves you distrust you or think you are a danger to him? Many of the interactions we have with dogs are misinterpreted: what we feel is friendly may be perceived as threatening by the dog. (See chapter 1 on communication.) Additionally, maintenance procedures are activities for which dogs are not naturally prepared. In a wild setting, dogs and their ancestors are not subjected to ear medications, eye cleanings, toothbrushing, and nail trims. A wild animal vehemently guards his feet because legs are used to escape and to hunt; injuries to them often lead to death. Similarly, the only reason a dog living in the wild would be picked up off the ground would be by a predator. These are naturally scary actions to dogs. When your dog rolls over onto his back or play bows and dodges away when you approach with the eye medication, he is trying to politely tell you to stop, that he is worried.

Another reason the dog may mistrust you is if he has had a previous bad experience with a procedure. Perhaps his ears are infected (or once were infected) and putting medication in the ears is quite painful. The dog does not necessarily understand that the medication will make him feel better in the future. He just knows that the procedure hurts *now* — and he's not going to let you do it again!

To add insult to injury, we often get frustrated and angry with our dogs when they behave in an uncooperative, or, especially, in an aggressive manner. This generally leads us to yell at or even spank the dog in an attempt to try to make the dog "submit" and cooperate. Our anger only makes the dog more fearful and distrustful. Now he's not only worried about the procedure, but also his typically sweet and loving owner is "going Mr. Hyde" on him — and those nail trimmers (or ear medication or whatever) signal the transformation. It's another good reason to run when he sees the trimmers come out!

So how do we deal with this problem? First, don't take it personally. The good news is that your dog is not trying to be dominant over you or take control of your life. Grooming resistance doesn't mean he is disrespectful. The bad news is that it *does* mean your dog has not been adequately prepared to feel safe and comfortable with you or someone else doing these procedures. But more good news: you can change this! If a zookeeper can train a rhinoceros to allow someone to poke him with a needle, certainly we can train our dogs to do the same.

Training Dos and Don'ts
First, DON'T try to trick your dog! For example, sneaking up on the dog and administering medication or trimming his nails while he is sleeping will *seriously* harm your relationship with him. Try this often enough, and it may also make your dog afraid to sleep in your presence. He may become hypervigilant when sleeping and begin to defensively snap or bite if approached or wakened. At times, distraction is an appropriate part of the prevention and retraining process, but subterfuge is never acceptable.

DO find a temporary solution to the problem while you are working through training exercises. For example, if your dog's ears need to be medicated, speak to your veterinarian about options for another form of treatment, such as oral medication or a long-acting topical preparation that the veterinarian may have to administer under sedation. If your dog's nails are in serious need of immediate trimming, speak to your veterinarian about having the dog sedated and the nails cut short, to give you time to work with your dog.

DO set up a systematic training plan to methodically work through the issue. Seek the assistance of a qualified behaviorist or trainer, especially if your dog is trying to bite.

DO plan to be patient and work through the problem at a pace that makes it fun and nonconfrontational for both you and your dog. The success you have with one maintenance procedure will help you address other handling issues more easily. As your dog's trust in you and his understanding of what will occur increases, he will become easier to handle overall.

Changing Your Dog's Opinion of the Procedure

For this to work, the training must be done in very small steps. The more afraid or uncooperative your dog is, the more slowly you will need to work through the process. If your dog has a severe reaction (screaming, yelping, struggling, snapping, or biting), plan to spend several weeks or more working through the problem. Your dog might not be aggressive, but if he is squirrelly all over, it makes the task mighty difficult!

What you will need: time, patience, a comfortable place to work with your dog, and, most important, some of your dog's favorite things — treats, toys, whatever he really loves. In a nutshell, you want to accomplish two things:

1. Pair the unsavory experience (such as toothbrushing) with something your dog really loves (such as chicken pieces), so he looks forward to the process.
2. Teach the dog to sit or lie still while you perform the procedure.

Start the training in a place and at a time when your dog is likely to already be relatively calm and relaxed. For example, if your dog is very active, training might best be done after his daily walk but before his dinner; this way, he is a little tired but still hungry. Eliminate other distractions; put other animals away in another room and send the kids off to play.

Using this process, you gradually teach the dog to sit quietly while you approximate — in successive steps — the handling that a maintenance procedure will require. After repeating each step, immediately reward calm behavior with a very yummy treat (keep them small so that you can quickly proceed to the next step). Remember not to go on to a more-challenging step until your dog is very comfortable with the previous step. Here's an example of how you might break a task into small steps:

1. Handle the appropriate body parts — legs and feet for nail trimming, head and ears for ear medication, head and mouth for toothbrushing, and so on.
2. Gently rub his teeth with your finger or bring the nail trimmers within a few inches of his feet.
3. Gently brush his teeth with your finger with toothpaste on it or touch his feet and toes with the nail trimmers.
4. Gently brush his teeth with a gauze pad wrapped around your finger or place the trimmers over a nail but without actually cutting the nail.
5. Brush his teeth with a gauze pad with toothpaste on it or gently cut one toenail.

When the dog is able to reliably and calmly accept one step, move on to the next. You can also apply this basic process to other procedures that you would similarly like your dog to adapt to.

Each step may involve multiple training sessions. The duration of the training sessions will be determined by your patience and how long your dog can stay relaxed but interested. Generally, sessions will run as short as five minutes or as long as thirty minutes. Predictability helps reduce anxiety, so doing the training sessions in the same place, at least

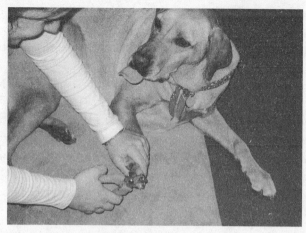

Trimming just the first nail. *Lore I. Haug, DVM*

for the first several sessions, can help. Most maintenance procedures will be easier to do if you sit in a chair or on the floor by the dog, so remember to start your training that way.

Your dog will catch on to the process faster if you use some type of marker signal to tell him the moment when he's done exactly what you want him to do. This could be a particular word (such as *yes, good,* or *sweet*) or a mechanical sound such as a clicker. Be generous also with calm and enthusiastic praise when he is successful.

Marker Signals

A marker signal is a unique sound, such as a clicker, whistle, or special word or noise, that is used to aid the training process. Initially, the sound you choose is always followed by a high-value reinforcer (usually a special treat), and this is repeated over and over until your dog learns to anticipate the treat after hearing the sound. You can use the sound to mark the moment when the dog does a desired behavior — for example, sitting still while you lift his upper lip. (See chapter 3 for more on clicker training.)

Remember that this training should be fun — for both of you! If, at any time, your dog gets nervous, aggressive, or acts as if he does not want to participate in the training session, stop. Next time, start fresh at an earlier step. Back up and make it easier and more fun. Proceed more slowly through the steps.

It is not uncommon for dogs to be easier to handle on one side than the other. So, for example, you may need to work longer on trimming the left paws than the right ones. The "bad" side might need extra work and extra patience on your part. Remember, you are not on a time schedule. Take your time. You might just work on one paw one day and the others on subsequent days. If you are doing this correctly, the whole procedure should be rather mundane for your dog.

How to Train Your Dog to Allow You to Brush His Teeth

Step 1: Sit in your chair with a bowl of high-value dog treats within easy reach (of you but not the dog!). Ask your dog to sit in front of you. Gently place your hands on the dog — one hand on the back of his neck and the other under his jaw.

Teach the dog to stay quietly while you gently hold his head.
Lore I. Haug, DVM

If the dog holds his head still, count one second in your head, use your marker signal (such as a clicker), or if using two hands, use a special phrase or verbal noise, then *pull your hands away* and immediately give him one of the treats from your bowl. This technique gives your dog two rewards when he holds still: you let go of his head and mouth, *plus* he gets the dog treat. Letting go of his head also gives him a little break, so he does not get too nervous or antsy.

If the dog struggles or wiggles a little, leave your hands resting gently on his head until he stops moving, then count one second, use your marker signal or phrase or noise, pull your hands away, and give him a treat. When your dog can hold still for one second three to five times in a row, move on. Ask him to hold still while your hands are on his head for two seconds, then three seconds, and so on, working up to five seconds. He has to be able to hold still at least three times in a row at each time duration before you increase your count. Remember to practice on both sides of his head and mouth.

Step 2: Now, repeat what you did in step 1, but begin moving your hands farther forward on your dog's head. Your goal is obviously to get your dog to allow you to touch and hold his muzzle as well as to lift his lips on both sides of his mouth.

Place one hand on the top of your dog's head and the other hand under his jaw or chin. Repeat your one-second count if he holds still. If he moves his head, keep your hands gently on his head until he stops, then count one second, use your marker signal or phrase or noise, let go, and give him his treat. As in step 1, increase your time count by one-second intervals after your dog is successful at least three times in a row.

Step 3: Move both hands forward on your dog's head so that one hand is gently covering his eyes and the other is under his jaw or chin. Do your count and use your marker signal, then reward him if he keeps his head still.

Step 4: Hold his head gently and use one of your fingers to lift his upper lip on one side of his muzzle. If he remains quiet and still for one second, use your marker signal or phrase or noise, pull your hands away, and give him his treat. What a good boy! As in previous steps, increase the time you ask him to hold still by one-second increments, and remember to practice on both sides of his head and mouth.

Lift the upper lip. *Lore I. Haug, DVM*

Step 5: When your dog will allow you to hold his muzzle, lift his upper lip, and pull the corner of his lip backward (so you can see the larger molar teeth in the back of his mouth), then you can begin "brushing." Hold his mouth gently, lift his upper lip, and use your finger to gently rub his front teeth for one to two seconds. If he holds his head still and is calm, use your marker signal or phrase or noise, let go, and give him his treat. Repeat on both sides of his mouth at least three to five times before trying to "brush" a larger area or farther back in his mouth. Rub only small areas of his mouth at a time so he gets frequent rewards during the process. As you practice this more, you can gradually rub larger sections of his teeth at one time.

Step 6: Repeat step 5, but use a small amount of canine toothpaste on your finger when you rub the teeth. (Do not use human toothpaste; only use toothpaste made specifically for dogs.)

Step 7: Repeat the training steps using a gauze pad wrapped around your finger to acclimate your dog to the additional friction and the feeling of something in his mouth besides just your finger. Remember to start with small sections of his teeth at first, and be sure he will hold still at least three times in a row before you move to a new or larger area. Continue to use your marker signal or phrase or noise and reward the dog each time he holds his head and mouth still.

Brush the teeth with a gauze pad. *Lore I. Haug, DVM*

Voilà! Now you and your dog can enjoy calm toothbrushing! Think of how much less stress you will have and how much healthier your dog's mouth will be. It will save on veterinary bills too, because your dog won't need as much professional dental care.

If, during any of the steps, your dog displays an aggressive response, such as growling, stop whatever you are doing and simply do not provide a reward. Wait a few seconds until your dog is relaxed again, and return to a previously acceptable step so you can now provide a reinforcer. Then proceed more slowly in working your way up to the step that elicited the aggressive response. If the aggression continues, please contact your veterinarian or a veterinary behaviorist for advice.

This systematic process can be used to teach your dog to lie still while you trim his nails or accept eye or ear medication, as well.

Avoiding Pitfalls and Staying on Track

- Remove all rewards or reinforcement for nuisance behaviors. That is, ignore the dog completely when he performs a nuisance behavior, and instead praise and treat the dog for sitting, being quiet, chewing on his toys, and other desirable behaviors.
- Be consistent. If jumping up on people is allowed on the weekends, the dog won't understand that the rules change during the week. Dogs don't discriminate between days or jeans and office attire.
- Be persistent. After repeated reinforcement (however unintended) of a nuisance behavior, the dog won't immediately abandon his original strategy. But sooner or later, the light bulb will go on and he'll understand the new and better way to get what he wants. And remember, dogs, like people, may revert to a strategy that worked in the past; just ignore him and ask for the new behavior.
- Appreciate your dog's dogness. Okay, dogs steal food and jump and do obnoxious things to capture our attention. They are dogs. But we couldn't teach them a high-five or snuggle with them on the couch if they were goldfish. And if we spend a little time teaching them which behaviors we like, we can get the best of both worlds — nice manners *and* devoted companionship.

What Did We Say?

Sure, changing a behavior sounds easy here. Admittedly, putting the steps into practice can sometimes be challenging. It helps if all family members are involved and practice a consistent training plan. Just keep in mind the basics.

- Manage the situation so the dog can't keep practicing and learning undesirable behaviors.
- Make sure your dog is getting adequate mental and physical exercise. Dogs aren't toys to be put out of mind and sight and then entertained only when we feel like it (see chapter 9).
- Put the dog on a say-"please" program that essentially involves giving the dog desirable things only when he is behaving calmly and politely.
- Begin a systematic training program to teach the dog to behave in a more desirable manner. Remember, you get what you reinforce, so it is important to give your dog things he desires only when he behaves the way you like. Don't take good behavior for granted.
- An ounce of prevention really *is* worth a pound of cure. So if your dog isn't having any of these issues, take some steps to keep it that way. Let him know when he's doing a great job for putting up with the weird and sometimes painful things you may subject him to.

8

Lassie and Timmy: Kids and Dogs
Creating a Family That Works

Valarie V. Tynes, DVM, DACVB

Carol was devastated. She had owned Sweetpea, a female Miniature Poodle, for four years when she became pregnant with her first child. Sweetpea had always seemed to have the perfect name to describe her demeanor — such a sweet and friendly dog.

Sweetpea was fine when the baby was first brought home, sniffing him but showing minimal interest. But when the baby began crawling, Sweetpea at first tried to avoid the baby and growled when he approached her. Carol was surprised but told Sweetpea, "No!" and then held the dog in her arms so that the baby could pet her. After some initial struggling, Sweetpea allowed this petting, but her ears were pinned back flat against her head, and the whites of her eyes were showing. Sweetpea trembled and panted.

Two days later, Carol heard the baby screaming and ran into the living room to see that Sweetpea had apparently bitten the baby on the head. Thankfully, the bite looked superficial. "Bad dog!" Carol yelled at Sweetpea as Sweetpea cowered under a chair. That evening when Carol's husband returned home from work, she sobbed as she told him what had happened. "I guess we are going to have to give Sweetpea away. I never thought she would be jealous of the baby, but we can't keep her if she is going to be mean to him!"

Sadly, this is a story veterinarians hear too often. Many dog owners do not realize that the gentlest, most beloved dog can see small children as threatening, and behave in a defensive manner that is perfectly normal from the dog's perspective. Many people expect every dog to be like Lassie — able to read every nuance of human emotion and behavior and respond to any command — but most dogs are not.

Facts, Not Fiction

Owning a dog has many benefits for children. Helping to care for a pet can help a child learn about empathy and compassion as well as the joys and challenges associated with caring for another being. Bringing an animal into the home, especially the average urban home, helps a child make a valuable connection with the natural world. The special companionship provided by a pet can greatly enhance the life of most any child. When children are old enough, they can also participate in the care and training of the dog and learn how to be responsible for another life. But those benefits are possible only if parents take an active role in ensuring that children know how to behave properly around dogs and that dogs are well socialized and trained.

Is That Really True?

One recent study found that almost three-quarters of dog-bite injuries to children could have been prevented if the parents and the children had been educated about safe and appropriate behavior around dogs. In other words, *most dog bites* (to children, in particular) *can be prevented.* The first step in doing so is understanding what is and is not true about dogs and children. Let's take a look at some common myths.

My dog is jealous of my child. When a dog attempts to insert herself between you and your child, it's tempting to interpret this as jealousy. But the dog is simply seeking some attention at a moment when she seems likely to get it. Often, the dog picks this time because you are displaying body language and using a tone of voice with your child that's a lot like the way you interact with your dog — soft eyes, crouching down, speaking in a happy voice. So the dog thinks it's time to be with you. In some cases, the dog may receive less attention when a family has a child, so it's normal for the dog to seek attention when she's getting less.

If the dog is also afraid of the child, and the child approaches at the same time that the dog is seeking attention and possibly comfort from you, the dog may growl or snap at the child — not out of jealousy, but because the dog fears the approach of the child. In fact, fear and the lack of appropriate socialization — not dominance or jealousy — are much more likely explanations for canine displays of aggression toward children.

Most children, due to their small size, interact with dogs at the dog's eye level, something a dog might see as threatening. The high-pitched voices of small children and their erratic movements can also seem very frightening. In the dog world, frightening interactions are avoided by growling or snapping to ward off the threat.

When Does a Wagging Tail Mean "Come Pet Me"?

As mentioned in chapter 1, a wagging tail indicates a willingness to interact; sometimes that may be in a friendly or happy way, but other times it can be in a defensive or aggressive way.

Young children are unlikely to be able to tell the difference and should not approach dogs who are unfamiliar to them without permission from a responsible adult. Older children can be taught to make sure a dog is "loose and floppy" in the rest of her body language before even considering an interaction with any dog. If in doubt, they should always err on the side of caution, which means they should walk away.

My dog is trying to be dominant over my child. Scientific studies of dog behavior have demonstrated that domestic dogs do not try to form hierarchies with humans. Most aggression directed toward humans occurs because the dog is anxious or afraid and is attempting to ward off something or someone that she sees as threatening to her safety. When dogs look away with tucked ears and tail while trying to avoid a child (the way Sweetpea did), they are clearly saying that they fear this little stranger. Since young children, and often parents as well, are unable to interpret this behavior correctly, they may continue approaching and attempting to interact with the dog, regardless of the fearful behavior shown by the dog. (For more information on interpreting aggressive responses, see chapters 1 and 10.) Tragically, this scenario often ends with the child being bitten. If that happens, the dog may no longer be trusted. The human-animal bond suffers as a result, and the dog may be euthanized.

Young children, who do not yet understand appropriate interactions with dogs, can do things that increase the chance that a dog's behavior will escalate from an aggressive display to an actual bite. In studies done in 2007 and 2010, veterinary behaviorist Dr. Ilana Reisner studied dog bites to children under eighteen years of age. Children under the age of six were most often bitten when they approached a dog who was near a resource (something important to the dog, such as food or a toy) or while the dog was resting. Usually the dog was not moving and was approached by the child. Children older than six were most often bitten when entering the dog's territory. And most children were bitten by a dog they knew.

By recognizing the early warning signs of guarding behavior, owners can prevent injury by avoiding the dog when it has a resource, separating her from the family while she is eating, or seeing a veterinary behaviorist for information on treating the problem. Once we understand what a dog might regard as threatening from a child, such as encroachment on resources or territory, we can create environments that are safer both for children and dogs.

What Does That Mean?

Resource guarding: Behavior a dog shows to another individual who is attempting to remove something the dog values. Resource guarding may occur even if the dog simply *thinks* someone is attempting to remove a valued resource. The behavior may be obvious, such as growling or snapping, or subtle, such as stiffening, lifting the lip, stopping eating or chewing, or hovering over the item the dog is trying to guard.

Safe refuge: A spot in the home where the dog can go to avoid situations that induce fear or anxiety. All family members are taught not to bother the dog in any way while she is in her safe refuge.

Fear response: Fear is a feeling of apprehension about a situation or object. The fear response in an animal is the behavior shown when experiencing fear. The response also includes physiological changes, such as increasing heart and respiration rates, as well as visual cues, such as flattening the ears, lowering the head and tail, and avoidance behaviors.

Avoidance behaviors: These behaviors are exhibited by dogs when they are afraid of a particular stimulus that they would like to escape. The dog may lower her head, flatten her ears, lower her body, and then actively try to back away from or completely leave the area where the scary stimulus is present. If a dog leaves the room every time a particular person or animal enters, she may be demonstrating avoidance behaviors.

Cowering: When a fearful or anxious dog tucks her tail, flattens her ears, drops her head, and lowers her body toward the floor, this may be described as cowering. It is as if the dog is trying to make her body look smaller to avoid the attention of someone or something that seems threatening.

Where Do We Begin When Children Enter the Home?

In Carol's case, Sweetpea is not jealous of the new baby. Even so, is Sweetpea a vicious dog who cannot be trusted around children? Should she be euthanized or rehomed? The fact is that Sweetpea did not grow up around children, so when the baby began crawling around the house, Sweetpea was naturally frightened of this strange newcomer who was nothing like the humans she already knew.

How can we help our dogs learn about children? As puppies develop, they go through a socialization period between roughly six and fourteen weeks of age (more about that in chapter 6). Puppies who are not exposed to a wide variety of people, animals, environments, sights, and sounds are more likely to be frightened or unusually reactive as adults when they are exposed to new or novel experiences, including children. Young human children behave very differently than adults do. They move rapidly and erratically, make high-pitched sounds, and approach dogs at eye level, which many dogs find inherently frightening.

Of course, not all dogs, even those who have not been socialized to children, will be afraid. But dogs with limited experience with children, or those showing signs of anxiety or fear, need owners to pay attention to the messages they send and keep them safe. Owners must allow a dog to avoid the child when she wants to. For example, using a child gate so that the newly toddling baby cannot chase after the dog helps to keep both the dog and the child safe. We must actively teach the dog that the child is safe to be around and actually predicts good things: new parents can toss treats to their dog and praise her when she approaches the baby in a calm manner. By providing positive experiences for the dog (play, feeding, and attention) when the child is present and minimizing these interactions when the child is not, we help the dog learn that good things happen when the child is around.

All dogs must have a safe place away from the child (such as a crate or bed in a less-busy area of the house), where the child is not allowed to approach or interact with the dog. Child gates are excellent for this, and no household with children and pets should be without at least one.

So what about Sweetpea and her behavior with the new baby?

When we're afraid, we generally look like we are afraid, and often we say so. Sweetpea did attempt to say she was afraid by growling and trying to avoid the baby. And no doubt she looked afraid as well. When Carol held Sweetpea and forced her to allow the baby to pet her, Carol was unintentionally heightening Sweetpea's fear. Sweetpea did not feel less frightened about the baby because he was stroking her; she felt trapped and helpless. It's likely she felt her only choice was to bite.

Sweetpea's owners, and any parents who want to do more to improve their dog's relationship with their child, should consult a professional behaviorist. The dog's behavior may be safely changed using appropriate behavior modification techniques. (See chapter 3 for more information about how dogs learn.)

Predatory Behavior

Predatory behaviors are used by an animal to find, chase, and kill prey. When a dog sees an animal she believes to be prey, she will initially become very silent and still. She will stare at the prey and then slowly and quietly begin to move toward it. If allowed, the dog will then grab the prey and shake it.

Unfortunately, some dogs have very high prey drives, and this can lead to them hunting small animals such as cats or squirrels, even when the dog is well fed. Some dogs may even behave in a predatory fashion when they see a very small dog. These behaviors can be very distressing for most dog owners, who do not perceive their dogs as skilled predators.

Of even greater concern is the dog who looks at small infants as prey. While this is relatively rare, owners should pay attention to their dog's behavior when they first bring home their new baby and when the baby first begins to crawl. If the dog stares intently at the baby and follows the child very quietly, parents should immediately consult their veterinarian for a referral to a qualified behaviorist.

How Do We Work with Dogs Who Are Afraid of Children?

It is critical that dogs who display signs of fear, aggression, or avoidance behavior *not* be punished for the behavior. Forcing a dog into any situation when she is showing fearful behaviors can make the dog's fear much worse. Punishment is more likely to increase fear and aggression, not make the dog feel better about the presence of the child.

The general health of the dog is also a factor in good relationships between children and dogs. Like people, when a dog is ill or is experiencing pain or discomfort from conditions such as arthritis or is accidentally hurt by the child, she may respond aggressively. Young children do not have good control of their motor skills and may fall on or step on a dog or pet the dog roughly. Children under the age of three or four do not yet recognize that others experience pain and discomfort, and often they inadvertently handle a dog too roughly, hurt her, and provoke an aggressive response.

Many problems between children and dogs can be avoided if adults better understand the nature of fear in dogs. Even dogs who grew up around children are likely to be afraid of them and show subtle signs of fear if they have not had good experiences with children. Parents should watch for the following behaviors and signs of fear:

- The dog slinks away from the child, cowers, tries to leave the room, or otherwise avoids the child.
- The dog tucks her tail or flattens her ears or looks away when the child approaches.
- The dog licks her lips frequently, yawns, or suddenly starts scratching or licking herself — signs of anxiety or nervousness — when the child approaches.
- The dog snarls or growls when the child approaches.
- The dog snaps at children.

If you see any of these behaviors in a dog, immediately remove the child to a safe area and confine the dog to an area where she can also feel safe. If you see these behaviors every time the dog is around children, seek assistance from a veterinary behaviorist or other qualified behavior professional, such as a Certified Applied Animal Behaviorist. If that is not possible, prepare to keep the dog separated from children at all times until the dog can be taught that children are not to be feared. And don't forget, painful interactions can occur when children reach for or grab a dog. Also, any dog can have a medical problem (dental disease, ear infection, arthritis) that makes her less tolerant of interactions with children.

Can a Dalmatian Change His Spots?

Willie, a six-year-old male Dalmatian, was seen by his veterinarian one Monday morning for euthanasia, after having bitten a child the day before. His veterinarian, knowing that Willie had been around many children before and had never shown aggression in the past, was shocked.

This was the story his owner, Paula, had to tell: A friend and her six-year-old son had spent the weekend at Paula's home. Several times throughout the weekend, the child had been admonished for pestering Willie while he slept or ate.

On Sunday afternoon, while everyone was in the living room watching TV, Paula noticed the child approach Willie where he lay sleeping on the couch. Since the adults were focused mostly on the television, they did not see exactly what happened next. But they turned when they heard Willie snarl and were just in time to see Willie lunge forward and bite the child on the face.

The bite was severe enough that they immediately rushed the child to the emergency room. Paula was shocked and very upset by Willie's sudden, vicious behavior and admitted that if an animal emergency clinic had been nearby, her next stop would have been to have Willie euthanized.

The veterinarian was really taken aback by this story. Before euthanizing Willie, he performed a thorough physical exam. What he found were ten bright red, crescent-shaped marks on Willie's face where the child had grabbed him and dug his fingernails into Willie's skin. When the owner realized that Willie had been harmed by the child, she understood that maybe his behavior was not so inappropriate after all. She chose to take him home, promising that she would never again put him in such a difficult situation.

Realistic Expectations

Tom and Mary Anne made an appointment to evaluate their two-year-old Labrador Retriever, Cassie. Tom was furious because Cassie had begun growling at their three- and six-year-old girls. Tom explained that he chose a Lab because "they were supposed to be so good with kids." His brother had a Lab who was "great with kids; he allows them to ride him and pull his tail and pretty much do whatever they want to him." Tom said he expected his dog to do the same.

Unfortunately, Tom's attitudes are common and represent the very unrealistic expectations many people have for their dogs. While some dogs may tolerate some rough handling from children, they are not appropriate interactions for children of any age. It's unfair to expect any dog to accept this sort of harsh treatment — even for dogs who do tolerate kids pulling on their ears or yanking their tail. The lesson the kids learn puts them in danger if they come to believe that all dogs can be handled roughly. At some point, while they are young, many children will come in contact with an unfamiliar dog, and they must be prepared to interact appropriately, for their own safety as well as the dog's.

In addition, if we expect children to learn about responsibility to others, compassion, and empathy, the lessons should start early, with

By approaching head-on, staring, and reaching over the dog, this child is approaching in a way the dog may view as threatening.

By avoiding eye contact and squatting next to the dog, the child is less threatening. The child is stroking the dog on the back using long, gentle strokes rather than patting the dog.

M. C. Tynes

their first experiences around animals. They can learn these lessons only if an adult teaches them. Therefore, although young children lack refined motor skills and may unintentionally interact roughly with a dog, the parents must supervise and teach kind and gentle interactions at all times.

Avoiding Pitfalls and Staying on Track

At home, infants and children should *never* be left unattended with dogs. A responsible adult should always be present supervising their interactions. The age at which a child may be alone with the dog varies, both with the individual development of the child and the temperament of the dog. Generally speaking, children under the age of five should not be alone with dogs, and children older than that may need varying degrees of supervision.

Teach children to be respectful of the dog's needs. As soon as they are old enough to take direction, children should be taught the following:

- Do not stare at dogs.
- Do not try to hug dogs; while the dog may tolerate hugging from adults, a hug may be unwanted and threatening from a child. Remember, hugging is not a natural behavior for dogs. Although many learn to enjoy the interaction, some do not, especially from unfamiliar people and children.
- Do not approach a dog who is eating or resting.
- A dog is a living, breathing animal and should be handled with kindness, gentleness, and respect, just like people.
- Use teaching resources made for children, such as *The Blue Dog*, a parent guide and CD available in the United States from the American Veterinary Medical Association (order online at www.avma.org/KB/K12/Pages/AVMA-Products-The-Blue-Dog.aspx).

Until children are old enough to be taught proper behavior around dogs and reliably act in a respectful manner, it is the parents' responsibility to keep dog and child separated when close, constant supervision is not possible. Obviously, this varies from family to family and dog to dog. Generally, very young children under five are not reliable in their interactions with family pets.

Often when a family seeks help from a veterinary behaviorist, the history shows several early signs of canine discomfort (head turning, avoidance behavior, snarling) in interactions between the child and the dog. These signs must never be ignored, but instead should be used as the basis for understanding the relationship between the child and the dog; they usually mean that intervention by a qualified specialist is needed.

WHEN AWAY FROM home, children and parents should know never to approach a dog who is loose and on her own. If the dog is accompanied by an adult, it is best to always ask permission before attempting to interact with the dog. If permission is given, consider these cautions to avoid frightening the dog and risking an aggressive response:

- Don't stare; stand with your side toward the dog, speak in a quiet, friendly voice, and allow the dog to approach first. Do not attempt to pet until the dog has sniffed and shown interest in interacting. (The previous photos show how not to and how to correctly approach a dog.)
- If the dog moves away, assume the dog does not want to interact; stop your approach and ignore her.
- Don't immediately extend your hand over the dog's head. Some dogs find this approach frightening.

If the dog shows interest and continues to try to interact, gently stroke her back, ears, or under her chin. Use slow, long strokes and avoid patting, because many dogs do not seem to enjoy this. If any dog growls at you, stop and slowly move away from the dog. If a dog runs at you, never turn and run away. Stand very still with your hands tucked under your arms or around your ears (see the photo). If you fall down, curl up in a ball with your arms wrapped around your head and neck and lie very still.

Remember, young children, especially those under the age of five and possibly until they are ten, should never be left unattended with dogs. No matter how gentle and well-behaved the dog, accidents can happen in the blink of an eye! Worse yet is that if a growl, snap, or bite occurs without an adult present, it is impossible to know exactly what happened.

Supervision may not prevent all aggressive encounters, but if some-

This boy is standing very still with his arms around his head, demonstrating the proper pose if a dog approaches you in an aggressive manner. *M. C. Tynes*

thing happens and an adult witnesses the episode, it can give the veterinary behaviorist valuable information — including whether the child hurt or frightened the dog and whether the dog is very intolerant of children approaching. This information can help the veterinary behaviorist better assess the situation and devise the best management and treatment plan, while realistically assessing the prognosis. In addition, if parents are always supervising, they can actively participate in teaching the child and the dog what to do and what not to do.

Never Use Punishment

Punishment and verbal corrections for the dog's avoidance and warning behaviors (such as looking away, licking lips, or growling) are not helpful and will not solve the problem. These things don't lessen the dog's fear, and in fact may cause the dog to associate the presence of the child with unpleasant outcomes — in other words, may make things worse.

Imagine if you were afraid of elevators and someone forced you into an elevator and then yelled at you while you struggled and fought to get away. Imagine if you trembled and sweated, and their response was a punch in the nose. Do you think this would help you feel less afraid of riding in elevators? At worst, dogs who are punished for exhibiting avoidance and warning signs of aggression may stop warning and proceed next time straight to biting.

Safe Refuge

While forcing a dog to interact with a child is a bad idea, allowing the dog to avoid the situation by giving her a way out is a great idea. Your dog should always have a safe refuge to avoid the excitement and stress associated with a busy family. Safe refuge for a dog can be anywhere in the home where the dog can go to avoid situations that induce fear or anxiety. The sanctuary can be a crate in an out-of-the-way place, a dog bed in a quiet bedroom or office — anywhere the dog can go to be on her own. What is important is that the safe refuge is always easily available to the dog and that the dog is taught that she can go to her safe refuge whenever she wants to avoid scary or uncomfortable situations. It is also critical that all family members are taught to respect the dog's right to separate herself from the family by not bothering her in any way while she is in her safe refuge. So the kids *must* be taught to leave the dog alone when she is in her safe refuge.

Planning a safe refuge for the dog *before* a new baby (or any child) arrives is an essential, necessary, and, for the dog, a welcome step. To begin training, separate the dog from you for a few minutes at a time while you are present nearby but otherwise occupied. This should be fun for your dog and should not make her feel anxious. Give the dog a special treat during these sessions and use a cue such as "quiet time" to help the dog understand what is expected. Gradually increase the amount of time the dog is left alone. Always give her treats when she is being quiet, and never respond to whining or barking or let her out of the crate or from behind a baby gate when she is complaining. (For more tips on crate training, see the appendix.) If your dog seems extremely distressed about being separated from you, contact your veterinarian right away so the problem can be addressed before the child arrives.

If the dog will not be confined, she could be taught to just go to a place and remain there, but she should not be disturbed and should be out of the way of children. Teach the dog to use and enjoy this quiet place by providing long-lasting chew toys or food puzzle toys (such as Kongs, Kibble Nibbles, and Tug-a-Jugs) in her safe refuge. Give the dog these toys when children are not present, to avoid potential problems with resource guarding. They can also be given as rewards for resting quietly in the safe refuge.

Plan Ahead

If you are getting a dog and have children or plan to have them, here are some things to keep in mind:

- Very small or delicate breeds, such as Yorkshire Terriers, Chihuahuas, and Toy Poodles, can easily be picked up and therefore easily injured by rough handling, which may occur inadvertently from small children with limited motor skills.
- Breeds with a tendency to chase moving things — for example, some of the sighthounds, such as Afghan Hounds and Deerhounds, and herding breeds, such as Australian Shepherds and Border Collies — may direct these breed tendencies toward children, who move quickly in play, requiring additional supervision and training. (See chapter 2 for more information about choosing a dog.) In addition, your veterinarian is an excellent source of information to help you choose the best pet for you and your family.
- If possible, acquire your puppy from a breeder who has children in the household or has arranged for frequent, gentle handling by children. Or you could rescue a dog who has spent time in a foster home where that family can tell you if the dog has been around children.
- Take every possible opportunity to expose your puppy to children of all ages and sizes during the first three to twelve months of her

life. Have children offer the puppy delicious treats upon meeting. Remember, supervise closely to be sure the kids do not play too roughly and accidentally frighten or hurt the dog.

- Teach your dog to go to a safe and quiet place where she will be undisturbed.
- Make sure your kids know to leave the dog alone when she is in her safe refuge.
- Plan to confine the dog while children are eating, so that she does not learn to lick or snap at children for food.
- Teach basic manners to your dog and have good verbal control of her behaviors, including "sit," "down," "stay," and "go to your bed."
- Teach basic manners to your kids about how to handle the dog and when to leave her alone.

Preparing Your Dog for a New Arrival

Planning ahead for how your schedule will change and implementing some of those changes before the arrival of a new baby can greatly decrease stress for dog and family, giving everyone time to adjust to the new schedule and environment. For example, what if Mom is the one who takes the dog for walks during the day but suspects she will not have time or that walks will be shorter once the baby arrives? Another adult can begin walking the dog on her regular schedule, decreasing the time allotted for walks, before the baby comes.

Life gets hectic when a baby is added to the family, and it may be necessary to separate the dog and child, particularly when the child begins crawling and toddling. Start by buying any equipment you may need for separation — baby gates or a crate for the dog. Then spend time working on teaching your dog how to be comfortable in her safe refuge. (See the section "Safe Refuge" earlier in this chapter.) Remember to start slowly.

Some baby equipment may seem scary to a dog, such as strollers, walkers, swings, playpens, play mats, and Pack 'n Plays. Try to introduce some of this equipment before the baby arrives, so the dog can become familiar with it. Remember, activity centers and swings are not safe places to leave a baby unsupervised while a dog is present. The dog should be behind a baby gate or in her crate when a baby is in one of these, unless a responsible adult is present and supervising. Supervising means *actually* being present, so if you leave the room, even briefly, a crib or playpen may be the safer place to put the baby.

New Baby Checklist

- Make any changes in the schedule or environment *before* baby comes home.
- Desensitize your dog to noises and items associated with babies. Consider using an audio recording, such as the ones available at www.soundtherapy4pets.co.uk.
- Practice walking the dog with a stroller alongside.
- Plan for controlled, careful initial introductions between the dog and new baby. (See the section "Bringing Home Baby" later in this chapter.)
- Consider denying the dog access to elevated surfaces (sofas and beds, for example) when the child becomes more mobile, by giving the dog her own separate and safe resting place instead. There is a greater risk of the child approaching the dog while she is resting on a couch or chair and possibly triggering a territorial or re-source-guarding response. The added concern here is that the child's face may be more vulnerable to a severe bite when the dog is elevated.
- Speak with your veterinarian if your dog has a history of growling or snapping around food, treats, toys, or unfamiliar people. Your veterinarian may refer you to a veterinary behaviorist before the baby arrives.

If you plan on sleeping with the baby in your bed but the dog currently sleeps with you, begin long before the baby is born to change the dog's sleeping habits. Give her a new dog bed, near your bed if possible, and with praise and patience the dog can learn to sleep in her own bed. This can be difficult at first, and sometimes tethering the dog where she can only be in her own bed will help with this process. Waiting until after the baby comes home to make these types of changes only makes them more stressful for everyone.

Some dogs are helped by getting them used to the noises associated with babies. This process of gradually getting accustomed to something new is called "habituation." There are excellent commercial recordings available to help with this. (See suggestion in the "New Baby Checklist.") These recordings include all kinds of sounds, including crying babies. Playing them at a very low volume while feeding the dog very special treats can help the dog associate good feelings with those sounds rather than associate feelings of fear or anxiety. Over time, increase the volume. If the dog acts anxious (panting, licking, ears back), you've pumped up the volume too far too fast. If you begin working on this several months before the baby is born, spending just a few minutes every day, the dog is likely to be much more comfortable with the sounds associated with the baby.

Dogs are very aware of smells in their environment and eagerly wish to investigate any new odor. Bring her some of the baby's clothing or blankets before the baby actually comes home, and allow the dog to sniff these items and familiarize herself with the smells associated with the newborn, including all baby-care products. Keep in mind, many dogs quickly adjust to these changes and no special arrangements will be needed.

If you have friends or relatives with babies or young children who are calm around dogs, invite them to spend time at your home so your dog can experience and adapt to the presence of young people. Having the parents of the infant, or the young children themselves, toss treats to your dog can help develop a positive association with children for your dog.

If you live in an apartment, condominium, or other home where it is necessary to take your dog for regular walks, especially for elimination, begin practicing walking the dog while also pushing a stroller. Bring the stroller into the home and allow the dog to become familiar with its presence. If the dog is afraid of moving objects, rolling the stroller back and forth while giving the dog treats may help associate the stroller with something pleasant. When the dog is comfortable with the presence of the stroller, begin walking her with the empty stroller alongside.

If the dog is a challenge to walk (tugging and pulling on the leash, for example), consider using a canine head halter (such as a Gentle Leader or Halti) or a no-pull body harness (such as Easy Walk or Freedom Harness). These devices are excellent aids allowing for good, safe control of the pulling dog. (See chapter 5 for more information about tools you can use to make walking the dog easier.) Also, use these walks to practice basic obedience skills with the dog. Improving the dog's responsiveness to requests such as "sit," "stay," and "come," before a new baby arrives, will make it easier for the dog to be safely included in family activities. If the dog continues to show signs of distress or makes walking with a stroller difficult, seek help from your veterinarian or a veterinary behaviorist for a more complete training program or for a referral to a qualified trainer.

If your dog exhibits excessive attention-seeking behaviors, such as pawing, barking, or jumping, these problems should also be addressed before baby arrives. If you have a dog who has previously shown signs of aggression around food, treats, or toys, consult a qualified veterinary behaviorist *before* trying any of the exercises described here. But remember, all dogs deserve to eat in peace and quiet. Find a secure room or crate to feed the dog to prevent interruptions during her mealtimes.

Older Dogs and New Babies

An aging or geriatric dog may have an especially difficult time when new children join the family. As dogs age and develop more aches and pains, they are likely to be less tolerant of any roughhousing or even accidental injury by a child.

Be empathetic with your senior dog. It's not fair to expect her to interact with children in the same way that a young dog might. It will be even more critical that the old girl has a safe refuge to get away from the hustle and bustle of a household with children. And always seek veterinary help to ease any pain or treat any illnesses in an elderly dog. (See chapter 14 for more about old dogs.)

Bringing Home Baby

When it is finally time to bring your little one home, careful planning can ensure that your dog's first exposure to the new baby is a positive one. It might be best for the new mother to greet the dog empty-handed while the other parent holds the baby, especially if greetings tend to be vigorous. Once the initial greetings are over and the dog has calmed down, it's time to introduce the dog to the baby.

Make sure that the introduction takes place when the baby is either sleeping or awake, but not crying. Have the dog on a leash with a responsible adult controlling the leash. The other parent can sit with the baby and allow the dog to approach and sniff the baby. If the dog is easily excitable or very nervous, do this gradually, with the person holding the leash frequently calling the dog back to them and giving treats while rewarding the dog for staying calm. If the dog becomes too excited, gently take her away and engage in some play with a toy, or give the dog treats in exchange for her responding to some simple requests, such as "sit." Or take her to her prearranged safe refuge.

- Never punish the dog in this situation for acting too excited or fearful. This will only cause her to associate unpleasant experiences with the baby. Simply remove her from the situation if she becomes too unruly and try a gradual introduction again the next day.
- Never force the dog to investigate the baby. Allow your pup to approach when she is ready but always under your supervision and control.
- Never dangle the baby in front of the dog for the dog to sniff. Allow the dog to approach and sniff the baby's legs. Dogs have an excellent sense of smell; even if the baby is several feet away and the dog is sniffing the air and showing interest, the dog is becoming familiar with the baby's scent in a very relaxed and nonthreatening situation.
- Give the dog treats while she remains comfortable in the baby's presence, to help reinforce a positive association with the baby.
- If the dog freezes or stiffens and stares intently at the baby for

more than a few seconds, calmly and quietly remove the dog and contact your veterinarian before attempting any further introductions.

Ted and Paula sought a behavioral consultation a few months after bringing home their first child, Shawn. They were concerned that their dog, Truffles, was moping around the house whenever Paula was busy with the baby, and when the baby was placed in his crib for a nap, Truffles became very excited and pestered Paula extensively for attention. Paula realized that she did not have as much time for Truffles as she used to and worried that Truffles would be jealous of the new baby.

They were really hoping that Truffles and Shawn would become good friends as they grew older together. Fortunately, Ted and Paula had been very careful about not leaving Truffles unattended with the baby, and Truffles had not shown any aggression toward the baby or shown any fear associated with the baby or any of the baby's items. There were several things that could be done to help Truffles view the baby in a more positive light:

- Pay more attention to Truffles when the baby is present rather than when the baby is sleeping or in another room. This can be done by talking to the dog in an upbeat tone and verbally rewarding her for calm, appropriate behaviors or tossing her treats just for approaching and behaving calmly. This way, Truffles learns to associate good things with the presence of the baby.
- Ignore all of Truffles's attention-seeking behaviors, such as pawing or jumping.
- Always walk Truffles when taking the baby out in the stroller. If possible, avoid walking Truffles at other times, so she associates the fun of the walks with the presence of the baby.
- Whenever it is necessary for Truffles to be separated from the baby by the baby gate, give her a very special long-lasting treat, such as a food puzzle toy, so she views these separations as pleasant distractions.
- Have a bowl of Truffles's food by the owners' side when sitting

and rocking or feeding the baby. Toss Truffles a piece of kibble every time she approaches and makes eye contact with you. Once she is doing that comfortably, ask her to perform a behavior she knows, such as "sit," and toss her a kibble for approaching, sitting, and making eye contact.

- Hide-and-seek is another fun game to play while holding the baby, especially if the baby is in a sling. Ask Truffles to sit and stay while you walk to another room with the baby. Then call Truffles, saying, "Where is Shawn?" in an excited, happy tone of voice. When Truffles finds you and the baby, toss her a treat.

Two months later, Paula reported that Truffles had really been enjoying the changes in the routine. She reported that Truffles seemed more comfortable just sitting quietly in the room when she was busy with Shawn, and that Truffles got excited whenever the stroller was brought out of the closet for a walk because Truffles knew that she would get to go out too. Overall, Truffles seemed more calm and relaxed around the baby. This was very helpful, and Paula said that she enjoyed Truffles's company more, too!

So Your Child Wants a Dog

Gloria had a few questions about her family's dog, Daisy. She explained in the behavior consultation that she and her husband had given in and adopted Daisy as a puppy from the local animal shelter when their sons were six and eight years of age, because "the boys just wanted a pet so badly." After Daisy grew up and ended up weighing sixty pounds instead of the forty they had expected, the boys lost interest and did not spend as much time with her. Now she is very unruly and spends most of her time barking at squirrels in the backyard, and the neighbors have complained.

Daisy was a very sweet but boisterous Labrador Retriever mix who received only an occasional walk or playtime with any of the children and was too unruly when other children came into the yard. After the behavior consultant took a complete history and observed Daisy with Gloria's two sons, it was apparent Daisy was a normal dog who was not getting enough exercise or mental stimulation for her age and temperament. Gloria did not have time to take her to training classes or teach her house manners, so she was no longer welcome indoors and Gloria wanted to find her another home.

Unfortunately, this is a common scenario. Veterinarians are asked almost every day to help find homes for dogs people no longer want to keep. Sadly, Daisy would have made a great pet for a different family. Like many busy parents, Gloria did not have time for a dog, and her boys, at six and eight, were really too young to be expected to be the sole caretakers of a dog. This story would likely have had a happier ending if Gloria and her husband had just said no and waited until their boys were older before acquiring a pet.

At some point in the life of every family, at least one of the children will beg for a pet. There may already be a pet in the household, but now the child decides they want one of their own. Or maybe the family has no pets and the child starts to notice that other kids have pets but he or she does not. What do you do when a child begins pestering you for a pet?

There are many aspects of a family's lifestyle to consider before you get a pet of any kind. (See chapter 2 for more on choosing a dog.) Here are a few questions you should ask yourself:

- Do I want a pet?
- Do I have the time to add another member to the family right now?
- Can I afford to take care of a pet?
- Am I ready to make sure the pet is properly cared for, even if I have to do it myself?

Many children will begin asking for a pet before they are actually old enough and responsible enough to be the pet's primary caregiver. Children mature at different rates, so you must decide how much of the caregiving you can reasonably expect of your child and how much you are prepared to do yourself. Generally speaking, if the child is twelve or older, he or she may be old enough to take responsibility for the day-to-day care of the pet. But a child younger than that will likely need to be assigned some particular duties, such as providing food or water with supervision, and you will likely need to perform other duties, such as taking the dog on walks, training her, and taking her to the veterinarian. You will likely need to supervise interactions between the pet and children under the age of eight or ten, especially when other children visit and your kids cannot be expected to take much responsibility for the pet.

You may want to get a pet for your child because having a dog can teach responsibility. But this is only possible if you have realistic expectations about the individual child's abilities and can monitor the situation for the pet's well-being and everyone's safety. And you must be prepared to pick up the slack when necessary.

Ultimately, no matter what the age of the child, you have the final responsibility for your pet, your child, and their relationship. So if you don't want a pet, be prepared to just say no.

The good news is that many older children find a dog to be the perfect companion — someone to play fetch or soccer with or to simply hang out with them while they play outdoors. Other children enjoy training a dog and teaching her tricks. Some find the simple presence of the dog to be calming and a companion to pour their heart out to when the day goes badly. Dogs make nonjudgmental best friends and can greatly enhance childhood. So when your child is ready to take on the responsibility of caring for a dog, or you can assume it for them, having a dog can be a wonderful experience.

Great Interactions for Children and Dogs

Children of different ages will be able to safely interact with dogs in different ways. The younger the child, the more adult supervision is necessary during these interactions.

Very young children, under the age of eight, can still enjoy interacting with their pet under parental supervision in these ways:

- Helping prepare the dog's food or treats
- Placing the food bowl down for the dog after the parent has filled it (and is still nearby), then stepping away

- Giving the dog food puzzle toys or other treats prepared by the parent
- Offering a food reward by tossing it to the dog on the parent's cue, while the parent is requesting behaviors from the dog, such as "sit" or "down"
- If the dog knows how to relinquish toys when requested, playing fetch with two toys to throw can be a great game.

Some children may feel more involved with their pet if you simply suggest they draw pictures of the dog to decorate your home. They can even draw pet pictures to hang over the dog's crate or sleeping area. Others love the dog to join them for stories right before bedtime.

One mistake new parents make is to reserve time for their dog when the baby or the children are sleeping, while focusing more on the baby and less on the dog at other times. The dog may then associate the baby with inattention and lack of activity. So, if possible, it is always better to try to include the dog in family fun and maybe reserve a little alone time for you and your partner when the baby is asleep, as opposed to using that time for your dog. In this way, the baby's presence signals to your dog that good things are about to happen.

As children mature and develop more motor skills, there are many games they can begin playing with the dog:

- Fetch games, where the child throws a toy for the pet to retrieve, are very appropriate for some dogs. You can teach your child to play this game with two or three different toys, so when the dog returns with one, the child can show the dog the other toy. Most dogs will readily drop one toy to retrieve another, thus avoiding a situation where the child is trying to remove something from the dog's mouth. Obviously, this game is only appropriate for a dog who likes to play fetch and shows no resource guarding or aggression associated with items she has retrieved.
- Hide-and-seek games can be stimulating for the dog and encourage active exercise for everyone. The child or children hide, and then you send the dog to find them. Reward the dog with toys, treats, or more play for finding the child. Similar games, where

you and your children hide a toy or treat and encourage the dog to find it, can also be fun and stimulating.

- Learning how to train or participating in basic positive reinforcement–type training exercises is another excellent way for children to interact with their dogs. The act of asking the dog for a behavior she knows, and the dog responding and thus earning a food reward, is a consistent, predictable type of interaction that really delights most children. Consistent and predictable interactions between the dog and the child will greatly increase most dogs' comfort level around the child.
- When a child is old enough to participate more actively in training the dog, some may enjoy learning how to do agility, flyball, and other types of canine sports with their dogs.

What Did We Say?

- Socialize your dog to young children during the first six months and beyond of the dog's life.
- Recognize the subtle signs of fear and anxiety in dogs, and do not force them to be around children if they act anxious or afraid of them.
- Teach children that they should never approach an unfamiliar dog and that they should never stare directly at dogs or attempt to hug or kiss them. Teach children to always ask a responsible adult, preferably a parent or guardian, before interacting with any dog other than their own.
- As children mature, you can teach them to recognize the body language of fear and aggression in dogs and to avoid dogs demonstrating those visual cues. (See more about how to recognize these signs in chapters 1 and 10.)
- Be empathetic with the dog who is not very comfortable with children. Don't force interactions when the dog shows signs of wanting to avoid the child.
- Teach children how to interact appropriately with dogs. Rough behavior and interactions with the dog should never be okay.
- Never leave a dog and a child under the age of eight together un-

supervised, especially if the dog is unfamiliar to the child or has shown any signs of discomfort around children in the past.

- Always provide the dog with a safe place to escape the chaos of life with small children. Teach children to leave their dog alone when she is eating, sleeping, or resting in her own bed, her crate, or her safe refuge.

- Confine the dog while children are eating so that she does not learn to lick or snap at children for food.

- Keep the dog's association with the child pleasant by giving her extra attention and treats in the presence of the child.

- Understand that some dogs may never be able to safely interact with children.

- Be prepared to keep the dogs and kids completely separated until the children are old enough to be empathetic and interact appropriately with the dog.

9

All Dogs Need a Job
How to Keep Your Dog Happy and Mentally Healthy

Mary P. Klinck, DVM, DACVB

Mark and Linda were at their wits' end with their ten-month-old Weimaraner, Finn. Recently, it just seemed as if he was always looking for something bad to do. He regularly got into the garbage; he stole and shredded papers. If they left anything on tables or counters (be it a pen or a ham sandwich), he immediately grabbed it and chewed it to pieces. The plush squeaky toys they bought him were disemboweled and turned to piles of fluff in seconds, and he even tore apart rubber and plastic toys. There were spittle and scrape marks all over their windows from his jumping and barking at any person or animal who passed by.

They just couldn't understand it. Finn was sweet as a little puppy, easy to housetrain, and the star of his puppy obedience class; he learned new things *so fast!* They took him for walks around the neighborhood once a day and let him out in their small yard for bathroom duties two to three times a day.

They had thought this would be a great time to get a puppy, because Linda worked from home and the dog wouldn't be alone all day. Weimaraners are so beautiful with their shiny silver coat and blue or golden eyes; Mark and Linda hadn't thought about the breed's behavioral tendencies. Now Linda was becoming increasingly overwhelmed by having to juggle her "real" work and attempts to minimize Finn's destruction. Both Mark and Linda were convinced that even when Finn appeared calm and well behaved, he was really plotting his next acts of vandalism.

Mark and Linda's situation is not unique. In fact, cute little puppies often grow up to be unruly adolescents between six months and two years (or more) of age. Owners confronted with this sort of situation frequently surrender these dogs to shelters; they never expect a dog to be this much work. Nor can they figure out how to fix problem behaviors like barking, jumping, pawing, and mouthing — behaviors that were adorable in a fifteen-pound, squeaky-voiced, uncoordinated bundle of fur with gangly legs and baby teeth. But now, at sixty-plus pounds, a sinewy, agile, strong-jawed, house-destroying barking machine, Finn is no longer cute.

Although Mark and Linda thought they were providing for Finn's needs by walking him and letting him out in the yard, this simply wasn't enough physical and mental activity for this type of dog at this age. What they saw as random acts of destruction were simply Finn engaging in normal play and investigation of his environment. What they saw as nuisance barking was Finn unable to contain his excitement when he saw animals and people with whom he wanted to interact.

What they saw as destroying dog toys, Finn saw as appropriate and, most importantly, *fun* use of the objects given to him. Finn wasn't plotting anything and didn't want to be a bad dog. He was bred to go out hunting all day, not to sit around waiting for something to happen. Finn was at his physical peak and had a keen, busy mind and strong motivation to seek out interesting things. He just needed something to *do* with himself.

Pet owners today lead busy lives. It is uncommon for people to be at home all day, every day, with their dog, and if they are, they are not usually free to provide continuous canine entertainment. Humans expect their pets to learn certain rules of the home: not barking excessively, not stealing or destroying objects that aren't theirs. We require our dogs to follow a routine we set for their food, water, bathroom opportunities, and exercise, and then we expect them to spend the remainder of their time resting and out of trouble. But these are not realistic expectations.

Dogs, depending on their life stage, breed or mix, and personality, will have different needs for exercise, attention, and mental stimulation. A puppy or young adult will usually be more "busy" than an older dog. While individuals within a breed can vary, a dog bred for hunting (such as a Weimaraner) or for herding (such as a Border Collie) will often be more physically active than one bred to sit with his owner all day (such as a Pug). That being said, some toy breeds are actually very active and need lots of attention, and some lines of hunting dogs are low-key and able to lounge around all day. However, some dogs are built to spend the entire day working outside with their owner, and they have the physical ability and energy required for constant thinking and moving for *hours*. Viewed from this perspective, it is not surprising that more active dogs are simply unable to make do with a leash walk and a few brief outings in the yard. Little wonder that they get into trouble in the house.

Facts, Not Fiction

Dogs are living beings with behavioral and emotional needs as well as basic physical needs. These needs don't go away because we are busy or distracted. Dogs can become bored or frustrated when they lack stimulation; they can also become stressed or overreactive when they have too much to do or too much of the wrong kind of mental stimulation. Either can lead to problem behaviors.

Just like people, dogs are individuals with different energy levels, interests, and physical abilities — all factors that determine what sorts and amounts of enrichment will be right for any given dog. Dogs need both mental stimulation and physical exercise. One can make up for the other to a certain extent, but most dogs need both, so more exercise won't necessarily fulfill all a dog's needs.

Mental stimulation can be provided in many ways. For example, social interactions with people or animals require mental energy; these can be low-key interactions, such as walking together, meeting new individuals, play, or training. Investigating an environment also requires mental and sometimes physical energy. Investigating their surroundings is important to dogs. Dogs do this with their nose by sniffing, with their mouth by chewing or eating, with their paws by scratching or digging, with their ears by listening, and with their eyes by looking.

Looking is last on that list for a reason. Dogs are "paws-on" creatures; preliminary investigations may be visual, but activities that involve direct contact with a subject of interest are better. Dogs evolved as scavengers and hunters. When we think of them this way, it makes sense that they have a hardwired need to check out their environment.

What Does That Mean?

Enrichment: Providing objects or having interactions with your dog that occupy and stimulate his thinking and/or physical activity. The overall goal is to help your dog use these activities to dissipate stress and relieve boredom.

Social enrichment: Providing an animal with opportunities to interact with people or other animals and to develop social relationships. Social relationships relieve loneliness, encourage thinking, and help develop and maintain appropriate social behavior.

Environmental enrichment: Providing new objects and other variations in the environment that encourage investigation and allow the animal to have a choice of activities. In some cases, environmental enrichment also includes enabling the animal to be alone, if that's what he wants.

Stimulation: A type of enrichment; stimulation is opportunities for thinking or physical activity that are available to the dog.

Exercise: The physical activity part of stimulation. Dogs will have different capacities for exercise, depending on their breed or mix, the size of the dog, his age, health, temperament, and other characteristics.

Mental stimulation: The thinking part of stimulation. These might be activities in which the dog works out a problem, hones his social abilities or physical coordination, or investigates his environment.

Lack of stimulation: Dogs may not experience boredom the way humans do, but they are affected by a lack of things to do. This results in an animal with unspent mental and physical energy that needs an outlet. A dog in this situation will likely be looking for things to do around the house or will be constantly bugging you for attention.

Overstimulation: Just as there can be too little stimulation, there can also be too much. People become overwhelmed when they have too much to deal with; so do dogs. What overstimulates an individual dog can vary from too many visitors in the home to highly exciting training classes to loud noises. This can lead to exaggerated reactions to benign events.

Interactive play: This is play involving social interaction. The term is usually used to distinguish solitary play from play with a person or another dog.

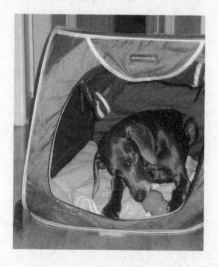

You can stuff food inside a Kong, and it also makes a good chew toy.
Mary Klinck

Too Much, Too Little, or Just Right?

It is important to remember that each dog will need and want different amounts and types of social and environmental enrichment. Similarly, how much is enough stimulation and how much is too much will depend on the individual. Some dogs will crave and excel at complex mental tasks, and some will prefer running around a lot without having to think too much. You will be able to tell, based on your dog's response to different types of enrichment, what combination works best for him. You can also expect his needs to change with age.

Jodie grew up with Labrador Retrievers but decided she would like to have a smaller dog, so she got a Sheltie puppy and named her Emma. Jodie took Emma to the dog park every day for her to socialize and to run around, but as Emma matured, she became less and less interested in playing with the other dogs. She clung to Jodie when they were at the park, and then when they returned home Emma chased and barked at Jodie's cat, causing him to hide under the bed. She would also come up to Jodie while she was on the phone or working on her computer and bark or paw at her.

In an effort to distract Emma and to give the cat a bit of breathing room, Jodie started putting Emma out on her balcony, which overlooked the street. She figured that watching what was going on would be sort of like TV for Emma. Within a couple of weeks, Emma began reacting violently when she saw passersby from the balcony, barking, spinning in circles, and jumping on the patio door and against the railing. Even when Jodie brought her indoors to stop her from bothering the neighbors, Emma continued to bark, spin, and jump at the inside of the patio doors for several minutes.

What happened? In this case, the enrichment and stimulation provided was not appropriate for the dog. Jodie meant well, but Emma was either not interested in or afraid of the dogs at the dog park. This prevented her not only from socializing with them but also from running around and exploring the park. When Jodie and Emma came home, Emma was stressed and still needed an outlet for her energy, so she sought attention excessively from Jodie and scared the cat by trying to play too vigorously with him.

Jodie again meant well by offering Emma the balcony as a form of enrichment. However, as happens with many dogs in similar situations, Emma began barking either as a territorial alarm ("Alert! There is someone approaching!"), or in frustration due to the lack of opportunity to interact with the passersby whom she could see but not reach.

What can we learn from Jodie and Emma? Not all dogs like dog parks. The time Jodie and Emma spent at the dog park would have been better devoted to another form of physical and mental stimulation, such as a leash walk during which Emma could sniff around and take in her surroundings, a training session, or a play session with Jodie or a single familiar dog. Emma should not have been left unsupervised on the balcony; her problem behavior escalated, possibly due to overstimulation without an appropriate outlet. When in the house, Emma should have some activity she enjoys to avoid understimulation and to help dissipate any stress or nervous energy. Such an activity, a food puzzle toy perhaps, would have to be more engaging to her than the cat.

How to Keep Your Dog Out of Trouble at Home

The tables on the following pages list some activities that can keep your dog busy when he is on his own and needs to expend mental and physical energy. Remember, you can use enrichment to limit boredom, encourage thinking, and help the animal cope with mild stresses. A variety of toys and also different types of resting or hiding places can be used to enrich an animal's environment.

Chew toys, as suggested in the table, are long-lasting edible treats, such as rawhides, or inedible toys that are filled or smeared with food that the dog has to work to obtain. Puzzle toys require the dog to think and try different strategies to obtain a reward. Don't worry, you don't have to spend an arm and a leg on toys or doggie sport classes; there are lots of inexpensive toys and activities.

Exercise and mental stimulation may be combined (for example, playing with other dogs in a park provides both exercise and the opportunity to practice social skills). Mental stimulation is a way to provide enrichment in situations in which an animal is confined or otherwise unable to be physically active. Training a dog to perform a behavior on cue is an example of mental stimulation because the dog must figure out what is wanted of him.

DON'T LIMIT YOURSELF to the examples in tables 9.1A and 9.1B. Check out other toys at the local pet supply store or things you have around the house. Even a few minutes of one-on-one playing or trick training can build your relationship with your dog and help him settle down at home.

And if you come up with a new trick or game, try it out! Just remember that it is always important to supervise your dog when you give him a new type of toy, to be sure he doesn't tend to consume inedible objects.

Table 9.1A: Solo Activities to Keep Your Dog Busy

Activity	Examples	Things to Consider
Basic toys	Balls; stuffed and squeaky toys; rope toys	Get your dog some of his favorite toys, and experiment with other types. Supervise to make sure he doesn't consume entire, or pieces of, inedible toys. Restuff and/or resqueaker his "emptied" stuffed toys a few times before throwing them out.
Chews and food toys	Inedible chew toys (such as a Nylabone); long-lasting treats (such as rawhide or a bully stick); stuffable food toys (such as a Kong); dry food/treat-dispensing toys (such as an Omega Paw Tricky Treat Ball)	Supervise to make sure your dog doesn't bite off and swallow pieces of inedible toys or large pieces of edible chews. For stuffables, try canned dog food, mashed fruit, cooked vegetables, or small amounts of low-fat cream cheese or low-fat, low-salt peanut butter mixed with dry dog food. Toys stuffed with food and then frozen last even longer! Be cautious when introducing a new food; some dogs have medical restrictions (such as allergies). Ask your veterinarian if you aren't sure.
Homemade toys	Cardboard, paper, flexible plastic containers (such as plastic water bottles); sticks	Avoid toxic materials and very hard or inedible objects (such as rocks) that your dog might consume or that can damage teeth. Supervise to be sure your dog is not consuming objects such as pieces of plastic, sticks, or cardboard. To help him distinguish clearly between dog stuff and your things, consider offering his toys in his own doggie toy box.
Games	Forage for food or treats	A dog doesn't have to eat out of a dish. Consider scattering his dry food or hiding treats in the yard, in his crate or bed, in his toy box, or elsewhere for him to find. This activity is not for dogs who guard food from people or other pets.

Table 9.1B: Interactive Activities to Keep Your Dog Busy

Activity	Examples	Things to Consider
Training	Practice a dog sport (see tables 9.2 and 9.3); tricks; other useful tasks (such as "go to your bed" or "put your toys away")	Although some experience or guidance is useful for training, you can also learn as you go. For trick ideas, look at books, websites (see Recommended Resources at the back of this book), and TV shows. Check to make sure training techniques are consistent with those discussed in chapter 3, and avoid aversive training methods.
Games	Fetch	Consider variations to increase the challenge (for example, different locations; or have the dog go over, under, around obstacles). For dogs who won't drop the object, use two toys or balls so you can exchange one for the other.
Games	Tug	To protect human fingers and household items, teach your dog "drop it" first. Use only the designated tug toy (not your socks!). Create a routine for how you start, play, and end the game, to make it easy for your dog to understand when it is tug time and when it isn't. If your dog tends to get overexcited and grab bits of you instead of the tug toy, reconsider whether you just need a longer tug toy (i.e., more space between teeth and fingers), need to play more calmly, or need to end the game earlier, *before* he gets so worked up— or whether this isn't the game for him (or you).
Games	Hide-and-seek; find your toy	A game or treat can be associated with finding the hidden person or toy.
Exercise	Walk, hike, or jog	This isn't a forced military march, is it? Let the dog explore (that is, sniff) a bit. Use appropriate control devices (see chapter 5) to make it enjoyable on both ends of the leash.
Being social	Doggie playdates	Not all dogs are sociable, and not all sociable dogs get along with one another. Don't always have your dog meet strangers at the park; make playdates with his canine friends.

"Real" Canine Jobs and Their Dog-Sport Counterparts

Many dog breeds were developed for specific purposes. Some canine jobs, including working with law enforcement, and the sports that have developed from them, are listed in table 9.2, along with the most common breeds or types of dog who perform them. When you are picking a canine sport for your dog, there are a few important considerations:

- Access to each activity will vary depending on where you live, sometimes making a particular sport expensive or inconvenient.
- Remember to evaluate the methods used by the trainer or training school, to ensure that they are appropriate (see chapter 3).
- Sports that are very physically demanding (involving running, jumping, pulling) also can result in injury to the dog. If your dog is young (under eighteen months to two years), his bones and joints are still developing and high-impact activities are not recommended. For older dogs who have an increased risk of arthritis or who may have other medical problems, it's best to consult with your veterinarian before beginning such training to make sure the activity is safe for your dog.
- Any sport involving interaction between the dog and another species (herding, hunting, earth dog, and others; see table 9.2) carries some degree of risk to the prey animal, ranging anywhere from mild stress to injury or death, depending on the activity and how it is performed. The dog may also be injured.

Table 9.2: Traditional and Modern Canine Jobs

Job Type	Dog Types	Sports	Details
Herding	Cattle dogs, Sheepdogs	Herding, stock dog, Sheepdog trials	The dog is trained to respond to the handler's cues to move herds, flocks, and individual animals.
Hunting	Terriers, Dachshunds	Earth dog	The dog follows the scent of a prey animal (such as a rat) through a tunnel and indicates when he has found the prey.

Table 9.2: Traditional and Modern Canine Jobs (cont.)

Job Type	Dog Types	Sports	Details
Hunting	Sighthounds	Hare coursing, lure coursing	The dog pursues either a live prey animal or an artificial lure over a course or open terrain.
Hunting	Scenthounds	Trailing, tracking, Beagling	The dog or group of dogs follows an artificial scent or a prey animal's trail and alerts the handler when the bait or animal is found.
Hunting	Retrievers, Spaniels, Pointers, Setters	Hunting, hunt tests, field trials	The dog is trained in the various skills associated with hunting birds, such as working with a mounted person or one on foot to find, indicate, and retrieve prey.
Pulling	Any medium to large breed (such as Siberian Huskies)	Mushing, drafting, carting, weight pulling	The dog pulls a sled or cart carrying goods or people. Recreational versions include weight pulling; pulling a person on skis (skijoring), a scooter (dog scootering), or a bicycle (bikejoring); or running or jogging (canicross).
Search and rescue	Any breed (usually large)	Search and rescue	The dog searches for missing or lost persons. Search-and-rescue teams often consist of extensively trained volunteers (i.e., ordinary owners with their well-trained pet dogs).
Law enforcement, protection	Any large breed (such as German Shepherds)	Police dog, Schutzhund, French Ring sport	The dog is trained in a variety of tasks (e.g., obedience, directed attack, defense of handler or object, tracking, scent detection or discrimination, agility).

Table 9.2: Traditional and Modern Canine Jobs (cont.)

Job Type	Dog Types	Sports	Details
Scent detection	Any breed	Narcotics or explosives detection, nose or scent work	The dog searches for and indicates specific scents, such as illegal or dangerous substances. Recreational tasks include finding specific items or the scent of a person on an item, or simply a "planted" odor (such as clove oil).

Other Canine Sports

Almost any activity you can think of doing with your dog probably already is (dog surfing!) or could become (insert your idea here) a canine sport. The list in table 9.3, which begins opposite, isn't exhaustive. You are limited only by your own and your dog's physical abilities, interests, and imagination. Some general considerations:

- An owner with restricted mobility may not be able to take part in all of these activities, but you may be surprised at the activities accessible to people with limited mobility or in a wheelchair (such as agility and canine freestyle; see table 9.3). Don't assume you can't do it; ask the instructor or ask people involved in the sport.
- Time commitments vary and may be flexible. Group class schedules are typically one hour once a week for a few weeks; condensed workshops may also be offered. Most sports will benefit from a few minutes of practice at home several times a week. Some require preparation prior to training sessions (for example, tracking).
- Some sports require specialized equipment (such as agility and flyball; see table 9.3), limiting practice at home. Some clubs allow their members facility practice time outside of class hours.

Table 9.3: Dog Sports

Sport	Description	Things to Consider
Conformation	The dog is judged on appearance (compared with an ideal written standard for the breed), walking and running on leash, and hands-on examination.	Dogs must be registered, intact (i.e., unneutered) purebreds.
Obedience	The dog learns to perform a variety of obedience tasks, ranging from simple ("sit," "down," "stay," "come," "heel") to complex (tasks at a distance from the owner, jumping obstacles, or retrieving specific articles).	Group classes are widely available, but obedience school training techniques vary. (See chapter 3 for desirable training methods.)
Rally obedience	A variation on regular obedience, this activity is based on performing obedience activities while the dog is walking at heel position. The dog must usually know some basic obedience ("heel," "sit," "down") beforehand.	Some mobility is needed (moving at a walking or slow running pace). Group classes are available in most areas.
Canine freestyle	Dog and owner perform choreographed movements (obedience, tricks); they "dance" together to music. The dog must know some basic obedience before starting.	Some mobility and ability to coordinate movements to music are needed.

Table 9.3: Dog Sports (cont.)

Sport	Description	Things to Consider
Agility	The dog learns to navigate a variety of obstacles that he must jump over, climb on, weave around, or go through. Owner and dog learn to communicate so that the dog can be directed to perform the obstacles in the correct sequence. The dog must know some basic obedience beforehand.	Some mobility is needed (moving at a walking or slow running pace). Certain basic exercises can be practiced at home, but the specific pieces of equipment and ample space required mean that practice is usually at the training facility. Group classes are available in most areas.
Flyball	It's a relay race; one at a time, dogs run down a lane, jump over a series of obstacles, and jump on a flyball box, causing it to eject a tennis ball. They return up the lane with the ball. The team with the fastest time for all their dogs to run the course wins. Basic obedience is a plus.	Not for the faint-hearted, this sport involves a lot of barking and occasional chasing or lunging of one dog after another due to high excitement and close quarters. Mobility is needed. The equipment required means that practice is generally at a training facility.
Flying disc	The dog chases and catches a flying disc (such as a Frisbee) thrown by the handler. The goal may be maximum distance of caught throws, or flashy style and tricks.	This sport can be practiced anywhere with adequate space; all the handler has to do is toss the disc. There are also organized leagues.
Dock jumping, dock diving	The dog jumps off the end of a dock into the water, chasing a thrown toy. This is usually judged either on jump distance (before hitting the water) or height.	Training may be limited by access to a dock from which to practice. Dogs must enjoy the water! There are traveling exhibitions that appear at pet expos and other events around the country, which often invite novices to try it out.

Table 9.3: Dog Sports (cont.)

Sport	Description	Things to Consider
Treibball	The dog pushes fitness balls (one at a time) into a goal. This is done off leash, requiring the dog and owner to learn to communicate for "steering" purposes. The dog should know some basic obedience beforehand.	This sport can be practiced anywhere there is adequate space and requires a little, easy-to-find equipment.
Tracking	The dog learns to follow a scent trail left by the footsteps of a human and to indicate objects on the trail belonging to the same human. Because the handler can't (usually) see the scent trail, that person must learn to read the dog's body language to know when he is on track.	Tracking generally takes place outdoors, requiring the dog and handler to be mobile and able to tolerate the elements (sun, rain, wind). Preparation time is needed to lay one or several tracks. Books are available to learn this sport on your own, but there are also clubs. This is generally a solitary activity, lending itself well to a busy or varied owner schedule.

How Do We Begin?

It is not hard to get going on finding just the right way to keep your dog happy, but it can take some trial and error, so be patient.

Plan Ahead to Fulfill the Dog's Behavioral Needs

We know that dogs need different types of enrichment and that each dog will be different in terms of what works for him. Think of your dog's likes and dislikes and of his energy level. What do you know your dog likes to do? Here are some examples of ways to channel doggie interests into acceptable activities.

In agility, the handler directs the dog to the obstacles in the correct order. This may be done by running with the dog nearby or from a short distance away. *Jacey D. Courneen*

Does the dog like to chew, or does he steal and shred items? This dog might enjoy food toys, puzzle toys, or safe recyclable items, such as cardboard. Food toys are handy in that they are inherently rewarding (food usually trumps nonfood household items).

Does the dog like to dig? Consider placing a sandbox or dirt box with toys or treats hidden in it in your yard. But be careful: Avoid the sandbox if your dog tries to eat sand. (Eating a little dirt is not so bad, as long as it is not enough to clump.)

Does your dog just seem to enjoy sniffing around outside — and possibly urine marking on things like trees? Consider taking him out on leash and just letting him choose the direction for a slow sniff walk, taking his time to investigate the environment and choose what smells to check out next. This is an opportunity for a thinking activity that can help many dogs unwind. An obedient heel position is not necessary; what you want is just a dog who walks nicely with you and doesn't pull you down the street.

Does the dog like to retrieve or chase objects? Play fetch, or consider a dog sport such as flying disc, flyball, or treibball. For fetch, you can try different kinds of thrown objects; it doesn't always have to be a ball. For instance, you can play fetch with something with an interesting bounce, such as a Kong on a rope.

Does your dog love the water? Many dogs enjoy running and swimming in the water. Consider water fetch or dock jumping, or simply go swimming with your dog or play fetch at the water's edge. This is physically and sometimes also mentally tiring.

Does your dog adore playing with other dogs? Find a fenced area and some dog friends for him to play with regularly. Like people, most dogs enjoy spending time with their friends more than they enjoy meeting lots of new individuals. Some dogs are real social butterflies and get along with everyone, but most would prefer to spend time with dogs they know. Consider that if you don't know the other dog, he may not be friendly (and might even frighten your dog).

These dogs have known each other for years, and they are having a great time playing chase at the beach. *Mary Klinck*

Does your dog really enjoy meeting new people? Seek out more activities for him to take part in with human friends. You can even teach him tricks to show off! He could also become certified as a therapy dog to visit elderly, ill, or disabled persons.

Does your dog just love doing things with you? *Does he love training? Does he have boundless energy?* Consider dog sports (see tables 9.2 and 9.3, earlier in the chapter.). A regular class will give you the opportunity to devote 100 percent of your attention to your dog for a relatively short period of time, and it will be mentally (and maybe physically, depending on the activity) stimulating and tiring for him. Training for dog sports using reward-based methods, such as treats and play, can encourage your dog to think and will strengthen your bond with him. In addition, he will likely come home happy and exhausted. If you are interested in a particular sport, go watch it in a class or a competition to see if it interests you and to assess whether your dog will enjoy it too.

Evaluate Your Dog's Response

You may think you have found the perfect activity for your dog, only to discover that he simply isn't interested or that he becomes overstimulated. How can you determine whether the activity is a good one for him?

If your dog shows apparent enjoyment during the activity and he gets into it with gusto, he probably likes it. Check out his body language; is it consistent with relaxed enjoyment? Make sure that the activity poses little or no risk of damage to property or injury to the dog. Does your dog seem more relaxed and satisfied after the activity? How can you tell? When it is over, he may be ready for a nap. The final telltale sign: your dog's overall behavior seems more relaxed and happy, he is happy to interact with you but less demanding of attention, and he doesn't seem to be searching for things (perhaps naughty ones) to do quite as much as before.

What signs will indicate this activity is *not* right for your dog? He isn't interested. Despite your best efforts, he avoids the activity or gives it up quickly. It may be that you can tweak it to increase his interest; give him an easier food toy or one with better food in it, or try a different sport or training facility). But this may not work. Another sign of disinterest is if he performs the activity in a way that risks damage to property or injury to himself. For example, some dogs can play with a ball in the house, but some destroy the furniture in the process; some dogs chew and play with rubber toys without damaging them, but some bite off and swallow large pieces, sometimes leading to intestinal obstructions. It's not right for your dog if he is stressed or frightened; watch his body language to tell. Is his tail down and his ears back? Is he panting and looking around anxiously? If your dog becomes excessively agitated, shows avoidance, or shows aggression to other dogs, to new people, or to you, it isn't the activity for him.

Finally, your dog should be interested in the activity but not more reactive or less able to relax than usual either after the activity or in general. He may indeed perk up due to the new and fun things in his life, but he should not appear to be more agitated after the enrichment is introduced. If so, he may be overstimulated or stressed by it.

Modify the Enrichment Offered and Reevaluate as Needed

If the activities you tried didn't seem right for your dog, then either try tweaking activities or switching to something completely different (if he didn't like going to class for a dog sport, try giving him food toys and puzzle toys to work on in the house). Like a lot of things in life, finding the most rewarding match will involve some trial and error.

Try New Things

If the activities you have selected seem to be good ones for your dog, don't forget that you should still reevaluate them from time to time and try new activities, in case your dog's interests change. Many dogs enjoy mild variation. For example, rotate the type of food or puzzle toys offered, or occasionally take him to a different spot for a walk or a play-date.

Providing Enrichment Around
a Busy Work Schedule

How should you manage your dog's behavioral needs when you have to go to work every day?

DO:

- Give your dog special toys or food toys to keep him busy while you are gone for the day.
- Provide enough exercise so that he will be fairly relaxed but not necessarily exhausted before you leave.
- Make sure your dog's physical needs are met — empty bladder and bowels, water available, enough food to stave off intense hunger — until you return.
- If you will be gone for a long time, consider using a timed feeder or getting a dog walker to take your dog out and maybe even to play with him partway through the day.
- Consider using a doggie daycare now and then if your dog enjoys it and it is convenient and affordable for you.
- Schedule a bit of time every day to give your dog your undivided attention in a context that both of you enjoy. It can be for a few minutes or a few hours. You will both feel better.

DON'T:

- Automatically interpret destruction of toys as a reason to withhold them from your dog (unless you fear for his health; for instance, if he tries to swallow big chunks of his Kong toy). It means they were useful and enjoyed!
- Overexercise your dog to make up for a lack of mental stimulation or to try to reduce distress when he is alone. This could lead to bone and joint injuries — and it won't make up for the lack of mental stimulation.
- Withhold water and all food while you are out all day. Your dog may misbehave because he is hungry, and water restriction can have adverse health effects.

- Skip training or playing with your dog when you only have a short time. A little is still better than nothing!
- Feel guilty that you aren't at home enough. Make use of the time you have with your dog; many dogs don't even have a home.

Avoiding Pitfalls and Staying on Track

Don't wait to see evidence of lack of stimulation before offering enrichment. Undesirable habits can form fast, and they can be hard to change. If you set up good habits in the form of acceptable outlets for your dog's behavioral needs right from the get-go, both you and your dog will be happier.

Sometimes we get busy or our schedule changes and we forget to plan accordingly for our pets' enrichment. Life changes may make it necessary to change the type of enrichment you can offer, so consider what you can do within the constraints of your schedule and environment.

Dogs sometimes become injured or have illnesses that make it impossible to provide exercise or other forms of enrichment. In this case, you should always consider how you can replace a particular activity with a new, acceptable one. For example, this could mean providing more chew toys or feeding most meals out of food toys when your dog is physically limited.

What Did We Say?

- All dogs require some form of enrichment. If you just want a soft creature to look at and to pet occasionally who will not place demands on your time and won't affect your schedule much, a dog may not be right for you.
- Dogs are individuals who have behavioral, social, emotional, and physical needs.
- A lack of activity or the wrong kind of activity may result in undesirable behaviors.

- Enrichment will contribute to well-being, reduce problem behaviors, and enhance your relationship with your dog.
- Creating the right enrichment environment will depend on your dog, his life stage, temperament, and physical abilities, as well as your own preferences.

Whether you are at home all day or work ten hours a day, make sure you provide enrichment. What you choose will depend both on your dog's needs and what works best for you and your family.

10

Aggression Unleashed:
Do Dogs Mean to Be Mean?
If Aggression Leads to More Aggression,
How Do You Respond?

Ilana Reisner, DVM, PhD, DACVB
Stefanie Schwartz, MS, DVM, DACVB

As a Jack Russell Terrier puppy, Maybelline seemed cute when she placed her front feet on her owner's knees. However, when Maybelline was two years old, this still-small but forthright girl was in the habit of jumping up into her owner's lap, placing her paws on her shoulders, and growling in her face. How should her owner react? And why did Maybelline threaten her owner during an affectionate interaction?

Sherlock, a young Giant Schnauzer, was taking a walk down a city street with his owner. His collar was attached to a long retractable leash because his owner felt it gave her pet more freedom. Sherlock's owner didn't want to curb the dog's spirit and believed obedience training would subdue his natural behaviors. But when Sherlock pulled her down on his way to a fight with a neighbor's Bassett Hound, she began to rethink her lack of control. Sherlock actually knew this Bassett Hound; they were playmates at a dog park where Sherlock played off leash a few times a week. Why had his attitude changed so dramatically when the dogs saw each other during leash walks, and how could his owner control such a large dog?

Flash, a striking black and white English Pointer mix, was adopted from a shelter several months earlier and had settled beautifully into his new home and family. At first, he seemed a little nervous in the presence of visitors in the house. Recently, however, he had begun to growl when anyone unfamiliar tried to make friends, and now he had lunged at a neighbor's pants leg when she walked past him in the living room. He was so good with his family; why would he act this way with their friends?

Growling at a person's face or lunging at other dogs while on a walk are potentially serious aggressive behaviors that can result in biting. Without a good understanding of dog aggression and proper responses to such behavior, owners often find themselves confused about what to do. The behavior may seem harmless at first glance, but is likely to be repeated in other circumstances and eventually grow to be a more serious problem.

Growling, baring teeth, and biting are part of every normal dog's behavioral repertoire. But that does not make aggression appropriate in most situations. Whether your dog tries to bite strangers who reach to pet her during a walk, unfamiliar dogs trotting by her, or the dogs and people in her own household, it is never acceptable behavior for companion dogs to bite.

Dogs are integrated into our lives and our families, yet sometimes our interactions with them can be dangerous. According to the Centers for Disease Control, 4.5 million Americans are bitten by dogs every year. Most of these bites do not require medical attention, and many dog bites (especially those inflicted by small dogs or family pets) are not reported to public health authorities. However, hundreds of thousands of people require medical attention, including emergency treatment and reconstructive surgery, for dog bites each year.

Why Do Dogs Behave Aggressively?

At its simplest, aggression can be defined as behavior that injures — or at least intends to injure — its target. Because there is a "cost" to aggression (that is, the biting dog might be bitten as well), the function of growling, snarling, staring, and even snapping and biting is to increase the distance between the aggressor and the target. Aggressive behavior can be seen in many situations, but in most cases it is motivated by fear or defense of things that have high value to the dog.

Aggressive behavior is part of the normal range of behaviors available to all dogs. But knowing that it is typical or understanding its evolutionary purpose is not enough when we are trying to manage aggression in our own pets. A critical piece in managing aggression — or any undesired behavior — is to understand your particular dog's motivation, fears, and reactivity. Each dog has a story.

Facts, Not Fiction

Is my dog aggressive because she is dominant? This is very unlikely. The perception that dogs bite their owners or other familiar people because they are competing for "alpha status" has largely been replaced by the realization that dogs bite for defensive reasons that are not related to a social hierarchy. Although this might contradict some of the information we receive from the Internet and other media, it is a conclusion based on the science of dog behavior. Behavior studies of free-roaming feral dog groups in India, for example, have shown neither a strong hierarchy component nor persistent aggressive interactions between members, except when breeding and raising their young.

Why do we no longer interpret biting as an expression of dominance? First, dogs who bite their owners most often look, in their body language, fearful and uncertain. Second, much of the outdated "dominance theory" of dog bites is based on captive wolf behavior, which is not analogous to either wild wolves or domestic dogs. People often respond to this misconception by asserting their own dominance and thereby put themselves at risk of being bitten by a fearful dog.

Should I punish aggression to nip it in the bud? You might receive confusing, conflicting advice about what to do if your dog snaps or bites. One of the more common pieces of advice is that such dogs should be punished for their aggression. Some suggest that the owner should assert dominance over a dog they perceive as challenging their authority. The dominance myth came about from two rationales, both of which have now been shown to be false. The first was that wolves living in groups have a dominance hierarchy that they maintain by fighting with one another. This assumption was based on early research in the 1940s, observing unrelated wolves living in captivity. The study found a great deal of fighting between group members. Fast-forward fifty years, when other researchers studied wolf packs in the wild. Those results turned the dominance theory of pack behavior upside down. A wild wolf pack consists of parents and their offspring, both newborns and juveniles. No fighting takes place within the wolf social group, but rather they all work together to increase their survival — no evidence of alpha status or aggression here!

The second false rationale deals with dogs. Behaviorists once thought that because dogs are descended from wolves, they will act like wolves in their social relationships. But since we now know that wolves don't act within a strict hierarchy, we should not assume dogs do either. Unfortunately, the damage was done. Dog training was already based on the assumption that the only way to train and "tame" a dog was to be confrontational — something we now know is not true.

So punishment is not your best course of action at all. Rather than reduce the risk of bites, punishment and so-called dominance activities (for example, the alpha roll, grabbing the dog and rolling him onto his back) *make it more likely that the dog will bite again.* In fact, there are several reasons *not* to punish a dog who has shown aggression. Again, dogs who growl, snap, or bite people are usually expressing fear and self-defense. That fear will only increase in the face of harsh treatment. Remember, punishing a dog who is already showing aggressive behavior is likely to result in a bite. And we have research to support this. Veterinary behaviorist Dr. Meghan Herron found in her study that aversive or painful treatment of dogs who already have a history of aggression will, in fact, lead to the handler being bitten. This is clearly a downward spiral that we want to avoid with our companion animals. As counterintuitive as it might seem, the best and safest reaction to aggression is to disengage immediately by stopping the interaction, turning away, and perhaps leaving the area.

Although punishment might stop or inhibit any behavior for that moment, the behavior itself will reappear at the next opportunity and might be driven by even worse anxiety and arousal than it was previously. In addition, if you want your dog to learn an alternative, unaggressive behavior in a similar situation, punishment will not teach that lesson.

Should I take my dog's food or move her off the couch to show I am in charge? You might have seen advice from various sources that says dogs should be expected to relinquish items on request, and that this should be taught by taking things away from them at an early age. This is misleading and sometimes unsafe advice; taking food and toys away from your puppy, juvenile, or adult dog only teaches her that her food or toys can be randomly removed at any time. This would be upsetting and create anxiety for any of us! These unfortunate efforts will make her more nervous than ever about you coming near.

Moving your dog can be dangerous too. It is common for dogs to growl, swing their heads, snap, or even bite when someone tries to physically move them from their spot on the furniture, from under a table, or any time the dog is resting comfortably. Dogs don't appreciate being pushed, pulled, or cornered any more than we do.

Harsh treatment and punishment are likely to increase, not decrease, aggression. This dog is hiding and clearly afraid of an encounter with a person.
Ilana Reisner, DVM, PhD

Types of Aggression

There are many types of aggression, and various systems have been suggested to classify them. However, there is still no consensus on terminology and whether it should refer to the target of the aggression or to the presumed function.

We'll mostly be discussing aggression where the targets are familiar people. In this context, it is useful to think about aggression as either self-defense or defense of valued resources. Defensive aggression can appear to be offensive when the dog is lunging and snapping at her target. However, aggression that appears offensive or self-confident can also be rooted in fear.

Functional categories of dog aggression include fear-related aggression, aggression related to territorial defense, resource guarding, conflict, status-related aggression (specifically referring to other household dogs), and pain and irritability associated with disease. Fear and defensiveness play a role in all of these functional categories.

What Does That Mean?

Aggression: Behavior that harms, or threatens to harm, another individual. Because aggressive behavior has a cost for the aggressor (who might get hurt as well), the function of aggression is often to increase the distance between the aggressor and the target.

Fear-related aggression: Aggression used as self-defense. Such aggression may be a last resort for dogs who otherwise cannot escape, or it can also be a preemptive behavior when they anticipate a threat.

Territorial aggression: Defensive aggression associated with the arrival of an intruder in or near the house, yard, car, or other area perceived by the dog as her territory. Territorial aggression is usually facilitated — made worse — by the presence of other household members. It is most common for territorial aggression to be associated with fear.

Defensive aggression: A nonspecific term that describes aggressive behaviors motivated by self-defense, territorial defense, and defense of resources.

Resource guarding: Defense of resources perceived by the aggressor as having high value. Examples are food, toys, resting places, and even owners.

Conflict-related aggression: Aggression directed toward owners (and family members) in contexts that create conflict between the dog's drives and her ability to inhibit the behavior. Triggers can include threatening postures by often unaware owners, punishment, physical manipulation, and other interactions.

Status-related aggression: Aggression between household dogs related to resources, social and physical access to desired locations, and postural provocations.

Pain-related aggression: Aggression that occurs directly as a result of pain.

Irritable aggression: Aggression associated with disease but not directly as a result of pain.

Predatory behavior: Behavior that is motivated by the instinct to detect, pursue, and kill for food. Unlike overtly aggressive behaviors, the objective of predatory behavior is *not* to increase the distance between the aggressor (dog) and the target (prey).

When they perceive a threat, dogs have limited options to stay safe. When possible, it is often safest for them to flee. This is clearly not possible when a dog is cornered in the living room, restrained on a veterinary exam table, or attached to a leash. If escape is not possible, dogs will often attempt to diffuse the threat with appeasing signals, such as lip licking, averting the eyes, turning the head, rolling over onto the back, or urination and other appeasement behaviors. If the threat persists — for example, if the unfamiliar person continues to reach out to pet the dog when she is uncertain about being touched — the dog threatens by stiffening, growling, baring teeth, or biting.

Defensive behavior stems from fear or uncertainty. A dog in defensive mode has options: run away, submit, or threaten in an attempt to use bravado to stop the unwanted social encounter. Defensive behavior functions to prevent an opponent or perceived menace from gaining an advantage, not to actually "win" the encounter.

Why Is Force-Free Training Important?

Most dog bites to people result from fear and self-defense on the part of the dog. Preventing and minimizing the risk of biting includes being sure that your dog is not placed in a situation in which she feels threatened enough to bite. Force-free training emphasizes positive reinforcement and avoids leash tugs, shock, physical manipulations, and threats. Keep these things in mind:

- Dogs have no agenda. They live in the here and now and will protect themselves if frightened.
- Dogs in our homes rely 100 percent on us, their human family, to feed, walk, shelter, and love them. It is important to extend this to humaneness in training.
- Any training method — including use of aversive tools, such as shock collars or other sources of pain — can result in a "well-behaved" dog who performs the commands, but may be quite frightened and unreliable. In fact, studies have shown that using these types of training devices and techniques increases anxiety in dogs and diminishes their interactions with humans who use them. Ethical and humane methods train just as effectively and result in less stress and, therefore, less risk of fear-related biting.
- Science-based training relies on well-established principles of learning. If your goal is to have a happy dog who is eager to do the things you ask her to do, use positive reinforcement to ensure this will happen.
- As their keepers and owners, we have a responsibility to ensure that our dogs are treated with kindness.
- Assuming that your dog disobeys to spite you or is out to get you is detrimental to your bond with your pet and is simply not true. If your dog does not respond to a request, it may mean she doesn't understand what you are asking, is distracted by something more important to her at the moment, or is too anxious or fearful to respond.

Is That Really True?

If your dog is allowed to sleep on the bed, walk in front of you, or run through a door before you, she will become alpha. This common misconception has resulted in unneeded harsh handling and confrontations between people and dogs. Using common sense, it is easy to see why a dog would *want* to pull on leash or run into the yard — there are things to see, bladders to empty, and squirrels to chase. This behavior can be resolved by teaching the dog to walk on a loose leash, with the help of a force-free trainer (see "Why Is Force-Free Training Important?"), and teaching her to sit before dashing through doorways (a great example of a "life reward," getting to do what she wants by complying with the request for sitting). As far as sharing a bed — if your dog has a history of growling, snapping, or biting on the bed, keeping her off is a safe step. If there is no history of aggression in the bed, however, it might be inconsequential. Veterinary behaviorist Dr. Victoria L. Voith found that there was no association between "spoiling behaviors," such as sleeping on the bed, and behavior problems. There is *no* evidence that allowing dogs on the owners' bed contributes to aggressive behavior.

My dog is aggressive toward strangers because she is protecting me. Unless your dog is specifically trained to bite (and release) on command, as military and police dogs are, it is very unlikely that her stranger-directed aggression is related to protecting you. It's much more likely that your dog is lunging at strangers because she is protecting *herself.* Having you nearby is probably increasing her tendency to be aggressive when frightened. Just as two dogs in a yard will bark at passersby more vigorously and vociferously than one will, your dog is most likely feeling that she has a backup when she is with you and so can be more overtly aggressive.

Rolling on her back means a dog wants a belly rub. What a dog means or wants when she rolls on her back is all about context. True, your dog might paw you for attention and then roll onto her back as a not-so-subtle hint. But this posture is also a common way for dogs to signal discomfort with an interaction — especially if your dog has any

Aggression directed toward strangers is usually motivated by self-defense, not protection of the owner. These dogs do not look welcoming, with their direct stares, closed mouths, and worried facial expressions. If someone reached for these dogs, they might bite.
Ilana Reisner, DVM, PhD

history of aggression. It's a canine appeasement signal, intended to tell you the dog is uncomfortable and needs you to step back and discontinue what you're doing. If such a dog were to get a belly rub, it is very likely she would escalate her defensiveness by biting.

How can you tell the difference? If your dog rolls onto her back after *she* initiates an interaction with you and is clearly seeking attention, it should be fine to pet her. However, if the interaction is initiated by *you* or another person (for example, you've called your dog several times to no effect, at which point you approach her and she rolls onto her back), it is safest to discontinue the interaction and walk away. If you aren't sure, don't rub the dog's belly; it's certainly not the way dogs interact with one another.

Socializing a puppy to children will prevent her from being aggressive to children when she grows up. Even well-socialized puppies and dogs can experience fear or pain or can guard high-value possessions. When children are too young or impulsive to follow the rules of dog management, it is safest to separate the dog so that *both* are safe. Alternatively, an adult can be assigned to actively supervise, preferably with a leash on the dog. If there is any history of aggression, the dog should be leashed or securely separated when children are present. (See chapter 8 for more information about children and dogs.)

The Difference Between Normal and Abnormal Aggression

Some behavior problems that bother owners may just be part of the normal behavior repertoire of dogs. The perception of the "problem" in these cases is in the eye of the beholder. A behavior might be normal for the animal but still unwanted or inappropriate for the human. In the case of aggression, it is also unsafe.

On the other hand, behavior problems can also be abnormal or atypical. For example, animals might bite when they are sick or in pain. Aggressive behavior might be manifested in abnormal ways. So how do you tell the difference between normal and abnormal behavior?

Growling, snapping, and biting serve important functions in the normal behavior repertoire of dogs and are used to communicate in social situations both to people and to other dogs. For example, growling with or without an inhibited bite (snapping, or biting with little resulting injury) serves to warn that more aggression might follow if the trigger is not removed. Here are several scenarios in which aggression, though unwanted, is within the normal limits of dog behavior:

- Maxine is lying on her owners' bed, and all are asleep. One owner wakes and leaves to use the washroom. When he returns and starts to get back into bed, Maxine growls at him. This is resource guarding, with the valued resource being either the bed itself or proximity to the owner.
- Howard, a recently rescued Beagle, is wet after being caught in a downpour in the yard. His owner lifts up his foreleg to dry his foot, and he bares his teeth at her. This is pain-related aggression if the paw is injured, or fear-related aggression at being restrained and handled.

- Bonnie and Clyde are barking vigorously at the fence, running back and forth as pedestrians walk by. Bonnie jumps onto Clyde and the two dogs fight. This is territorial aggression, with the aggression redirected to the other dog because the dogs cannot get direct access to the primary target.
- A dinner guest is petting the host's Golden Retriever for several minutes. He leans over to kiss the dog on the head and is suddenly bitten on the lip. This is fear-related aggression; the guest continued an interaction that was uncomfortable for the dog.

Apart from its function in normal dog behavior, aggression may result from almost any aspect of disease. In addition, fever, nausea, joint pain, and other health problems can increase irritability and, therefore, biting.

Some aggressive behavior, however, appears to be exaggerated and perhaps unprovoked and does not fit into the expected pattern of dog behavior. Dogs showing abnormal aggression might behave in a way that is unpredictable and exaggerated in response to the trigger. This kind of response is sometimes described as an impulsivity disorder or as "rage syndrome" — a term that is often used by dog owners and even trainers but is not recognized by behavior scientists. While a "normal" aggressive dog may bite when the owner pushes her off the sofa (a recognized provocation for dogs) but not at other times, an "abnormal" dog may bite when the provocation is as subtle as a pat on the head. These abnormal dogs may be less likely to warn with a growl and may become extremely emotionally aroused — along with trembling, dilated pupils, and even disorientation.

A study by this chapter's author, Dr. Ilana Reisner, showed that aggressive dogs have lower levels of serotonin metabolites (brain neurotransmitters associated with mood) in their spinal fluid than unaggressive dogs. The neurotransmitter serotonin has been associated with mood regulation and a delay or inhibition of acting in potentially self-harmful ways. In its absence or dysfunction, dogs and other species might be more likely to act impulsively and aggressively.

Serotonin dysfunction is just one example of many physiological problems that might lead to aggressiveness. Highly stressed or anxious dogs are physiologically on edge because of abnormal function of the hypothalamic-pituitary-adrenal (HPA) axis (the connection between the brain and the adrenal glands), which results in release of corticosteroids, the fight-or-flight body chemicals. In this state, behavioral arousal is intense and dogs are likely to defensively bite without "rational" warning or inhibited behavior. Aggression by anxious dogs thus often appears abnormal. Ultimately, such behavior is maladaptive and even self-destructive; it certainly doesn't help the dog live a normal canine life.

Always Start with a Veterinary Visit

Behavior changes should always raise a red flag that the dog may be sick or in pain. If your dog's behavior — including activity level, any unusual aggression, nervousness, social behavior, or change in appetite — is new, different, or simply doesn't make sense, start by making an appointment with your dog's veterinarian for an examination and health assessment. It is common to discover that biting dogs have joint pain, ear infections, or other health problems. In fact, disease is almost always expressed by a change in behavior. Only when your dog's physical health has been addressed can you focus specifically on the behavior changes.

Problems such as infection, cancer, and even trauma, all of which can affect the brain, can also change an animal's behavior. To complicate things further, aggressive behavior resulting from disease can persist long after the disease has been treated and resolved — especially if the behavior resulted in the dog getting something she wants. For example, a dog with a painful ear infection may growl or bite when her ears are touched. Because this behavior is rewarded (growling makes the hands — and therefore the pain — go away), it might persist even after the ear infection has cleared up. Ultimately, then, aggression as a behavior problem and as a manifestation of disease can be closely linked, and it may be unrealistic to try to consider them separately.

Aggressive Signaling

As human animals, we negotiate, discuss, argue, and manipulate verbally but place less emphasis on the nonverbal social signals we exchange during our own interactions every day. Our dogs cannot speak, but they have developed a complex language through physical body postures, movements, vocalizations, and facial expressions, as described in chapter 1.

It is most common for territorial aggression to be associated with fear. This dog is guarding a doorway but looks uncertain and afraid, with lowered ears, direct stare, and a worried look. *Ilana Reisner, DVM, PhD*

Dogs are very good at observing us, their human family members, and reacting to even subtle changes in expression or movement. Unfortunately, we are not always as accomplished at reading our dogs, which often results in unwanted responses from our canine companions. We have to retrain ourselves to pay close attention to their body language — and vocal cues too.

While canine social signaling has some genetic basis, learning is also involved. As discussed in chapter 2, socialization is the early basis for the normal development of social behaviors. Puppies who are orphaned or removed prematurely from their littermates may have limited opportunities to learn the important "rules" of appropriate social behavior and may misinterpret signals given by other dogs or may signal ambiguously. These social deficits may remain, and these dogs may not do well at the dog park or in other group-play situations.

Dogs signal (or warn) their aggressive intentions to avoid the possibility of injury associated with fighting. The purpose of aggressive signals, one might say, is to increase the distance between the dog and the target of the aggression, thus decreasing the likelihood of an active and perhaps injurious confrontation. Growling, stiffening, snarling, and snapping can serve that purpose well.

However, overt aggression and biting do occur, largely because those more subtle signals were either not perceived or were disregarded by the target, or the event happened too quickly for the dog to assess the outcome. For fearful and anxious dogs, this may result in an aggressive response. If people are the target, miscommunication is usually the problem. Fights between dogs might result when at least one of the dogs is anxious or inappropriate in her social interactions.

Dog Fights

Dog fights can be sudden and severe. Triggers of fights between household dogs are often related to misread social cues or resource guarding. Other triggers include excitement and crowded spaces. As with bites to humans, fights with other dogs are often related to fear and defense.

Although there are exceptions, many bites during a dogfight are actually inhibited, at least to some degree. In other words the combatants could do more damage, but consciously control how far they go. That being said, such altercations should be interrupted because dogs can injure each other severely. However, it is always a risk to personal safety to interfere with a fight. Therefore, rather than using your hands or legs, try to interrupt fighting by throwing a blanket or water on the combatants or by inserting a handheld baby gate or large cushion between them. Once the fight has stopped, safely separate the dogs and contact a qualified behavior professional for advice on how best to manage the problem.

The Big Picture

In life, we often look at the big picture before focusing on the details, and we can do this with dog behavior as well. It is important to observe the dog's overall body language before narrowing in on specific body parts, such as the eyes or the position of the ears or tail. If you focus only on the dog's mouth or ears or tail, you might overlook other, equally important cues.

Dogs signal with every part of their body, right down to the hair follicles. When a dog goes on alert, the hair along the back of the neck and between the shoulders may stand up (raised hackles). This is part of a mechanism that expands the dog's silhouette, making her look bigger and more menacing to ward off a potential threat. Piloerection is not a voluntary response but rather is a sign of arousal, fear, or uncertainty; it tells us something about the emotional aspect of the behavior.

DOGS CONVEY THEIR internal motivation and inclination toward aggression by facial expression and body postures. Still, it can be a challenge to pick up on the signals our dogs try to convey. Signaling may be too quick or subtle for us to detect. Even a change of breathing pattern, for example, can indicate discomfort. In addition, dogs may be physically incapable of communicating their moods or behavioral inclinations because of characteristic breed traits for flattened faces or floppy ears (see "Breed Differences in Signaling"). Therefore, you must pay attention to *all* the clues, from the tip of the nose to the end of the tail (assuming the dog has a tail — and if the dog doesn't, she will be even more challenging to read).

In addition to the dog's behavior and signaling, it is equally impor-

Snarling (baring teeth) is part of every dog's potential behavioral repertoire.

Ilana Reisner, DVM, PhD

tant to consider the context of aggression. Who were the people present or nearby at the time the dog behaved aggressively? What immediately preceded the aggression, and where did it occur?

Congruency is the term behaviorists use to mean all the dog's signals are consistent. *Congruent signals* mean the dog is comfortable with her current decision about how to understand a situation and how to react to it. An open mouth with relaxed gaze and wagging tail are signals of a socially comfortable dog giving congruent signals.

Incongruent signals mean the dog is conflicted about the risks of a situation and how to react. This dog's behavior could change at any moment. A wagging tail with a lip curl and a low growl conveys incongruence; this dog is in conflict about what she will do next.

Why is it so important to observe and understand your dog's social signals? Because they provide the most direct path to the dog's current emotional state as well as her intentions. By watching our dogs, we can see that aggression is always provoked in some way, and it can often be anticipated and therefore avoided. Some communications are rather subtle but still detectable. Dr. Jacqueline Neilson presents a useful table on canine social signals in chapter 1 (see table 1.1 on page 9).

Breed Differences in Signaling

There are breed differences in a dog's ability to display social signals:

- Breeds with long, dangling ears or docked tails (Cocker, Brittany, and English Springer Spaniels, and others) cannot use these body parts very well to signal their social inclinations.
- Shar-Peis and Pugs and some other breeds have reduced and folded ears and limited ability to move them.
- The ears of Doberman Pinschers and Great Danes, among other breeds, are still traditionally altered with plastic surgery (although this is becoming less popular around the world). Cropped ears create a misleadingly aggressive look because the ears are artificially erect.
- Curly-coated breeds such as Poodles cannot signal arousal with raised hackles (piloerection).
- Some short-nosed breeds, such as Bulldogs (English and French), Boston Terriers, and Pugs, may be physically incapable of a lip curl, which can be an effective warning signal of aggression.
- Breeds such as the Akita and Chow Chow have fairly stoic facial expressions and may give abbreviated or inconspicuous displays (such as lip curls with growls), leading some people to comment that they might attack without warning or provocation.
- Dogs with permanently curled tails, such as Chow Chows and Shar-Peis, have more trouble lowering or tucking their tail than Labrador Retrievers and other straight-tailed breeds.
- The Old English Sheepdog has floppy ears, a bushy coat, and hair covering her eyes and cannot transmit the full set of signals that a German Shepherd can.
- Dogs with long hair around their face, eyes, and lips may have dilated pupils (indicating high autonomic arousal, or activation of the "fight or flight" system) or may snarl (show their teeth) without it being evident.

Why Is Reading My Dog's Signals So Important?
Your ability to read your dog is critical to being able to predict her behavior. *Most dog aggression is provoked and predictable,* so it is key to

learn the signals and understand the context. In fact, if you watch your dog's reactions to the world around her, including people, other dogs, and all kinds of environmental stimuli, you will have a better idea of her progress as you help her maneuver through potentially frightening situations. For example, your fearful dog might show initial nervousness and even avoidance when particular people approach on the sidewalk: her tail might go down and her pace might slow, her ears move backward, her eyes widen, and she might lick her lips. These are all signs of discomfort with the situation she is in, and you can't ignore them.

How should you respond? This would be an excellent time to give the approaching person a wide berth while talking softly and reassuringly to your dog. Rather than slowing or forcing her to walk close to the person, you can effectively avoid escalating her fear by walking briskly in another direction, behind a parked car, or across the street. If you have picked the correct course of action, your dog's body language will show *decreased* concern by walking fast again, tail held higher, ears relaxed. Offering some food to redirect her worry is an excellent distracter as well.

By watching your dog carefully, you can anticipate the triggers of her fear and, ultimately, prevent the fear from escalating into aggression. Remember, this is not "giving in" to your dog, but rather respecting her emotional state and allowing her to learn to trust you to protect her from harm and let you make the decisions about what is or is not a threat.

Ultimately, you must be proactive, stay alert to your dog's signals, and protect your dog from situations she can only respond to as a dog. By doing so, not only do you protect your dog and avoid unwanted behavior like biting, but ultimately you will also form a stronger relationship as she learns that she can trust you to decide what is best for her.

Is Aggression Always Provoked?

All dogs, however calm or tolerant they may seem, have the potential to bite. That does not make them "mean." Meanness really does not apply to our canine companions. There is no revenge or malice in dogs; they are merely using canine tools to respond to social situations.

Aggression can occur in response to many different triggers, such as the desire to keep possession of a favorite toy, a response to the approach of an "intruder" in the yard or house, or to a too-vigorous brushing of a matted coat. But these triggers are not always obvious. Maybe you just didn't see that unchewed rawhide chip three feet away from the dog under the sofa, or you thought your dog was tolerating the combing because she was standing still for it.

To those who don't know dogs, and sometimes even to those who do, aggression can indeed appear to be impulsive and unprovoked. However, in the majority of cases, once you understand what sets off an aggressive dog, her behavior becomes foreseeable and avoidable. The truth is that most aggressive behavior is provoked — at least from the dog's perspective — and predictable but may not occur every time a dog encounters a specific trigger. It is this lack of effective communication between us and our companion dogs that sometimes makes their behavior seem unpredictable.

Resource guarding is especially difficult for humans to understand. Traditionally, dogs are likely to value and guard food or food-related items, such as rawhide chews or food bowls. But it is important to view "value" from each individual dog's perspective. Dogs might guard a resting spot or bed, the bathroom trash, even their valuable food-giving owners.

Noticing the provocation, however, can be difficult. It can be challenging to pick up on all the subtle behavioral signals of some aggressive dogs. As discussed earlier, some dog breeds, and individuals within any breed, are rather stoic, or their signaling apparatus (or body language) has been tampered with by breeding, disease, or plastic surgery.

If this describes your dog, it would be wise to schedule an evaluation with a veterinary behaviorist, who can help you by getting more details about the aggression and then offering a diagnosis and a treatment plan. Remember, aggression is not a training problem but rather a problem of how the dog perceives what is happening to her and how she responds to that perception. As a result, aggression needs appropriate intervention to address the specific cause.

Most bites to younger children occur during a "positive" interaction, such as petting or hugging. Note that the dog here does not look comfortable or relaxed.

Ilana Reisner, DVM, PhD

We can protect our children and our dogs by being aware of the differences in how they look at the world. A resting or eating dog may not want to be bothered, or hugged and petted, and young children may be unable to read those signals, which can then result in biting.

Management: How Do We Begin?

Even though we all love our dogs, we must acknowledge that they might, in certain situations, bite. In fact, any dog, including the floppy-eared family pet you share your bed with, may bite. As with any of life's risks, the likelihood doesn't necessarily mean you should not take that chance — *if* it is outweighed by the benefits. Veterinarians, who must sometimes do unpleasant things, like touch a painful paw, are certainly aware of this. What can you do in day-to-day encounters to prevent aggression and, especially, biting?

- **Know your dog.** Each dog is an individual with her own temperament and sensitivities. Aggressiveness is influenced by physical health as well as the dog's reactivity, experience, and personality (including genetic temperament). Do you have a reactive or resource-guarding dog or one who is frightened of noises? Consider this when weighing your dog's risk for aggression and plan accordingly.

- **Be aware that the risk of aggression may increase with behavioral maturity.** Behavioral maturity occurs *later* than physical maturity. If your puppy or immature dog seems frightened or nervous in the face of unfamiliar people or situations, there may be an increased chance that she will express that fear through biting when she is a mature adult, at one to three years of age. Scheduling an appointment with a veterinary behaviorist when things first change will give you the information you need so that you know what to do.

- **Know, avoid, and lessen *your dog*'s triggers for biting.** An everyday situation might be meaningless to one dog but a grave threat to another. For example, consider what happens when you approach an unchewed rawhide bone lying near your resting dog. While your dog might open one eye at your approach and then go back to sleep, your neighbor's dog might guard the bone with a growl and a lunge.

- **Be aware of canine communication and body language.** Dogs usually signal their fear, arousal, and uncertainty. It's a good idea to watch your dog's face, eyes, head, tail, and body posture to decipher what she is saying. Generally speaking, it's not good to assume your dog will accept certain people, dogs, situations, or events. If she seems nervous, take your dog away from the situation as soon as you can.

- **Understand the typical provocations of aggression for all dogs.**
    - Pain
    - Punishment
    - Defending oneself
    - Being disturbed while resting
    - Physical manipulation, pushing, pulling
    - Being disturbed while in a denlike area
    - Being disturbed while on a high-value bed

- Defending the home, yard, car, and other territory
- Being approached when behind a fence, in a car, or in a crate
- Defending high-value resources that are approached, touched, or removed

The following are some behavioral management tools to help you deal with aggression realistically and safely.

Safety

The best strategy for dealing with aggressive behavior is to prevent it from happening in the first place. But if you are faced with a growling or lunging dog in an emergency situation, it is important to remove yourself from the interaction as quickly as possible. Remember our earlier discussion about punishment and how it can escalate aggression? If your own dog is growling at you or attempting to bite, turn and walk away.

After you have safely removed yourself, consider the situation. If the trigger is simple to figure out (for example, you were reaching to clip on a leash when your reluctant dog had withdrawn into a corner), it can be equally simple to avoid the problem the next time (call the dog to you rather than cornering her). In some situations, avoidance is the solution.

In other cases, and when it is safe to do so, it is also important to work with the dog to teach her to accept such approaches or interactions. Changing the mood of the interaction from exasperation to cheerfulness can help. A tossed handful of treats can coax food-loving dogs out of their hiding spots, and the same food can be used as a lure to move the dog to the door. Rather than defending herself from an angry owner, your dog would now view the situation as much safer and more enticing.

The Resource-Guarding Dog

If your dog claims ownership of an item that isn't dangerous, such as a tissue from the trash, you might decide to just let her have it. Don't take it away unless you are confident that your dog is unconcerned when "her" things are taken. A good strategy when you *need* to take something away is to offer something else in trade. This method can be effective, but it is important to be careful. Dogs are awfully quick, and they can take the treat you offer, return to the item just as you reach for it, and still inflict a bite. A better strategy is to throw the delectable treat a distance away so that the dog has to leave the item behind. You then have a chance to pick it up before the dog can return. Or try the two-treat method of trading with one treat to get the dog to come to you and then luring her away into another room with the other. Shut the door and return to safely discard the item.

Keep in mind that you are simply redirecting your dog's attention away from something you want to take away. Once your dog is a safe distance from the item, any food given is not likely to be linked with the thing she abandoned. Is this bribery? In a way. But there is nothing wrong with bribing or enticing a dog to move from one place to another. In fact, it is a humane method of moving a dog who might otherwise be reluctant or confused. You can always take it a step further and teach your dog to relinquish items when asked.

What about food-guarding dogs? It is very important that, first, you *do not* take your dog's chew toys or food away while your dog is engaged in chewing or eating. Second, for safety, dogs who guard their food should be fed in a secure, separate location without interference. Third, with puppies (with whom it is still safe to attempt handling exercises), try to associate your approach and touch with *adding* a delicious treat. Teach your puppy that your presence is thrilling and wonderful — not something to be feared.

Moving Your Dog from One Place to Another

A helpful and safe strategy is to *teach* your dog to move from one place to another on cue. Again, as an emergency measure, a handful of tossed food can do wonders to transform a fearful, reactive dog into one who is focused on kibble. For a longer-term solution, take the time to teach cues such as "off" (the bed), "come" (from anywhere, anytime), and even "go to" (a particular spot). Using positive reinforcement to teach these tasks will result in a happily compliant dog and will avoid the need to reach for the collar of a reluctant or nervous dog. (See chapters 3 and 7 for more information on training.)

Making Interactions Predictable and Safe

For any dog, but especially for those who are nervous or anxious, it is important to establish a routine and predictable vocabulary. As discussed in chapter 7, make it a point to ask your dog to sit before she gets all sorts of things she may want. Instead of food, we are using the "life reward" of the open door or the tossed ball. These exercises are not intended to force "payment for services," but rather are an excellent way to make our dogs' lives as predictable as possible. By asking them to sit before getting positive things for themselves, we teach them to look to us for guidance and allow *us* to make decisions for them. With enough repetition and consistency, they are only too glad to hand the responsibility for their well-being over to us. Just as we try to teach impulsive children to say "please," we are asking our dogs to do the same thing before they receive things.

For nervous dogs, this is critical for several reasons. First, stress is increased when dogs don't know what to expect at any given moment, and our goal is to reduce their stress so that we can also reduce the chances of fear-related aggression. Second, nervous, worried dogs (like many of us when we are anxious) are motivated to take care of themselves by taking the situation into their own paws.

Safe Haven/Refuge

This has been discussed in other chapters in this book, but it is worth just a short mention here. If your dog has learned that her place is safe when things are calm, it will be much easier for her to go there when things are chaotic and she should not be part of the action. A safe haven allows your dog to take a break from the chaos of parties and playdates and provides safety for both your pet and your visitors. Use this area to keep your dog away from triggers that are known to cause aggressive responses. (For more on safe havens/refuges, see chapter 8.)

Avoiding Punishment

Harsh treatment and punishment are not necessary when you're managing your dog's behavior, and at worst are likely to increase anxiety and aggression. There is no need to use leash pops (a quick tug on the leash), shock collars, alpha rolls (flipping the dog onto her back), dominance downs (physically restraining the dog on her side), growling, hitting, or other aversive interactions with dogs. Such treatment is not recommended for *any* canine behavior problem, but it is particularly ill-advised in managing aggression.

Meeting Your Dog's Daily Needs

All dogs must have their needs met. Make sure to meet your dog's daily needs for social interaction, exploration, exercise, and play. This does not need to be a two-hour walk; it can just be a short stroll — a five-to-ten-minute sniff walk a few times a week. Dogs love to sniff and chew and should have safe outlets for those behaviors as well. Finally, dogs need to be with their people on their own terms. Some dogs like petting and stroking, but some do not. Please realize that your dog may be happiest just sitting at your feet while you read your e-mail, or lounging on your bed. But find a way to safely interact with your dog that is satisfying to both of you.

When More Than Management Is Needed: Behavior Modification and Control Tools

When you schedule a consultation with a veterinary behaviorist, once a diagnosis and prognosis have been established, she will discuss a treatment plan specifically designed for you and your pet. This plan will include several measures, including the management interventions discussed in the previous section.

Behavior modification plans should be designed to do these four things:

1. Change the underlying emotion that is driving the unwanted behavior, in this case the aggression. This means instead of being anxious or afraid, your dog would be relaxed and happy.
2. Understand how the dog's response varies as different aspects of the stimulus that triggers her aggression change. This could be the intensity, the distance, the sound, or any number of stimulus variables that affect the intensity of the dog's response. These must be understood and factored into creating a successful treatment plan.

3. Teach your pet a new response to the situation. This can only happen when training sessions are correctly structured to avoid a full-strength exposure to the stimulus and the full-strength response. Your dog only learns when she is calm. If your dog is calm and under control, you can be calm, too.

4. Reward the right response, which is usually done with delectable food rewards and perhaps play.

Keep in mind that even with a behavior modification plan, some situations may never be safe for your dog and must always be avoided (see "Unsafe at Any Time," below).

Another useful adjunct to treatment is control devices, such as head collars, harnesses, and muzzles. These tools can give you better control, make the dog feel more secure, and provide safety for people who might come in contact with your dog. (See chapter 5 for more details on how and when to use these tools.)

Unsafe at Any Time

While successfully managing aggression issues can result in a significant decrease in the frequency and severity of aggression, there are circumstances that can be consistently high risk and should always be avoided. This is especially true for anxious, highly reactive, or easily aroused dogs. Here are a few of the circumstances you may need to avoid virtually all the time:

- Large gatherings of people in your home, particularly if you are unable to closely supervise and manage your dog's behavior. If gatherings like these occur, your dog must be safely confined elsewhere.

- Visits to your home by young, active children, because young children can be unsettling for an anxious dog. If children will be visiting your home, your dog must be safely confined elsewhere.

- Workers or service personnel in your home; they usually move quickly around the home, carry tools, and make loud noises. To be safe you must confine and isolate your dog during these events every time they occur.

- Leaving your dog alone in a yard (fenced or unfenced). This situation allows your dog to choose how to react to people or dogs going by or approaching the yard. This can lead to aggressive, territorial responses. Always be in the yard with your dog and keep her engaged in activities so she is less likely to focus on passersby.

- Electronic fencing as a fence replacement in your yard should never be used without your close supervision. Electronic fencing does not prevent people or animals from entering your yard while your dog is loose there. If sufficiently motivated, highly reactive dogs can run through the fence.
- Off-leash dog parks are stressful for the fearful, anxious dog; dogs and people can approach at will. While being off leash may allow your dog to flee from other dogs and people, the potential for fights between dogs or aggression toward people can be a significant risk.

Counterconditioning and Desensitization

Counterconditioning means teaching a new response, and desensitization means learning to experience the stimulus without displaying the unwanted response. Sometimes these behavior modification techniques are needed to improve a dog's behavior.

Nancy and Ed brought in Tucker, an eight-year-old ninety-pound Labrador Retriever, for a behavioral consultation because he lunged and barked at other dogs while on walks. Nancy was frightened by his behavior, and one time Tucker pulled Ed to the ground. Not only was his behavior frightening, it had become dangerous. Tucker was showing fear-based aggression toward other dogs.

The first step was to restrict all walks to a time when it was unlikely they would encounter other dogs. Next, Tucker was fitted with a head collar to give Nancy and Ed additional control. They and Tucker were taught a calming cue: Tucker would look at Nancy or Ed and get a food reward when he relaxed. The relaxation had to be complete — a soft, calm dog; relaxed ears, eyes, face, body, and tail — not anxious in any way.

They also charted his responses on a sliding scale: When would Tucker look at the approaching dog? When would he bark? When would he pull? When would he lunge? Using the lowest level of response (looking at an approaching dog), they began to work on counterconditioning and desensitization. When Tucker first saw a dog on a walk, usually about half a block away, Nancy or Ed asked him to sit and relax. As the dog got closer, maybe by twenty or thirty feet, Nancy or Ed continued to feed Tucker treats. Before Tucker would escalate to another level (in his case, barking), they put the treats away and left by crossing the street or turning in the other direction. Over time, other dogs on a walk could get closer, but often Nancy or Ed just crossed the street anyway, before Tucker could respond inappropriately. Tucker, Ed, and Nancy learned how to manage the dog's responses and their walks so he could be safe and not anxious.

Can Aggression Be Cured?

Because behavior is a complicated expression of many components — physical and emotional health, social and physical environment, genetics and temperament, and of course, learning — it is simplistic to think in terms of "curing" a behavior problem. Many behavior problems are best viewed as chronic conditions (like diabetes or asthma) that require understanding and long-term management.

Most important, remember that aggression is part of the normal behavioral repertoire of dogs. Any dog is capable of biting, *whether or not* the dog has a history of biting. It is part of their normal social communication. When we accept that idea, we might then have a more-realistic view of aggressive behavior as normal defensiveness or resource guarding. It cannot be *cured*, because its potential never entirely goes away. Instead, veterinary behaviorists focus on the *reasons* for biting, acknowledging the risk and then lessening that risk as much as possible.

Can Medication Help?

Some behavior problems are more challenging than others to treat. This is particularly true when the behavior is at least partly temperament related (that is, genetic) rather than solely a result of learning.

In some cases, training your dog and changing the environment and your management are not enough to significantly change the problem. In those cases, drug therapy might be a helpful addition to the dog's treatment plan. Its usefulness depends on several factors, including the veterinarian's or veterinary behaviorist's assessment of the individual dog and the particular goals and expectations of your family. Remember, only veterinarians are qualified and licensed to recommend and prescribe drug therapy for dogs.

When might drug therapy help?

- When there is underlying anxiety. Anxious dogs may not respond to behavior modification as well as dogs who are not anxious, simply because stress hinders their ability to learn. Management of the problem might hit a plateau and go no further. Stress can also easily override the effects of learning. When you think about it, anxiety and depression are forms of pain, and your pet deserves relief from suffering.
- When it is not possible to control the stimulus — such as claps of thunder — that cause fear-related aggression. As an alternative, the dog's reactivity might be controlled instead.
- When the character of the aggressive behavior is explosive. Some dogs appear to go "from zero to sixty" in a flash and are reacting to underlying physiological changes. This is related to an adrenaline rush and results in the dog experiencing extreme stress. In such situations, medication can help regulate the dog's reactivity so that she is better able to listen to the owner and perhaps even have self-control.
- When the behavior is related to a physical problem. For example, irritability and aggression can be linked to pain, whether acute (sudden onset) or chronic (long term). Treatment with pain-relieving medications can sometimes help reduce the aggression.

If your veterinarian or veterinary behaviorist has determined that there is a compelling reason to use medication, it may be a useful adjunct to the behavior modification plan. You should know that using medications to treat aggressive behavior is considered to be "off-label use," meaning that no drug has been licensed or specifically approved to treat aggression. Many of the antianxiety drugs used in dogs were first developed as antidepressants for humans, before being adapted by the veterinary behaviorists for use in animals.

Medication must not be administered without a thorough assessment of the behavior problem, along with an understanding of the safety measures required for the dog. The dog must be handled and managed as if she might bite, and behavior modification (training, changes in the environment, and management) is a critical part of the process.

When the stimuli that are triggering aggression cannot be managed, drug therapy is a risky strategy. While it may diminish arousal and reactivity, it may not make the dog safe in those situations. Aggression in these cases cannot be "cured" by drug therapy, but medication may help to ameliorate the dog's reactivity so that you can get her under control *at a safe distance from the target of aggression.*

It's also important to understand that any behavior-modifying drug has the potential to *increase* aggression and arousal. Just as people who are taking antidepressants might feel more nervous and more anxious than they did without the drug, dogs can experience agitation and even irritability on medication. Because of this potential, it is most important to have a systematic plan in place so that safety issues, prevention, positive reinforcement–based training, avoiding provocations, and other steps are taken along with the medication.

Aggression presents a complex situation when it comes to using behavior-modifying drugs. Behavior-modifying drugs can be useful in management, but it is important to remember that aggressive behavior cannot be "cured" and that the risk of biting cannot be entirely eliminated. Dogs who bite will continue to be dogs who bite, and dogs who threaten to bite *can still become dogs who do bite.*

Does Your Dog Have the Right to Say No?

Like us, dogs are sentient beings who can feel frightened, stressed, or contented. Life with dogs is a lot simpler if we think of their needs as well as our own and attribute some autonomy to our complex companions. Dogs will express their reluctance or ambivalence through their actions and body language. If a family member or unfamiliar person initiates an interaction and the dog does not reciprocate by approaching, it is best to leave the dog alone. This is true whether your child wants to hug the family dog who is sleeping on her bed or couch or whether a stranger approaches with his or her own dog to "say hello." If your dog does not jump off the couch to play with your child, let the dog sleep in peace and keep your child from interrupting her rest (or separate them with a secure gate). If she stiffens or growls when other dogs approach, lead her the other way. Rather than assuming your dog feels up to such interactions or, worse, assuming she *should,* allow your dog to say no and quietly discontinue or interrupt the interaction.

Can You Choose an Unaggressive Dog?

There is at least some genetic basis to personality and temperament. You should always choose a dog whose parents do not display resource guarding, fearfulness, or aggression to people — if it is possible, of course, to know the personality and tendencies for aggression of the dog's parents or other relatives. It is not clear, however, whether aggression to other dogs predicts aggression to people. If there is some aggression in the parents' history (such as growling over a bone when approached), consider whether this aggression is expected, predictable, and mild. Even aggression that is all these things might be unacceptable for a family pet.

What about the breed itself? Although breed generalizations are often made, the characteristics of individual dogs within each breed are too inconsistent to be meaningful. There are many books written about specific dog breeds. Golden Retrievers, for instance, are often portrayed as ideal family dogs, but the truth is that every family is different and every individual dog within any breed is different, too. If you are determined to have a purebred dog, it is most important to find an ethical and responsible breeder who takes temperament as seriously as you do. Look at breeds other families have and talk to breeders and handlers at dog shows. (See chapter 2 for more information on choosing a dog.)

Can We Work Things Out with This Dog?

Your dog doesn't have to be perfect, but she should be perfectly safe for you and your family. Sometimes, even in the best of homes with the most conscientious and experienced pet owners, there are dogs who cannot be safely kept in the home, either because of human-dog mismatch (that is, mismatching the owner's expectations, personality, or skills) or because the aggressive behavior is too difficult to manage. Some cases in which a dog may not make an ideal pet include the following:

- Dogs who are not well socialized to people or children perhaps because of social isolation, neglect, or abuse may be extremely difficult or impossible to rehabilitate so that they can comfortably and safely live with people.
- Dogs with a history of extreme arousal and uninhibited aggression may continue to have aggressive outbursts and remain a danger to family members.
- Owners who are unable or unwilling to follow the treatment plan recommended by a veterinary behaviorist. While it is possible that some of these dogs might respond better to being in another home, there may be liability or other concerns in rehoming animals with known aggression.
- Cases of serious aggression may persist even after treatment by veterinary behaviorists.
- Large dogs can be particularly difficult to handle if they are aggressive to people.
- Homes that are not a good fit for dogs, generally speaking, might include those with family members who have special needs and might interact unsafely with the dog. This would include aging family members with dementia or people of any age who cannot reliably follow guidelines or rules.

How to Decide What to Do with Your Aggressive Dog

Although it is hard to give up on someone you love, sometimes life presents limited choices. Factors that may lead you to choose not to keep your dog include when your dog's aggression has been evaluated by a veterinary behaviorist and given a poor prognosis (that is, a poor expected outcome for improvement), or if you have explored all the options and have seen little or no improvement, or if your dog's aggressiveness presents an ongoing threat to your safety and well-being. In any of those cases, this is not the dog for you.

A study of behavior-related euthanasia in dogs who were aggressive to their owners, conducted by Dr. Ilana Reisner, showed that certain characteristics make such dogs more difficult to keep in the home. These include larger size, lack of predictability in the aggression they show, and aggression in situations that should not seem provocative, such as petting or walking nearby. These characteristics seem to make sense and are likely to cause strains in the relationship between dogs and their human family. Unfortunately, the problems you have with your dog are likely to be repeated in a new home (though this is sometimes not the case), making rehoming a poor option. In addition, liability issues must be considered.

Avoiding Pitfalls and Staying on Track

It is important to realize that any dog has the potential to behave aggressively. Proactive interactions are critical for each and every pet owner, whether your dog has shown aggressive tendencies or not. If your dog is aggressive and you are determined to keep her despite the risk, however small it may be, you need to foresee high-risk situations and be prepared to prevent them as much as possible.

Aggressive behavior is not a training problem; there are many well-trained dogs who bite people. Therefore, if you choose to keep your dog, a consultation with a board-certified veterinary behaviorist, when possible, is the first step. This will give you a diagnosis, a realistic view of expectations, and a treatment plan for you and your family to follow.

To keep your dog safe and others safe, you must think proactively *for the life of the dog.* Avoid identified triggers and high-risk situations.

For example, dogs who fight with other dogs should not go to the dog park; dogs who are afraid of new people should not greet strangers (and the strangers should not be permitted, no matter how much they insist it will be fine, to approach and pet the dog!).

If you must walk your dog in areas where you will encounter the situations that cause aggressive responses, walk at low-traffic times of day. You may wish to walk the dog with a basket muzzle (see chapter 5). Such a device allows her to pant and get treats for counterconditioning or for good behavior.

Don't leave your dog unattended *anywhere,* even in your own backyard. In addition, anticipate problem situations, so that your dog won't be set up to make a decision you will both regret.

What happened to Sherlock, the dog we talked about at the beginning of this chapter? Fortunately for everyone involved, no one was hurt that day. Sherlock's owner stopped using the long retractable leash and switched to a four-foot leash to give her better control. She gradually introduced a head halter rather than a neck collar when walking with Sherlock. To help give Sherlock direction, she also started practicing the obedience exercises they had learned in training class using sit-stays and down-stays throughout the day. Sherlock became much calmer once he was comfortable with these more-appropriate responses to everyday situations, and he actually felt better with the predictability that his owner's control added to his life.

Always get help from a qualified professional such as a veterinary behaviorist. With appropriate diagnosis and behavioral interventions, aggressive behaviors can often be safely managed and improved.

What Did We Say?

- Aggression is almost always provoked, even if the triggers are too subtle for humans to notice.
- Dog owners must be proactive, staying alert to their dog's signals and protecting their dog from situations they can only respond to as dogs.
- Don't focus on just one element of a dog's social signaling.
- Do pay attention to a dog's face, ears, tail, vocalizations, and over-

all body posture to better understand what she is signaling and perhaps how aggressive she could become.

- Even the best dog could behave aggressively under the right set of circumstances; always *think proactively to protect your pet* from situations that are beyond her control or ability to interpret, except from a dog's perspective.
- Always consult with a board-certified veterinary behaviorist or ask your primary-care veterinarian for a referral to a veterinary behaviorist or other well-trained professional, such as a Certified Applied Animal Behaviorist, if your dog shows any aggression, so that you can get a diagnosis, safety assessment, and treatment plan.
- Aggression can often be managed, but it can never be "cured."

11

Loyalty Gone Overboard:
Separation Anxiety
The "Velcro Dog" Dilemma

E'Lise Christensen, DVM, DACVB
Karen L. Overall, MA, VMD, PhD, DACVB, CAAB

Malcolm was the perfect companion. He'd been adopted from a breeder after Malcolm retired from a stellar show-dog career. He was charming and friendly with people and other dogs. He spent many of his days at work with his owner, Charles. However, whenever Charles left him home alone, mayhem resulted. Malcolm barked all day and chewed and scratched up pillows, furniture, and rugs.

Charles loved Malcolm dearly but was angry and frustrated at the dog's inability to stay home alone. He believed Malcolm was vocalizing and destroying items out of spite because Charles had not brought him along. Charles tried punishing Malcolm by dragging him over to the destroyed items and scolding him. When that didn't work, he put Malcolm in a crate to stop the destructive behavior, but this seemed to actually make things worse.

When Charles came home to a crate full of urine, he realized Malcolm might not be "angry"; he might be suffering and scared. Charles decided to videotape Malcolm's home-alone behavior. He was horrified to see how right he was. When he was alone, Malcolm dug at the crate door, urinated on himself, and whined. He drooled profusely. He didn't stop until he was so exhausted that he couldn't stay awake anymore, a few hours after Charles left.

Charles discovered what veterinary behaviorists already know: many dogs who destroy or rearrange items, vocalize, injure themselves, salivate excessively, pace, and engage in other problem behaviors when alone are experiencing a serious type of suffering — separation anxiety.

Bonding in Dogs

It's great when our dogs run to greet us and seem to follow us around. In fact, for many people this is one of their favorite parts of having a dog. After all, we don't just fall for their huge eyes and soft coat; unconditional adoration is pretty heady stuff. For us humans living in a complicated social world, isn't it nice to come home to someone who just can't wait to see us?

Being social and bonding to people has probably been genetically selected as dogs evolved to become man's best friend. Some of this increased bonding may have been due to humans purposely breeding sociable dogs, or it may be because dogs who were naturally social with people had better access to protection, food, and other resources. Regardless, people had a hand in creating a species that is uniquely bonded with us.

These days, this unique bond can undergo stress from busy schedules that leave sensitive dogs without companionship, and that's the problem. In essence, over thousands of years we may have helped create the anxious little creatures who today keep pet-sitters in business on Friday nights or keep the dogs' family watching TV reruns instead of going out to the movies.

It can be normal for dogs, especially puppies, to show some distress when they're separated from attachment figures, such as dependable dog or human companions. This distress should be brief (less than a few minutes) and not too intense (for instance, the dog may whine a little, but then be happily able to eat). The signs of distress should diminish over time as the dog or puppy learns the daily schedule and can predict the return of those he is missing.

Dogs with separation anxiety are not just sad or disappointed when they are left alone. They do not learn to tolerate absences, the way less-anxious dogs do. Instead, when left alone, they experience extreme distress that frequently doesn't improve unless it is treated.

Even people who adore their dogs must leave them alone sometimes. When people leave their dogs alone, they don't expect or want to come home to pools of urine, piles of feces, a shredded couch, or complaints from the neighbors about the mournful wailing that occurs in their absence. For people whose dogs suffer from separation anxiety, though, these complaints are part of daily life. These behaviors put the human-animal bond in jeopardy, leaving these dogs at risk of abuse, abandonment, and euthanasia.

Rescued dogs are thought to be more likely to have separation anxiety. We don't know whether this is due to the trauma of the relinquishment itself, the time spent in the shelter, or whether their separation anxiety was the reason they were abandoned in the first place. Many people do not report separation anxiety behaviors to shelters or rescue groups when they hand over their dog, because they are afraid the dog will be euthanized as a result. Unfortunately, this means that there is no accurate count of shelter or rescue dogs suffering from separation anxiety.

What Is Separation Anxiety?

Dogs with separation anxiety have a behavioral disorder and show physical, physiological, or behavioral signs of distress *only* in the absence of their people or when they cannot get to their people because a door is closed, a gate is up, or they're otherwise physically separated. Occasionally a dog will exhibit signs of separation anxiety *only* when a *specific* person is absent or not accessible.

Most of these dogs are *fairly* normal when home with their people. They will not always insist on being in the same room with their people and will play normally with other pets. When left alone, though, the troubled dog won't engage with other pets; normal household dogs may avoid these frantic dogs when they are in the depths of their distress.

Occasionally a dog is not so normal and becomes a "Velcro dog" — one who can never, ever be parted from his people. In the worst manifestation, he may need to be always touching someone. These much less common hyperattached dogs may have no life separate from that of their people.

The most commonly reported behaviors associated with separation anxiety include urination, defecation, destruction, and excessive vocalization (usually barking or howling). These are the signs people recognize most easily. Dogs with separation anxiety may also show many other signs that are usually not noticed by pet owners without a video of their dog. Drooling, panting, freezing (becoming immobile), withdrawal, and changes in problem solving and other cognitive behaviors are less commonly noted because they are less apparent and simply can't be observed if you're not home. Unfortunately, dogs displaying these signs may never be diagnosed.

So how can you tell if your dog is exhibiting these less obvious behaviors?

Urine and saliva can evaporate while you are gone, but a small, handheld black light will make urine fluoresce. If you move the light slowly and low over the floor or carpeting, the places where the dog has urinated will light up.

If your dog has salivated, the fur may be stained a rust color (this may not be visible in dogs with dark coats). If you're not sure if your dog salivates when you are gone, run your hands over his legs and chest. If he was salivating, you'll feel stiff, stuck-together hair that's thick with saliva residue.

You may not know if your dog barks or howls all day long unless someone complains or you notice that the dog is actually hoarse. Voice-activated recorders are now cheap and will record barking dogs, as will the memo feature on answering machines. But the best way to learn if your dog is barking (and the best way to learn if he is pacing, shaking, freezing in place, and so on) is to videotape him. *Videos enable dogs to tell us about their day.* Dogs who are panting, pacing, rigidly sitting in a fixed position, or whimpering when no one can hear them are profoundly distressed and suffering. Videos give these dogs a voice and provide you with the behavioral information you need to help the dog.

Common Signs in Dogs with Separation Anxiety

- Urination
- Defecation*
- Salivation
- Destruction*
- Panting

- Pacing
- Freezing/immobility
- Trembling/shaking
- Vocalization*

*These signs are easiest for owners to recognize.

Videos of the dog when you are gone provide the best information for you and your veterinarian to share. You will want to video the dog from a few stationary locations (include at least the door by which people exit and the dog's favorite resting place). Also video the dog when you are home, so you can compare the happier dog to the distressed one. This is an important step, because it will help you identify behaviors you wish to change and those you wish to reward. The behaviors of concern listed under "Common Signs" will just pop out when you compare videos.

In general, behavior problems are most easily fixed if they are caught early. You can video your dog once or twice a year to make sure he's not showing signs of separation anxiety. If he is, you can get help immediately rather than waiting for it to get bad enough for you to see clinical signs.

Is That Really True?

As is true for most behavioral problems involving dogs, there are a lot of myths about separation anxiety and its treatment. Here are some of them:

- People who travel for their job sometimes say they are gone so much that their dogs are beginning to develop separation anxiety.

Yet breeders and veterinary staff who raise or work with puppies often tell people to teach the dog to learn to be alone so that he doesn't develop separation anxiety. So which is it?

- If you just got a dog, someone may tell you not to "spoil" the dog by letting him sleep in your bed, because then you won't be able to leave him alone.

- If you have a busy life, someone will tell you that your dog destroys things because you are on the go too much to have a dog. If you have a quiet life, other "experts" will suggest that the dog is destroying the house because you don't have enough to do and you "spoil" the dog, making him "too bonded" to you.

- If you have just one dog, people tell you that, of course, the poor dog shrieks while you are gone because he's lonely and because you focus too much on him. If you have more than one dog, people tell you that you have too many pets, so there's no way to pay enough attention to the dog with the problem.

- If you change from working at home to working in an office, you may hear that your dog urinates on the rug out of "spite" because he is angry that you leave.

- If your dog is "remodeling" your house, people may say your dog is bored and needs a job or more things to occupy him — even though he never plays with or eats the food from his food toys until you come home.

- Dogs need "limits." You should crate your dog, regardless of his reaction, when you are gone.

- Rescuers, shelters, and rescue sites often speak of Velcro dogs. These Velcro dogs are portrayed as good pets for people who really want attention from their dogs: "He'll always be by your side, and you'll always know where he is."

These contradictory characterizations often cause confusion and frustration for dog owners, resulting in either failure to get help in managing this condition or, worse yet, getting the wrong type of help, and not focusing on addressing the underlying anxiety.

Facts, Not Fiction

Data collected from trials to approve medications for the treatment of separation anxiety have helped to clarify what we do know — and can be surprising. The results put to rest many concerns arising from the rampant misinformation on separation anxiety.

Who the dog lives with or what the families do does not matter. Solo dogs and those who lived in multidog and multipet households were equally represented in the medication trials. Also, separation anxiety is not contagious: dogs who lived with a dog who had separation anxiety did not develop it themselves.

Marital status and whether the family had children had nothing to do with whether there were separation issues. Dogs with separation anxiety were just as likely to come from homes where everyone worked outside the home as they were to come from homes where someone was usually or always home.

Research also showed that separation anxiety is not caused by dog owners but is due to many factors. Some clients doted on their dogs, and others had dogs who were just part of the general business of the household. As has been shown in other studies, "spoiling" the dog did not affect whether separation anxiety developed. Some owners of dogs with separation anxiety allowed the dogs to sleep in their bed; some did not. Some people fed premium dog food, some did not. Some people barely groomed their dogs, others had clothes for them. The clothed dogs may have occasionally looked embarrassed, but dressing up the dog did not cause the separation anxiety.

There is no breed disposition for separation anxiety. The proportion of purebred and mixed-breed dogs did not differ from that of the general animal hospital population to which the affected group was compared. No breed was found to be more likely to have separation anxiety.

Dogs who were adopted as adults, strays, or rescues were not more likely to have separation anxiety when compared with the numbers of adults, rescues, and strays in the overall hospital population. There appeared to be no one "right" breed or source of dogs that would guarantee dogs free of separation anxiety.

More exercise and activity is not all they need. The vast majority of these dogs are neither understimulated nor deprived; they are not bored, either. Separation anxiety even affects dogs who have dog doors and access to the outside world! Videos reveal that affected dogs ignore the invitations of other dogs to play with them, do not use food toys, and do not eat food that they would otherwise gobble. Dogs who dig their way through walls and doors or who escape by breaking windows not only injure themselves physically, sometimes severely, but after doing so often seek out someone — anyone — who is home or who will sit with them.

These dogs are not distressed because their owners are not "dominant" enough. There is no research supporting the idea that owners cause separation anxiety in their dogs.

Myths that seek to place blame interfere with the dog getting help — an accurate diagnosis and appropriate treatment. Dogs with separation anxiety are distressed. They are *not* angry and behaving spitefully. Instead, they are behaving in a frantic manner that *they cannot control.*

These dogs are not punishing you for leaving them alone. Instead, they are responding physically and behaviorally to the profound distress — and sometimes panic — they feel when they are separated from their people. Malcolm, the dog at the beginning of the chapter, was punished for his destructive and vocal behaviors because his owner felt he was being spiteful — until he realized how much Malcolm was suffering.

What Does That Mean?

Separation anxiety: Significant distress that accompanies a dog's anticipation of being separated from family members and that continues when he is left alone. Some clinical signs are vocalization, destruction, house soiling in dogs who are otherwise housetrained, drooling, panting, and pacing. Many of these dogs exhibit clinical signs of panic when they are left alone.

Panic: A sudden, intense feeling of terror, accompanied by strong physical signs, such as a racing heart, agitation, stomach upset, escape behaviors, and panting. Panic may occur even if there's no specific, identifiable trigger.

Desensitization and counterconditioning: Treatment processes that are meant to be gentle and gradual and incorporate learning. These techniques involve exposing the dog to the situation that causes fear or distress, but at such a low level that the dog does not react with distress, and then gradually increasing some aspect of the exposure the dog finds distressing (this is desensitization). At the same time, the dog is taught a behavior that is favorable and fun and is incompatible with exhibiting the undesirable behavior (this is counterconditioning).

Anxiety: Apprehensive anticipation of dangerous, dreaded, or fear-inducing situations. Anxiety is usually recognized in dogs by signs of hypervigilance (the dog is easy to startle and is excessively watchful), restlessness, increased muscle tension, and trembling.

What Do We Really Know?

You've had a long day at work. You're looking forward to getting home and relaxing with your dog. You hope the new crate you bought for your dog is comfortable. It should be. It's large, and you put it in an airy spot; it has a blanket, a water dispenser, his favorite chew toys, and a food puzzle toy filled with the peanut butter he loves.

You chose the crate because, as your hours at work grew, you were beginning to come home to destroyed books and papers. And then the edge of the sofa was chewed. Your dog is young, your hours long; maybe the dog is just looking for something to do while you are gone. Someone recommended the crate and the toys. Your dog seemed to enjoy going in the crate for treats during the weekend, but this is the first day he was left alone, locked inside.

You open the front door and — the dog jumps on you! You look around and the house is a complete mess. Not only are books and papers chewed, but pillows and cushions are shredded. And the crate?

The blanket is strained through the bars, the water dispenser upended, the food toys have been ignored, and the bars of the crate are bent so the door hangs open.

And your poor dog! His gums are bleeding and he broke a tooth. His nails are broken and a pad is cut. There is blood on the rugs. What is wrong with your best friend? Can it be fixed? You love your dog but you *must* go to work. So you call the veterinarian.

Common Patterns of Behavior

Many dogs with separation anxiety show some common patterns. Your dog may fit one of these categories:

- The dog is distressed only if left totally alone but does not have a problem if he's at doggie daycare or with a pet-sitter.
- The dog is distressed only if left by one special person or a few people and is not helped by daycare or a pet-sitter.
- The dog is home with a person or people but becomes distressed when he is denied access to them (such as by doors or gates).
- The dog experiences schedule changes. For example, the daily schedule changes from fixed to erratic, or early to late. He can be alone without problems for six hours but not eight hours.
- For dogs with other coexisting anxiety-related conditions, the dog experiences the same or similar signs when exposed to a scary event (such as fireworks or thunderstorms).

It is often said that puppies need to be taught to tolerate time alone and that crating is a great way to do this. While appropriate crate training may not cause harm, it is not necessarily protective against separation anxiety. If a dog is behaviorally healthy and normal, the dog will take time away from people and other animals on his own, and some may select secluded areas, even a crate, for that time.

Early, classic research in the 1950s and 1960s shows that by two to four weeks, pups start to follow one another, and by five weeks they will rush an opening in a dog run as a group. By five weeks of age, if allowed to explore, dogs will begin to go off by themselves, honing exploration skills that continue to develop rapidly through fourteen weeks of age.

So if your dog is normal, he will seek circumstances where he can be alone and circumstances where he can be social, unless an overprotective human prevents him from doing so.

A study published in 2011 shows that dogs adopted at thirty to forty days (about 4.5 to 6 weeks) were more likely to be destructive, bark excessively, show fear on walks, react to noises, act possessive of toys and food, and exhibit true and excessive attention-seeking behavior from their people, compared with those adopted at sixty days (8.5 weeks). The take-home message from this finding is *not* that dogs must be "taught" to be left alone, but rather that, when possible, *puppies should remain with their parents and littermates in an environment where they are safely encouraged to explore and learn from the world around them until they are at least eight weeks old.*

While human behaviors may not cause separation anxiety, how humans behave around their dog can be *essential* in helping the dog recover from it. Well-adjusted dogs may not need to be taught to be comfortable being alone, but dogs with separation anxiety need to be taught, through a gradual and punishment-free process, that they can be calm when alone.

You must be careful not to encourage any anxious behaviors, while also gradually teaching the dog that he will be happier if he is calmer. You will have to learn to watch the dog and identify his anxious behaviors so that you do not unintentionally reward any of these by exhibiting what you think of as "normal" behavior (for example, petting the dog if he nudges you). This advice does not mean that you deprive the dog of anything. Instead, focus on rewarding calmer, more independent behaviors so your dog learns that these are desired and he feels better when exhibiting them. Only when dogs are calm can they learn new things, including how to be home alone.

To make this approach work, you need to know how your dog will respond to strategies designed to protect him, such as crates, gates, and being taken to doggie daycare. Crates and gates can make some dogs feel secure but may make other dogs feel trapped. If the dog feels trapped, his separation anxiety will likely worsen and he could panic.

If your dog loves his crate and voluntarily takes himself off to it for naps, to chew on toys, or to eat, and you can close the door and remain out of the room for an extended period without any sign that he is anything but ecstatic, a crate may help in your general approach to treating separation anxiety. If your dog dreads the crate, has to be dragged into it, sits in it wide-eyed and worried to the point that he never touches his toys, food, or water, the crate is going to make him worse.

This is the food bowl of a dog with separation anxiety who was crated to prevent destruction. The dog destroyed anything put in the crate—and the crate itself. Note that the dog *chewed through and pierced stainless steel*.
K. L. Overall

If you are uncertain, make a video of the dog in the crate. Then you'll know exactly how your dog is reacting.

There is some evidence that dogs who are reactive or phobic about noise — those who react in a fearful or panicky way to noises such as storms, guns, fireworks, and engines — often also have other problems involving anxiety. It appears that abnormal neurochemical responses under one set of circumstances may make it more likely to have abnormal neurochemical responses under other conditions. Noise reactivity may alter the way brain neurons communicate, so if you are worried about any behaviors that your dog is exhibiting, please make sure the dog is completely screened for all behavioral problems, since anxiety disorders in dogs are often co-morbid (meaning they occur together). For dogs to improve, become happy, and have an excellent quality of life, we must address all of their issues.

How Do We Begin?

Seek professional advice if you think your dog is suffering from separation anxiety. Your veterinarian is a good place to start; she can first make sure that there are no medical problems that may be contributing to the distress. Then, by taking a behavioral history, she can determine whether the diagnosis of separation anxiety is appropriate for your pet. If your veterinarian is not comfortable treating separation anxiety, she can refer you to a veterinary behaviorist for diagnosis and treatment or call one for a consultation.

If your dog has been diagnosed with separation anxiety, there are many simple and effective treatments that you can start right away. These include avoiding absences when possible, teaching your dog to be comfortable while alone, teaching your dog to relax in general, and relieving anxiety with medication if your dog must be left alone. If you begin working on all of these at once, you should start to see improvement, in all but the most severe cases, within four to eight weeks. Some dogs may improve to the point at which they are able to be calmly left alone, regardless of the type of absences they experience. Others will have improvements in the number, intensity, or frequency of clinical signs but may require some form of management over the long term.

Make Sure You Have the Right Diagnosis
Get a video of your dog when he's home alone and share it with your veterinarian or a veterinary behaviorist. This is critical to making sure you're not barking up the wrong tree on your treatment plan. Ideally, be prepared to record for several hours. If you can't get a video, don't let that stop you from seeking help for your dog.

Why? Treatment for separation anxiety isn't likely to hurt your dog even if you've got the wrong diagnosis. But if you aren't treating the real problem, your dog might not improve.

Signs of Separation Anxiety

These signs may occur when the dog **anticipates being left alone:**

- Watching the owner closely
- Following the owner from room to room, often with a tucked tail
- Showing a "worried" expression: eyes wide, forehead wrinkled, facial muscles tight
- Panting, pacing, whining
- Salivating
- Not eating, or refusing food

These signs may occur when the dog **is alone:**

- Barking, whining, howling
- Destroying items that carry a strong human scent (shoes, remote controls, eyeglasses, clothes) or exit points (doorjambs, flooring in front of doors or windows, curtains, doorknobs)
- Rearranging items
- Urinating or defecating in the house
- Sweating paws (you may see the paw prints on hard floors when you return)
- Signs of pacing (scratched floor, worn carpet)
- Vomiting
- Diarrhea
- Drooling
- Freezing and shaking, being unable to move

Get a Pet-Sitter

In a perfect world, dogs with separation anxiety would never be left home alone until their separation anxiety had been successfully treated. You don't necessarily need to hire a traditional pet-sitting service for this. Use some creative thinking to find company for your dog when you have to be away.

Why a sitter? Throughout the treatment, your dog will improve *gradually*. However, life will inevitably require you to be away. If you leave your dog in a situation where he is anxious, his improvements may be slower or his clinical signs may worsen. Everyone needs to get out once in a while. We all have family and work commitments. When you must be away, first find company for your friend, then go and have a great time knowing he and your home are safe.

If you're not sure how to find company for your dog, ask your friends and family. Many are happy to pet-sit for free or for a smaller charge than traditional pet-sitting services. If your dog does well at daycare, this is another option. Some offices will let you take your pet to work, and some dog walkers will keep your dog for an entire day of canine bliss.

Make Greetings and Exits No Big Deal
Greet your dog calmly and only when he's relaxed and quiet. Ignore jumping, barking, licking, and general *frantic* cuteness. Be vigilant about your own pattern of responses and make sure your response to any behavior from the dog can only be helpful to him. This will ensure you are only rewarding (through petting him, talking to him, and looking at him) calm, relaxed behaviors.

Leave quickly, quietly, and calmly. Don't make a fuss. Get your stuff ready long before you need to leave — at least a couple of hours, if possible — so that you aren't rushing around during the last several minutes before your departure. If you interact with your dog, do so in a relaxed way. Speak calmly, and if you pet him, pet in long strokes or a couple of gentle scratches rather than roughhousing.

Talking to your dog in an excited or worried tone or petting him in an agitating fashion can get him worked up. When you are about to leave, keeping cool can help him be as calm as possible.

Work It
Make sure your dog has adequate exercise. For some dogs, a long walk or game of fetch an hour or so before absences can be helpful. For others, a leisurely sniff walk is equally effective and desired.

Exercise alone won't cure separation anxiety, but adequate exercise and mental stimulation can improve your dog's overall health and lower anxiety. Additionally, it can help him rest while you are gone. However, don't go overboard; you can wind up with a dog who is in better shape and needs even more exercise to help him to relax.

No Punishment

Don't punish your friend for mistakes that happen while you are gone, even if you think he looks guilty. Current research indicates that the "guilty look" can appear simply in response to your angry and frustrated body language. Don't fool yourself into thinking that sheepish behavior is an effort to make up for destroying your couch. Your dog is likely just using dog language to avoid a threat.

When you punish, remember that you are punishing what is happening *right now,* not what happened forty-five minutes ago or even five seconds ago. Since signs of separation anxiety happen while you are gone, it's impossible to punish at the right moment. But even if you were able to punish at exactly the right moment, it's a bad idea because punishment can increase anxiety and fear and make it harder for animals to learn.

Punishment does not make fear go away. In fact, it may make your dog afraid or conflicted about your return. Can you imagine what would happen if you were in a similar position? Let's say you were home alone and so frantic about a missing friend that you couldn't sleep or eat. Would it really help your anxiety if your missing friend showed up and yelled at you for worrying and skipping your meals? Probably not. You'd probably feel a mixture of relief that your friend was back and confusion about why she was so angry. What a mess!

Reward Calm Behaviors

When you are home, encourage calm behaviors from your dog by talking to him in a quiet voice or giving him a short, calm petting session (long, smooth strokes) whenever he isn't showing signs of agitation, tension, or fear. Keep in mind that many dogs get excited if you speak to them in high-pitched, repetitive tones or pet them in short, quick strokes. Go for whatever helps your dog relax.

Not all dogs with separation anxiety shadow their owners or hang out close to them when they are home. But it's great for those dogs who do so to be rewarded for resting and staying at a distance sometimes.

Make Departures Fun

Although you shouldn't get your dog amped up just before you go, it's a great idea to give him something to do while you're gone. Scent games (such as finding hidden items) and food-filled puzzle toys are excellent options for keeping dogs busy while you're away. Set them out just as you are leaving. Whether or not your dog has separation anxiety, this type of departure routine can be great enrichment for dogs.

Many dogs with separation anxiety won't play with toys or eat while they are home alone. But if your dog will eat or play when alone, put something fun out for him every time you leave. Whatever game or toy you are planning to use, it can be helpful for the dog to learn to enjoy it when you are home for several sessions before you set it out for him when you are leaving.

Separation anxiety is *not* about boredom, but keeping your friend busy can help him learn that it's not scary when you leave — in fact, it's pretty darn fun. For those dogs who don't eat while you are gone, it's still a great idea to leave an easy food puzzle toy. If your dog begins playing with a toy while you're gone when he hadn't before, you can tell he's likely starting to feel better about being left alone.

But be careful: if you only set up these games or food puzzle toys when you are leaving, these toys can actually become one more departure cue for your dog. This means some dogs might associate the presentation of the toy with your departure. Instead of playing with the toy happily, they may get anxious as soon as they see it, since it means you're leaving.

Cue and Treat

There are many cues that let your dog in on the big secret that you've got to leave. In fact, it's probably easier to keep a secret from your spouse than from your dog. That's because dogs pick up so quickly on nonverbal cues.

Every dog uses different cues to tell him that you are heading out, but some common ones are picking up keys, handling handbags or backpacks, putting on jackets or shoes, wearing work clothes instead of weekend clothes, putting on makeup, and approaching the door. You can change the meaning of these actions by doing them at random times when you are home, so your dog learns they don't necessarily mean you're leaving. With practice, your dog will learn that these cues could mean anything. Picking up the keys could tell your dog that you are going to watch TV, do the dishes, take a nap, or do anything *but* leave. What we are using here is habituation: the dog stops responding to a situation just by being exposed to it many times.

It's smart to work on departure cues because you won't be able to avoid all of them. So you might as well teach your dog that they sometimes mean something besides an absence. Ideally, they should mean something fun. If you don't do this work, then every time you pick up your keys or put on your work shoes, you're setting your dog up to be anxious about your departure.

To make the most progress, practice only when your dog is relaxed, and make sure you're not leaving for at least a couple of hours after your practice sessions. Also, try to limit the number of cues you perform before an actual absence by getting things ready far in advance or keeping trigger items out of sight whenever possible. Watch your dog for any signs of distress: panting, worried facial expression, or pacing. If you see these, you are doing too much.

For calm dogs, you can bump up your plan a bit by teaching the dog that these cues mean treats. For instance, pick up your keys, jingle them, and toss a small treat. Don't talk or make a big deal out of it. Repeat up to ten times a day, as long as he is interested in eating the treats.

When your dog hears your keys and looks over at you excitedly for a treat, you know you have done the job. Now start practicing on a different cue. Just make sure that when you do leave, you toss a few treats for him. If your training has worked, he'll gobble them right up. The dog has just learned that keys mean treats.

Are You Going Too Fast Practicing Departure Cues?

If your dog shows signs of anxiety during or after departure cues and does not revert to calm behaviors between repetitions, you're working too fast and could make things worse. For the best assessment of how your dog is doing, video him at his most relaxed and compare it with a video taken when you are practicing a departure cue and for the ten minutes after. If your dog is not returning to his relaxed state within a few minutes — *at the most* — you should either abandon this technique, "soften" your departure cue, or simply get some hands-on professional help.

Softening your departure cue means making it less loaded. For instance, if your dog becomes agitated for thirty minutes when you pick up your keys, then stop practicing all cues for at least a few days. Restart with a set of keys that is tied tightly together with a rubber band so it doesn't jingle, which will make picking up the keys less noticeable. If this doesn't help your dog, let your veterinarian or veterinary behaviorist know. It will probably be best to abandon the work for this departure cue and work on a different one instead for a while.

Teach Your Dog to Relax

Anxious dogs can actually be taught to be more relaxed. You can teach your dog to relax using massage (there are books and DVDs on dog massage). Once you notice that your dog is taking deep breaths and has relaxed muscles during the massage, start to say the word "relaaaaax" (speak low and slow). Gradually, you can start saying "relaaaaax" earlier and earlier in the process. Eventually, the word itself becomes a cue for your dog to relax, because he's learned a wonderful massage is coming.

Another way to teach your dog to relax is to work with him on basic cues, such as "sit," "down," "stay," and "look," for three to five minutes in the morning and three to five minutes at night. At first you will reward him every time your dog performs the cue. But once he has the idea, switch to only reinforcing the most relaxed versions of each cue. For instance, if you ask him to sit and he sits in a nice, relaxed way, that will be the sit you reward. You are looking for soft muscles all over his body, slow tail wags, sighs, blinking eyes, deep breaths, and so on.

If your dog can't be taught to relax with you at home, how can he learn to relax when you're not there? Having some scheduled time to focus on relaxation can help him be calmer throughout the day. This means he may be less hypervigilant overall about your departure cues and absences. Once your dog learns to relax on cue, you can very carefully incorporate distractions (such as you approaching the door and returning to your dog) into your relaxation work.

Practice Your Departures

Many people get the idea from reading about separation anxiety that it is easy to teach a dog to be comfortable with your departures by leaving the dog over and over for longer periods each time. However, several veterinary behaviorists no longer routinely recommend this technique. Often, these types of departures are done improperly and quickly exceed the dog's comfort level, and so instead of being helpful, they make some dogs worse.

If you decide that you want to try working with departures, *video the dog while you are practicing.* If you see *any* signs of anxiety, you are moving too far, too fast. For instance, your dog should continue to happily engage with his toy while you are practicing your departures. If he looks up and abandons his toy, you've gone too far, too fast. It's a good idea to use a video camera or a baby monitor for all practice departures, so you know what is happening in your absence.

Here are some guidelines for practicing departures.

Step 1: Get an easy food puzzle toy, meaning that it's pretty easy for the dog to get highly valued treats to fall out or to lick out something gooey. Stuff the toy with yummies your dog really, really loves; this calls for the heavy artillery, like all-natural peanut butter or liver snacks.

Put the food toy on the ground with your dog and let him eat the food, then pick it up when he's finished. Repeat at least once daily at any time of day for at least seven days straight. This toy will only be available for practice departures until your dog can happily stay alone; never use it when you go to work or will be gone long enough to upset your pet. When your dog is eagerly looking forward to this treat and can settle in with it for several minutes (at least ten minutes, but up to thirty would be better), you can start practicing some departures.

Step 2: Get out the food toy, put it down in front of your dog, and walk toward the door. Do not touch the door, but get close to it. Come right back and sit down. As long as your dog is ignoring you and eating his treat, repeat up to five times. If you do these repetitions within a few minutes of each other, you can leave the toy down. If you are only practicing this one at a time, then pick up the toy when you return from the door. The goal here is for the dog to associate the special toy with you leaving but coming right back. (If you have a dog who guards his food, removing it may not be possible in this exercise.) When you can approach the door without your dog showing signs of distress at least ten to twelve times over several days (for instance, you practice three to five times a day for ten days and he shows no distress at least ten to twelve times you do this), you can actually touch the doorknob and wiggle it on your next session, repeating the same technique as before.

Step 3: Add another small increment of going out: turn the doorknob the whole way, for instance. After ten to twelve repetitions over several days, during which your dog is able to concentrate on his food puzzle toy, you may increase the intensity slightly. Do the same at each tiny stage of the process of going out the door. Increase the intensity in very small stages over the course of several days to weeks, repeating as before.

- Opening the door but not going out
- Opening the door, going out, and coming right back in
- Opening the door and walking out for one second, then coming right back in
- Opening the door, walking out for two to four seconds, then coming in

- Opening the door, walking out, closing the door, and coming in
- Opening the door, walking out, closing the door, and staying outside for a few seconds, then a minute, then a few minutes, then several minutes, and eventually up to sixty minutes

Once you can stay out of the house for at least fifteen to thirty minutes without any signs of anxiety, you can leave the area entirely using your car, or, if you live in an apartment, going downstairs, but quickly return before your dog can become anxious.

Many dogs who can be left alone for an hour or two can be left alone the rest of the day, but some cannot. How do you know? *Video!*

Signs That You're Going Too Fast Practicing Departures

Going too fast in trying to treat your dog's separation anxiety can slow you down and even make your dog worse! So how can you tell if you are making this common mistake? Watch your dog for any signs of anxiety, such as the following:

- Excessive watchfulness
- Breathing more quickly
- Worried expression, furrowed brow
- Sweaty paw marks on the floor
- Urination, defecation
- Vomiting, diarrhea
- Excessive greeting behavior
- Unwillingness to play games or eat treats from toys that your dog normally enjoys
- Excessive salivation
- Pacing
- Sitting, standing, or pacing by the exit point
- Shaking or trembling

If you are going in tiny, tiny increments, as you should be, you should never see any of these signs during practice departures. If you do, you must back up to at least one step before you noticed any signs of agitation, and stay there until your dog has been able to remain calm for several repetitions in a row.

Keep Things Quiet Inside

Use a white-noise machine or classical music to keep your dog from being startled by noises outside the home. Some dogs are easily startled even when they're relaxing — for instance, they may jump at noises from outside. When this happens, some dogs who have been resting can get anxious and start exhibiting signs of distress. Background noise can keep this from happening. Also, just as classical music is relaxing for us, studies show that it can be relaxing for dogs as well.

Put Your Dog to Work

Ask your dog to sit whenever he wants food, petting, play, the opportunity to go outside — whenever he wants something you can provide. Structuring your interactions helps anxious dogs predict their social environment. When the social environment is predictable, dogs may feel less anxious. So, before you pet your dog, give him the "sit" cue, and as soon as he sits and looks calm and attentive, pet him in a way you both enjoy.

Ease Suffering with Antianxiety Medications

Many dogs with separation anxiety benefit from medication that both eases the anxiety at the neurochemical level and helps the dogs learn new and calmer behaviors. Talk to your veterinarian or veterinary behaviorist as soon as possible to decide if antianxiety medication should be coupled with behavior modification as part of your individualized treatment plan.

While Malcolm, the dog in our first example, got better without medication, even though his separation anxiety was severe, the process took several months. During that time Malcolm suffered during absences, even though Charles was working intensely on behavior modification. This suffering was needless, given that serious side effects of antianxiety medications are rare.

Separation anxiety rarely improves immediately. It can cause significant, prolonged suffering while people implement behavior modification. Stress about neighbor complaints, threats of eviction, household destruction, concern about the dog's welfare, and many other issues make time of the essence in these situations. Some dogs with separation anxiety will be given away or euthanized without appropriate treatment and speedy improvements.

Appropriate antianxiety medications could have relieved Malcolm's suffering immediately and helped his behavior modification plan work faster. After all, no matter how hard you work on behavior modification, when your dog repeatedly feels such intense panic when you're absent, it's difficult for him to learn that being alone can actually be just fine. Unless you can guarantee that you will not have to leave your dog alone during treatment (and sometimes even if you *can* guarantee it), antianxiety medication should be considered so your dog doesn't have to suffer while you are gone.

Doing Everything Right, But Getting Nowhere?

You're not alone. This happens with some separation anxiety cases. This means it's time to reassess your dog's medication and your behavior modification plan. At this point, it can also be really helpful to get an exceptionally skilled, certified pet-dog trainer on board to help. This should be a trainer who works frequently with a variety of difficult behavior cases and ideally works in concert with a veterinary behaviorist.

Remember, punishment has no place in the treatment of separation anxiety. Only work with trainers who use dog-friendly positive reinforcement methods.

Your dog's charming personality won't change for the worse on the right medication. The best medications for separation anxiety are not sedatives. They are medications specifically for antianxiety. Some are given daily, while others are given as needed. Your dog should not become a "zombie" or seem doped up. While it's true that some medications can have sedative side effects, these effects are usually very mild and are usually gone within a few days to a week. Besides, it's better for a dog to be a bit drowsy for a short time than to feel absolutely and desperately panicked for the long term.

The goal of medication is to improve quality of life, decrease suffering, and improve the dog's ability to learn, by relieving anxiety. If your dog begins medication and you feel the effect on his behavior is not good (for instance, he no longer wants to play, sleeps excessively, or stops eating), of course you must report this to your veterinarian or veterinary behaviorist. The solution could be as simple as adjusting the dose or changing the medication. The goal is an improved quality of life for your dog.

Now that there are two FDA-approved medications to treat separation anxiety (Clomicalm from Novartis Animal Health, and Reconcile from Elanco), we have more data than ever on how well these medications work. The research and drug trials for these medications revealed many useful things about treating separation anxiety. First, dogs on both a medication and a behavior modification program might improve (show diminished signs of anxiety and panic) within a week. Second, even dogs on a placebo actually improved over the course of the trial, showing us that behavior modification is an important component in treating separation anxiety and should be used together with medication.

Thanks to these studies, we know these medications rarely have serious side effects. The most common are mild — temporary sedation, decreased appetite, and vomiting or diarrhea. If there are side effects, they are almost always minor and ease within a day or two of stopping treatment or adjusting dosage. Remember, your dog's health history must be reviewed with your veterinarian before using any medication, and, of course, only your veterinarian can and should prescribe all medications.

While serious side effects are rare, it is common for veterinary behaviorists to recommend premedication laboratory work. This generally includes a complete blood count, serum chemistry, urinalysis, and in some cases a thyroid assessment. This enables them to assess each dog's individual baseline values and screen for medical problems that may contribute to anxiety disorders. Often they will recommend that you recheck the laboratory work during treatment, too, to make sure your dog is doing well on the medication.

While Clomicalm and Reconcile are the only two medications approved by the FDA for treating separation anxiety in dogs, veterinary behaviorists have a variety of other medications to pull from their tool chest when these two are not effective for individual patients. Since these medications take a few weeks to be at their most efficacious for many patients, it is common for veterinary behaviorists to also provide a fast-acting option from one of several classes of medications. These other, fast-acting drugs are typically given as needed before absences when a dog with separation anxiety must be left alone; in severe cases they may be given daily. These medications can stop the suffering of separation anxiety the day they are given.

Most veterinary behaviorists recommend that you stay home with your dog the first time you give a medication, so you can watch for any side effects, such as sedation or, rarely, increased agitation or anxiety. If all seems okay, video your dog while you are away to help you and your veterinarian assess whether the medications are helping.

It might take some time to find the right medication and dose to help relieve the suffering of anxiety in each dog. While many dogs respond favorably to the first medication trial, some need to try multiple medications before finding the best choice for them. Because these dogs are suffering significantly, the process of working with your veterinarian or veterinary behaviorist to find the right medication is worth the effort. Pheromones may diminish anxiety for some dogs. See chapter 5.

Avoiding Pitfalls and Staying on Track

Practice your behavior modification strategies every day. It takes only a minute or two to fill food toys (they can be filled in advance and stored in the fridge for when you need them), a minute to work on teaching your dog that keys mean treats, three to five minutes of basic relaxation work twice daily, and barely any extra time to set up some music and structure your interactions. You don't have to do everything every day, but practice something every day so that you can keep your plan moving along.

While implementing a behavior modification program, do your best to avoid leaving the dog home alone, if at all possible. If you must leave your dog alone and vulnerable to separation anxiety, it's important to discuss antianxiety medication with your veterinarian so your dog doesn't have to suffer.

Don't get a new pet to treat your dog's separation anxiety unless you really, *really* want another pet. Sometimes a companion pet will help only temporarily, or not at all.

Be careful when you are practicing departures. Don't push the program too fast or you could accidentally make your dog more anxious about being alone and, especially, about the process of being left. The goal of practice departures is for your dog to be calm the entire time. If your dog starts to show signs of separation anxiety while you are practicing departures, you are moving too fast. Take a couple of days off. Just give him the food puzzle toy without leaving, as you did in the beginning, and then restart your work at least a few steps back from the point at which your dog became agitated. Pacing, panting, whining, barking, and rearranging things are all signs that you are moving too fast.

Make sure to check in at least weekly with your veterinarian or veterinary behaviorist. If your dog is not making progress, your veterinarian needs to know. The goal is to avoid suffering. Give all medications as directed by your veterinarian or veterinary behaviorist. If you feel your dog is experiencing a side effect, contact the veterinarian immediately to discuss other options.

What Did We Say?

- If your dog shows *any* of the clinical signs of separation anxiety, contact your veterinarian or a veterinary behaviorist right away to make sure you have a complete and accurate behavioral diagnosis.
- Make a video of your dog home alone and bring it with you to your initial appointment. For comparison, you can also include some video of your dog when he is not alone.
- Don't punish the dog, especially for behaviors that happen when you're gone.

- Strongly consider antianxiety medication to ease suffering and speed improvements.
- Focus on calm departures and returns.
- Reward calm behavior in general.
- Understand that "spoiling" dogs doesn't cause separation anxiety.
- Remember that confinement can exacerbate separation anxiety in many dogs.
- Know that dogs with separation anxiety are not bored and, in fact, rarely play when left alone.
- Dogs with separation anxiety are not spiteful. They are just trying to cope.
- Treatment can improve separation anxiety in over 70 percent of cases, and much improvement may happen within eight weeks. The sooner you get started, the better!

Dogs like Malcolm can be helped, and they can become calm and happy. With a well thought out plan for behavior modification and a medication plan prescribed by a veterinarian, most dogs with separation anxiety can improve, and you might actually be able to go to the movies on a Friday night once more without coming home to a disaster zone and a frantic fuzz ball.

12

I Know It's Going to Rain, and I Hate the Fourth of July
Dogs Who Are Phobic About Sound

Emily D. Levine, DVM, DACVB, MRCVS

Darni was an adorable little Shih Tzu who loved just about everything except loud noises, especially thunder. Her fear was so intense that she would shake, tremble, pace, whine, vomit, and have diarrhea whenever the weather was stormy. Darni's family was distraught and had tried many traditional training techniques to help her. Unfortunately, Darni was getting worse with each storm season. Her owners loved her very much and did not want to see her suffer any more. Fortunately, they were referred to a veterinary behaviorist for help.

Darni was four years old and had been suffering from noise sensitivities for two years. After the behavior consultation, it became apparent that Darni had a phobia of storms. However, her high level of fear and anxiety made it impossible for her to respond to behavior modification exercises without the help of antianxiety medications. With the use of appropriate medications, Darni's family was able to implement behavior modification recommendations and her fear of storms was greatly reduced.

Now, although Darni still does not love storm season, she is able to lie down, calmly walk around, and appear just a little worried as opposed to being panicked. For Darni and her family, this is a huge improvement in everyone's quality of life. Darni's family, who once thought there was no hope for their dog, are now firm believers in never giving up.

What Are Noise Phobias?

Fireworks, thunder, and gunshots, oh my! These are some of the most common noises that incite fearful responses in dogs. Anyone who has a dog who is afraid of noises knows just how difficult this can be for both the dog and the family. Why are so many dogs scared of noises? One study found that 33 percent of dogs who show noise-related fears were also reported to have experienced a traumatic event associated with noises. But what about the other 67 percent?

There are many theories as to why some dogs are afraid of noises while others are not. A study led by veterinary behaviorist Daniel Mills at Lincoln University in the United Kingdom looked into the causes of noise sensitivities. The study discovered that, in addition to their having had traumatic experiences, dogs with chronic stress and dogs who were not exposed to noises in early life in a responsible, nonscary way are more likely to be sound sensitive. Dogs who do not respond well to stress may have a genetic predisposition to being afraid of noises.

Unfortunately, the research into this particular area is in its infancy. Until we learn more about why and how these fears develop, it is most important to know that there are currently treatments out there that can be very effective. So don't give up.

Facts, Not Fiction

Is reacting to noise really abnormal? After all, who hasn't jumped or startled at a large crack of thunder or when someone drops a tray of plates in a restaurant?

In fact, reacting to noises is very normal. Evolutionarily speaking, it is a mechanism for increasing survival. If you hear a sound that might represent danger and you flee from that sound, you survive. In fact, sound travels so fast in the brain that it will often bypass the thinking parts and go straight to the part that makes an individual flee. So if this can be a normal response, what constitutes an abnormal reaction to noise?

For a noise response to be healthy, it is important that any reaction to a noise is short-lived and that recovery from the noise is quick. One should not exhibit a sustained response to the noise, even if the noise is sustained. Most of us have the ability to get used to certain noises that our brains learn to ignore because they do not represent danger. This process is called habituation. The ability to habituate requires normal functioning of many parts of the brain, because habituation is a learning process.

A healthy response for a dog would be to have a startle response to a surprising noise, pause for a moment, and then be able to recover within seconds. If this noise repeats itself over and over (for example, traffic, beeping, fireworks, thunder), the dog should get used to or habituate to the noise. If the dog is unable to habituate to the noise, this can lead to serious sound sensitivities and other serious anxiety issues.

It has been suggested that noises that evoke an immediate defensive response (meaning you need to prepare for danger) may not be as easy to habituate to as noises that evoke a simple orienting response (meaning you turn to look at the source of the noise). The most common noises that elicit a fearful response in dogs — gunshots, fireworks, thunder, and engine noises — are all loud (seventy decibels or greater), lack a specific sound pattern, and are impulsive (consist of short bursts rather than sustained tones). These noises may be more likely to cause an immediate defensive response because they are sudden and loud.

As mentioned earlier, biologically, some noises will bypass the thinking part of the brain and incite a fear response so the animal can react quickly. This makes sense from an evolutionary perspective. *If* there is something in the environment that might indicate danger (a loud, sudden, unfamiliar noise), it increases your chances of survival to just act (run away) rather than take the time to think about running away.

What Does That Mean?

Phobia: A persistent, abnormal, intense fear of a stimulus that is out of proportion to the stimulus

Sound sensitivities: The anxiety, fear, and phobia associated with sounds

Stress: A term that is broad and nonspecific; most behaviorists agree that the basic function of stress is to maintain a physiological and psychological balance so that individuals can react in a healthy, normal manner to life's changes and stressors. Stress becomes counterproductive when the physiological response is sustained or activated too often.

Distress: A behavioral and physiological response that has harmful effects on an animal's welfare, both physiologically and emotionally

What Are Sound Sensitivities?

Is your dog anxious, fearful, phobic, stressed? Is she simply not intelligent because she has not yet learned that sounds won't hurt her? (Gunshots may be the exception here, but most people and their dogs are not walking through the woods in a hunting zone during hunting season.)

Fear, anxiety, stress, and phobia are not the same things. There are important differences among these reactions, but they do share similar neurobiological pathways. The nervous behaviors a sound-sensitive dog shows are a result of these underlying neurobiological pathways being activated by the scary noise.

Common Behaviors Sound-Sensitive Dogs Display During Noise Events

- Panting
- Pacing
- Drooling/salivating
- Trembling/shaking
- Destructive behavior
- Hiding
- Remaining very close to a person
- Barking, whining, howling
- Inability to settle

- Defecating, urinating, vomiting
- Behaviors that may cause self-injury (excessive licking or chewing body parts)
- Escape behaviors, trying to get outside or inside (running, climbing on furniture, scratching at doors and windows)

In some cases, escape behaviors, self-injury, and physical responses such as urinating may be much worse when the dog is home alone without people.

Is That Really True?

There are many myths that surround noise sensitivities in dogs. Some of the more common ones are the following:

- She is stupid.
- She should just learn to get over it.
- She will get better as she gets older.
- She just needs to be better trained.
- She just needs to be told who is boss.
- Getting another dog who is not scared of noises will help her.
- She learned it from me because I am scared of noises.

One of the more aggravating myths is that the dog is stupid. *Intelligence has nothing to do with anxiety.* There are plenty of very intelligent people who are afraid of spiders, flying, heights, and so on. In fact, from an evolutionary perspective, one could argue that it is intelligent to have fears about things that may hurt you. Often, the body's biological fear responses intentionally bypass the thinking part of the brain and tell you to act, so intelligence is not a factor. If you are in trouble, this is not the time to assess your options. If a man is running toward you with a gun, you would not debate whether you should use your cell phone and waste valuable minutes to call for help or use the nearby stairs to get away, even though it could aggravate your arthritis. You'd just *run!* Sometimes it is safer to just react.

When the emotional system is kicked into high gear, you, a dog, or a cat are not in the proper mental state to think or learn. Intelligence has *nothing* to do with noise sensitivities.

Do dogs grow out of noise sensitivities? Although there are dogs who can have mild reactions and eventually habituate to noises, it shouldn't take years. In general, the only time dogs seem to grow out of noise sensitivities is when they reach an age where they:

- have hearing loss and can no longer hear the noises that scare them;
- start exhibiting signs of cognitive dysfunction (see chapter 14);
- develop a painful condition such as arthritis and can no longer pace and show other physical reactions, which is mistaken as a sign that they are no longer anxious.

If you have a dog who has noise sensitivities, do not wait to see if she will grow out if it. Get help. It is not fair to the dog to just try to wait it out. More often than not, the reaction actually gets worse, not better.

Is there a connection between noise sensitivity and training? Being trained just means a dog has learned what certain words or hand signals mean and will comply with certain requests. Often it is essential that dogs know how to perform certain behaviors so they can be used with a behavior modification plan to help lessen the dog's anxiety. But having a better recall or a perfect sit does nothing to alleviate noise sensitivity.

In fact, if you have a dog who is pacing and you tell her to lie down and she does, she may no longer be pacing but she may still be very anxious. The anxiety doesn't go away just because you're not seeing it. Do not assume because a dog will obey that she is not anxious or that an anxious dog just needs to be better trained.

One of the most potentially damaging myths is the idea that the dog should be punished for the anxious or fearful behavior. The idea that a dog should be punished often stems from the belief that the dog is "being bad" or is "trying to be dominant" by not listening to you when you tell the dog to stop a certain behavior (pacing, whining, and so on). But being anxious has absolutely *nothing* to do with dominance or control. Using punishment will make the animal more anxious and fearful in the long run. Certain punishments may make a dog stop pacing because she is more scared of you and the punishment than she is of the sound, but the pacing behavior is simply being suppressed. The dog is still anxious on the inside and has now learned that storms (or other noises) are even scarier because she gets punished during them.

Punishment can range from verbal corrections to physical corrections. *Punishment is* never *okay to use on a fearful, scared, or anxious dog.*

Will getting another dog help to alleviate noise sensitivities? In a recent study, researchers found that having a dog who is not noise-sensitive together in a home with a noise-sensitive dog did not help to reduce the reaction of the noise-sensitive dog. There are many stories of canine patients with noise sensitivities who live in a home with a dog without noise sensitivities, and the unfearful dog has no positive influence on the fearful dog. Please do not take on the responsibility of another dog if the sole purpose is to see if the new dog will help the original dog with a noise-sensitivity issue.

I am afraid of noises and storms. Am I to blame for my dog's noise sensitivities? There are at least two studies that have found that a person's fearful response to noises does not cause a dog to become scared of noises.

In 2005, researchers Nancy Dreschel, DVM, PhD, and Douglas Granger, PhD, looked both at fear behaviors and cortisol levels of nineteen dogs exposed to thunderstorms via sound recordings. Cortisol is a hormone that causes an increase in glucose production, and higher levels of it have been associated with high levels of arousal. The results showed that cortisol levels in dogs increased as much as 200 percent when the dogs heard the thunderstorm noise, and, of course, the dogs also showed fear-related behaviors. The way their owners behaved had no effect on these results. In addition, a 2007 study looking at 2,458 noise-fearful dogs found that there was no association between the presence of a fearful human and the presence of a fearful dog.

Signs That You Need to Seek Help for Your Dog's Noise Issues

- Your dog exhibits some or all of the common behaviors seen in sound-sensitive dogs, and they last throughout the entire duration of the noise event.
- Your dog has become an amateur meteorologist and has learned to predict the approach of a storm; she begins showing anxious behavior well before you know a storm is coming.
- Your dog starts to react to signs such as rain or gray skies, because she predicts a thunderstorm might occur. (In some cases, dogs will refuse to go outside even when it is sunny, in fear of a storm approaching.)
- Your dog takes thirty minutes or longer to recover from a storm or loud noises.
- Your dog starts to react to additional noises, other than the one she was originally scared of.

How Do We Begin?

The best way to prevent your dog from having noise sensitivities is to responsibly expose her to a variety of different sounds when she is young. You can still do this if you have adopted an adult dog. You want to expose your dog to a variety of sounds, initially at reasonable intensities, and make sure these exposures are fun.

If you are out on a walk and hear sirens, give your dog treats during the siren sounds. Any time it rains or thunders, make sure to play a game your dog enjoys, like fetch or tug of war. In addition, you can always give your dog a special, extremely delicious treat during storms so she associates those noises with something fun. Can you imagine what fun it would be if every time it rained someone came to your door with a chocolate cake and a thousand-dollar check? You would surely be eager to answer the door in bad weather. With the right rewards, you can encourage pups to be excited about playing in the rain.

Another way to responsibly expose the dog to various sounds is to buy a CD with various noises and play the sounds at low levels while playing with your dog or giving her treats (see "Behavior Modification Using a Noise Recording"). Another study by Dr. Daniel Mills at Lincoln University evaluated the efficacy of using noise recordings along with dog-appeasing pheromones (see chapter 5) to modify fearful behaviors. The end result: Exposing dogs to noise recordings of the fearful stimuli in a specific manner helped reduce their fear of fireworks. One year after the study, the owners reported that their dogs remained improved.

Dr. Sharon Crowell-Davis, a veterinary behaviorist, and colleagues also looked at using noise recordings, along with medication, to help dogs who were fearful of thunderstorms. The results, once again, indicated these treatments helped reduce the dogs' fear of storms.

Behavior Modification Using a Noise Recording

1. *Goal:* Create a location the dog will associate with calm, relaxing events.

   Technique: Create a safe haven. This can simply be a towel / blanket / dog bed that the dog associates only with positive, calming activities, such as massage, calm obedience exercises, etc. This is counterconditioning — teaching a new response. The owner may wish to spray this area with dog-appeasing pheromones, such as Adaptil (Ceva Animal Health). The owner should create this safe haven well before actually starting to use it as part of the *desensitization* and *counterconditioning* process.

2. *Goal:* Expose the dog to the sound she is sensitive to at a very low level, so that the only reaction you may see is a mild orienting response or very mild signs of anxiety that go away after ten to thirty seconds.

   Technique: Have a CD player with the speakers elevated and spread apart to mimic a more natural event. Play it at the lowest volume level that elicits either no sustained response (this may not be possible) or a very transient orienting or anxiety response. Ideally, the dog will be at her safe haven when you start, to help keep her anxiety or fear levels low.

3. *Goal:* Try to change the dog's perception of what that noise means by associating the low-level noise with something positive.

   Techniques: As the noise recording is playing, start giving the dog high-value treats. If it is a rain or wind sound, give treats constantly. If it is fireworks or thunder, it may be desirable to wait to give a treat until after the loud bang. Other methods of counter-conditioning and desensitization include using games as a reward, such as playing ball or tug if the dog is motivated by this. If the dog likes to work, have her do sits, downs, etc. during the noise recordings.

4. *Goal:* Make the event more realistic by slowly increasing volume.

   Technique: Once the dog does not show any signs of anxiety or fear at a low level and is willing to engage in another activity (food, games, commands) and has body postures that indicate she is not anxious or fearful, the volume on the recording should be increased and the dog allowed ten to thirty seconds to habituate to that increase in volume before efforts are made to engage the dog by giving treats, doing a calm sit, down, or stay exercise, etc. Once the dog does well, an attempt to escalate to a play game can be made. As the owner proceeds through training, the volume of the recording should be increased based on the individual dog's behavioral progress, until loud sounds can be played effectively.

5. *Goal:* Make the event more realistic by adding in other elements.

   Technique: Once the dog is used to loud sounds, other stimuli associated with that noise event can be associated with it at low levels. For example, to mimic a storm, someone may wish to spray water on a window to mimic rain hitting a window.

Research by the author, Dr. Emily Levine, suggests that these techniques are most helpful when CD training begins at least two months prior to "noise season" and that the individuals do the training up to eight times per week.

(Adapted with permission from the *BSAVA Manual of Canine and Feline Behavioural Medicine,* 2nd edition, © BSAVA.)

Part of exposing your dog to noises responsibly is not putting her in situations where she will be bombarded with intense sounds before she is ready to cope with them. For example, don't take your young puppy to a fireworks display or to a rock concert. You don't want the sounds to be continuous or too intense, as this could be traumatic. Because it is possible that sound sensitivities are inherited, when you are getting a dog from a breeder, ask if the parents have ever shown sound sensitivities.

What Should I Do with My Terrified Dog During a Thunderstorm?

What you *should* do and *can* do may be two very different things. If the suggestions here do not help, seek help from your veterinarian or veterinary behaviorist for your dog.

• If your pet is scared during a thunderstorm, try offering her a new toy that resembles her favorite type of toys. So if she likes to chew the squeaky out of a squeaky toy, give her a new squeaky toy; if she likes to rip the stuffing out of a stuffed animal, give her a new stuffed animal.

Food puzzle toys like these can help distract a scared dog. Be sure to fill them with something your dog finds especially yummy. *Donna Nuñez*

- Play her favorite game (tug, chase, or whatever your dog loves).
- Give her a special treat to work on — a long-lasting bone or a food puzzle toy stuffed with yummy food (something tasty like peanut butter, not boring, dry kibble).
- Create a cozy place for the dog to rest, such as a closet corner or a bathroom, and see if she does better in that environment. Ideally, you should create this "zen" environment by teaching the dog to go there on request when there is no scary noise. Associate this location with calming activities, such as massage, and giving the dog treats for remaining in a calm, relaxed down position. (See chapter 8 for more information on safe havens or refuges.)
- Close the windows and cover them well to block the flashes of lightning and soften the sound of thunder and rain.
- Try a training session with the dog, such as asking her to review behaviors she already knows, like "sit" and "down," or have her perform tricks. Use a very high-value food as a reward.
- Some dogs may do better outside, so if you are up for it, put on your rain gear and go for a walk.
- Turn on some classical music (find some good examples at throughadogsear.com) to help drown out the sound of the rain and thunder with a calming sound. (Some dogs may prefer rock and roll!) You can also try a white-noise machine.
- Spray dog-appeasing pheromones (see chapter 5) on a blanket and massage your dog on the blanket, using long, slow strokes. Make sure you spray the pheromones on the blanket fifteen minutes before using it. Or during thunderstorm season, keep a pheromone diffuser plugged in all the time and have your dog wear a pheromone collar.
- Some dogs feel calmer when a family member puts a leash and perhaps a head collar on them and holds the leash. (If this does not help your dog calm down, take it off immediately.)
- Some dogs may feel more comfortable in a crate. Keep in mind that a crate is not calming for all dogs, and many dogs will become much more anxious when crated; using a crate is not appropriate for those individuals.

- If you know a storm is coming, try to engage your dog in activities *before* she gets too anxious.

Can Medication Help?

Sammy is an eighteen-month-old male neutered Lab mix who was so scared of noises (car sounds, construction sounds, things dropping, footsteps heard in the apartment above) that he would not go outside. His owners had to carry him to the elevator in their building to get him to leave the apartment. When in their home, Sammy stayed in their bathroom most of the time because there were too many noises in the apartment that scared him. This was clearly a debilitating problem for Sammy, and his quality of life was considerably compromised.

Sammy's owners were distraught and had been trying to use some behavior modification techniques to help. After implementing some behavior modification, they did see minimal improvement, but they clearly needed more help.

Because immediate relief was needed, fast-acting antianxiety medications were prescribed; he was also started on some similar but longer-acting medications.

Within a few days, the family saw Sammy doing things he had not done in a long time, such as following them out to the elevator and outside all on his own. Even though treatment had just started for Sammy's behavioral disorder, his early positive response gave everyone a lot of hope and a lot of smiles!

There are many dogs who can learn to tolerate loud sounds when you make the proper efforts to prevent anxiety or with behavior modification techniques. However, there are dogs like Sammy who simply cannot overcome this fear without the help of medication. Medication is very helpful and sometimes essential in reducing the level of fear, anxiety, or panic so that the behavior modification exercises can work.

It is very difficult for anyone to learn at a time when they are frightened and very emotionally upset. Imagine if you were scared of heights and someone asked you to go to the top of the Empire State Building with a calculus book and said, "While you are up there, read this book and then tell me what you learned." Not realistic, is it?

Let's think about what is happening when you are scared. Your body is pumping out adrenaline. This is the hormone responsible for the initial fight, flight, or freeze response. It prepares the body to go into survival mode. When you are in survival mode, your body is not concerned with day-to-day processes such as digesting food, reproducing, or learning new concepts that seem unnecessary at that moment.

Just like us, animals can't learn anything when they are really scared. And learning not to be scared is a form of learning, too! This is when medication can be especially helpful. Medication can reduce the fear so a dog can learn to play games, eat treats, and learn through behavior modification exercises that she does not need to be fearful. The goal is for the dog to create new neural circuits in her brain and learn on her own not to be fearful of the situation. Then, in the future, she may not need medication.

There are various medications that can be used, and you should always consult with your veterinarian or veterinary behaviorist as to which are best for your pet. Unlike for separation anxiety, there are no FDA-approved drugs to treat noise phobias in dogs. Only one study by veterinary behaviorist Dr. Sharon Crowell-Davis examined using clomipramine and alprazolam for dogs suffering from storm phobias. She found this combination of medications to be useful. There are also other medication options that may be more appropriate or just as effective for your dog.

Medication to Avoid: Acepromazine

Acepromazine is *not* an ideal medication for noise sensitivities. This is a sedative, not an antianxiety medication. It also has the potential to make some animals more sensitive to noises. So, in a worst-case scenario, the dog is sedated to the point where she can't move, but her brain still perceives the noise, and the drug does nothing to lessen the dog's anxiety.

Part of the decision about which drug to use must be based on your pet's medical history and what other medications she is currently taking. As beneficial and necessary as medications can be for noise sensitivities, medications are never risk free. Only a veterinarian is qualified and licensed to prescribe medication for your beloved dog. A qualified trainer or dog behavior consultant may suggest your pet would benefit from medication, but that professional does not have the training, the experience, or the legal authority to recommend specific medications.

Thundershirts, Bathtubs, and Storm-Defender Capes

There are nonpharmaceutical options for treating sound sensitivities. *There is no one-size-fits-all magic product that is a cure-all for all dogs,* but there are some products that can be helpful for some dogs and they are certainly worth trying.

The Thundershirt is a body wrap that fits snuggly on the dog. Exactly how it works to calm is unclear, but some dogs benefit from it. In 2011, there was a small study that showed the Thundershirt can reduce some anxious behaviors. Ten dogs were selected to be tested on various indicators of anxiety. These indicators included observed anxiety behaviors, time spent in a hiding box, blood cortisol levels, and heart rates. Dr. Gary Landsberg found there was a 50 percent decrease in the likelihood of a dog entering the hiding box when wearing the Thundershirt, and a decrease in the overall observed anxiety behaviors.

Milo looks dashing in his Thundershirt. *Donna Nuñez*

Storm fears are more complex than other noise fears, because there are several aspects of a storm the dog may be responding to other than just the noise itself. Some behaviorists speculate that the electrostatic change in the atmosphere is one of the triggers that elicits a fear response in some dogs. The Storm Defender, a capelike wrap, has a light metallic lining that reportedly protects against that charge.

There are no studies identifying which dogs are better candidates for the Storm Defender, but dogs who seek out hiding places where there is a lot of plumbing and metal, such as bathtubs, showers, or cars, may be helped by it. There was a small study in 2009 with two groups of dogs — those with a real cape (Storm Defender) and those with a "placebo" cape (a similar cape but not the actual Storm Defender cape). There were thirteen dogs in the Storm Defender group and ten dogs in the placebo-cape group. Both groups had similar anxiety scores pretreatment, and both groups showed improvement while wearing these capes, but the group with the Storm Defender showed a higher percentage of improvement. Dr. Nicholas H. Dodman concluded that more research is needed on why the placebo capes helped at all, but Storm Defenders may very well help some anxious dogs.

Music therapy is another option. Playing music can help drown out the sounds of the scary noises with sounds that can actually help some dogs feel calmer. There are various aspects of music that can influence behavior, such as resonance, rhythm, and pattern identification (harmonic complexity). Through a Dog's Ear (throughadogsear.com) makes music CDs that take into account the critical musical elements that can reduce a dog's heart rate and have a calming effect.

Avoiding Pitfalls and Staying on Track

- If using a noise recording, play it at least two months before an event (see "Behavior Modification Using a Noise Recording").
- Have your dog's favorite toys and treats ready to redirect her attention.
- Practice relaxation exercises in the dog's safe haven.

- Have calming music ready to play.
- If you know none of these things have helped in the past, make an appointment with your veterinarian or veterinary behaviorist to discuss pharmacological or other nonpharmacological interventions.

What Did We Say?

- As soon as you get your puppy or dog, begin to responsibly expose her to sounds.
- If you are getting your dog from a breeder, ask if either the mother or the father has a history of noise sensitivities.
- Dogs who have noise sensitivities should be treated humanely and with respect. They are not stupid, nor are they trying to be dominant. They should not be punished. They are experiencing an involuntary emotional and physiological reaction to noises that they perceive as frightening.
- Your approach to a serious behavior problem like noise sensitivities should be no different from your approach to any other malady your dog develops: Seek out help, advice, and treatment from a qualified individual, who will help you formulate an appropriate, humane, and comprehensive plan to help you and your dog.
- Some dogs respond to treatment very quickly, while others require more time.
- A behavior modification program using sound recordings is a very effective treatment for noise sensitivities, but it may not work for all dogs.
- Medication can be very helpful and even *necessary* for some dogs. Medication advice should be taken only from veterinarians or veterinary behaviorists.
- There are nonmedication aids that are worth trying. For more information on alternatives, make an appointment with a veterinary behaviorist.
- Dogs deserve to live without fear and panic, and there are plenty of humane solutions to help them do so. Implement responsible

noise training for your puppy. Think of it as a behavioral vaccine. If you do this, your dog is less likely to develop noise sensitivities.

- If your dog does develop noise sensitivities, know that there are professionals out there who can help, and do not give up!

13

Tail Chasing, Leg Licking—Can't You Stop?
Compulsive Behaviors

Melissa Bain, MS, DVM, DACVB
Marsha Reich, DVM, DACVB

Rachel loved Harley, a two-year-old neutered male Border Collie she adopted six months earlier. They did everything together — hiking, biking, long daily walks, and toys. And, boy, did Harley have toys, including those he had to work to get food out of. Rachel trained with Harley twice a week for agility and other sports and continued with his training every day. Their relationship seemed just perfect.

Over the holidays they visited her family, and all went well until the day they visited her sister's home. While there, Harley took a very strong interest in the niece's flashing shoes and the flashing lights on the Christmas tree. The whole family thought it was cute and laughed when he chased after the lights. "Look at Harley chase me!" the niece called happily while she ran around the house with her special shoes.

The next day Rachel was not so happy when Harley pounced onto her in bed, chasing the filtered light streaming in through the windows. She was able to distract him pretty easily, but by the time they returned home, his behavior had escalated and she had to pull him away from any flickering light or moving shadow. Her roommates thought it was cute, until one of them tripped over Harley when he chased after the light coming from the open refrigerator.

Rachel was at a loss as to what had happened. Harley used to be such a great companion. Now he would even ignore her on walks if he saw shadows from the sun filtering through leaves or a glimmer of light bouncing off a hubcap. He would leave his food toys to rush over to chase the light on the floor coming from the open microwave. Throughout these episodes, he never looked worried or stressed, but he became less and less connected to Rachel.

Rachel brought Harley to her veterinarian to see if she could find anything physically wrong. After getting a history, her veterinarian considered a neurological disorder or a problem with his eyes. Harley passed a complete physical examination with flying colors, so the veterinarian referred Harley and Rachel to a veterinary behaviorist. After a visit, Harley was diagnosed with a compulsive disorder. While this term conjures up images of people who wash their hands a lot, it is different in animals.

A diagnosis of compulsive disorder is made when the animal cannot seem to control a repetitive behavior and is often unresponsive to interruptions. The behavior is often in response to a trigger (such as lights and shadows), but not always. It can have a profound effect on the animal's quality of life and interfere with a dog's normal ability to function day to day.

Certain breeds may be more likely to exhibit specific types of compulsive behaviors. For example, Border Collies, like Harley, are devoted to herding other animals. Perhaps, due to their drive to be working with livestock, they redirect the herding behavior toward a

Harley sees a light high up in the room and wants to chase it. *Melissa Bain*

seemingly inappropriate target. In Harley's case, he replaced sheep with lights and shadows. Redirecting is performing a behavior toward an object that you wouldn't normally direct that behavior to, because the normal object isn't there.

Facts, Not Fiction

Compulsive behaviors appear to arise from normal activities, such as moving (spinning, tail chasing, fence running, pacing, light or shadow chasing), grooming (licking or sucking an area of the body), eating or licking objects, or vocalizing, and seem to occur at continuously high levels. It often appears that the dog has no control over beginning and continuing the behavior, and the behavior can be self-injurious. These behaviors are repetitious (the same behavior occurs over and over). You might hear that your dog is exhibiting these behaviors because he is bored, doesn't get enough exercise, is looking for attention, or has an inappropriate relationship with you. None of these is correct for an animal with a true compulsive behavior.

So what does cause repetitive behaviors, and when do they become a compulsive disorder? Repetitive behaviors (behaviors that occur over and over) can be due to a number of problems. One of them is that the dog has a true compulsive disorder, as Harley does. However, repetitive behaviors can also be explained by underlying medical problems, attention-seeking behaviors, or ways to cope with another problem behavior or stressor. Sometimes a combination of these causes is behind your dog's behavior.

Why compulsive disorders occur is not well understood. There may be alterations in neurotransmitters in the brain — the chemicals that communicate information from one neuron to the next. Some of the neurotransmitters thought to be involved are serotonin, dopamine, and endorphins. In some dogs, frustration or conflict (when the dog can't do what he wants to do) seem to help trigger the compulsive behavior, and the behavior may then be maintained by these neurotransmitter changes.

Regardless of the underlying cause, owners often end up at their wits' end trying to get to the bottom of their dog's behavior. They try a lot of training, like Harley's owner, and feel that they can do no more to help their dog. They are stressed, the dog is stressed, and this escalates the frustration, which can interfere with the relationship they have with one another.

Table 13.1: What Does That Mean?

Diagnosis	Definition	When It Is Displayed
Compulsive behavior	A behavior that is constantly repeated without an apparent purpose, often without a specific context. The animal can potentially have an underlying anxiety disorder.	In many different contexts, scenarios, and locations. Can be very difficult to interrupt. Usually interferes with normal daily functioning.
Attention-seeking behavior	A behavior animals perform for owner attention. Attention could be something positive (petting, getting a treat). It can also be something aversive (yelling, tugging on a leash): at least it got the owner's attention.	Only when someone is present or might come into the area where the animal is. These types of behaviors are maintained by the owner paying attention to the pet in response.
Stereotypic behavior	A behavior that is constantly repeated, with a possible purpose of relieving stress related to housing or feeding conditions. These are quite similar to compulsive disorders and may even be the same.	Generally, when a confined animal (zoo and laboratory animal and perhaps even a pet) is not able to perform the full range of species-typical behaviors due to the environment
Displacement behavior	A behavior that is often repeated, but usually starts when an external stressful event occurs. When performed excessively and out of context, it may become a compulsive disorder.	In response to a stressful event, such as with separation anxiety or fear of unfamiliar people or dogs

Table 13.1: What Does That Mean? (cont.)

Diagnosis	Definition	When It Is Displayed
Seizure	Sudden abnormal electrical activity in the brain that can cause abnormal movements, some of which can be repetitive in nature	Can be displayed at any time. Cannot be interrupted.

Is That Really True?

Does your dog just need more exercise? Some of Rachel's friends told her to get some sheep for Harley to herd — easier said than done for someone living in the suburbs. "Increase his exercise," "give him a job," "give him more toys at home" — she'd heard it all. Without quitting her job, Rachel would find it difficult to squeeze much more time into exercise. Besides, Harley had dozens of different toys in the house and yard that he was no longer playing with because he was chasing the lights. Compulsive behaviors aren't just excess energy.

Are all repetitive behaviors compulsive disorders? Occasionally a medical problem can be mistaken for a compulsive disorder. Jasper, a male neutered Coonhound, was seen by a veterinary behaviorist when he was fourteen months old because he was licking the floor. When the problem first began, he would lick and leave a trail of saliva on the floor every morning, and by early afternoon he seemed like a normal dog. Over a few months the problem increased to licking the fence outside for hours, stopping only when his owner gently pulled him away. When we saw Jasper, his veterinarian had already started him on sertraline (a medication that increases serotonin), but it didn't seem to be helping. His bloodwork and stool sample were all normal.

Jasper seemed nervous throughout the appointment. Eventually he started to lick the floor. He was drooling and leaving long, wet saliva streaks. A detailed history revealed that Jasper always had a "grumbling" stomach. The owner also thought he ate a lot and defecated a

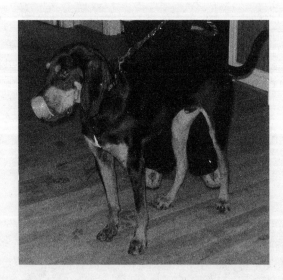

You can see Jasper's paw prints where he walked through saliva after he licked the floor. *Marsha Reich*

lot — more than the three other Coonhounds she had — and that his stools were not normal but were much softer and not formed, like pudding.

There was a concern that a medical issue might be at the root of his problem. Over the next couple of weeks and months, several interventions were tried, including a special diet to rule out a possible food allergy, and Zantac, an antacid, to help with his stomach issues. After two weeks with no improvement, an examination of the gastrointestinal tract was performed and intestinal biopsy samples were obtained. The biopsies showed mild inflammation of his stomach and small intestines. The veterinary internal-medicine specialist suspected that an unusual neurological disorder involving focal (in one place) seizures was causing his gastrointestinal problem. When Jasper was treated with antiseizure medication, he began to improve. It has now been two years since the treatment began, and Jasper remains about 70 percent improved.

Is tail chasing always a compulsive disorder? Tail chasing is another problem that can look compulsive but might be a medical problem. Rocky and his owner had their first appointment when he was a five-and-a-half-year-old German Shepherd. Rocky had a long history of tail chasing, beginning at six months of age, and of chewing the top of his tail (where it is connected to his body) from the age of one. He sometimes developed sores from biting at his tail. Rocky had a complicated history of allergies, separation anxiety, and thunderstorm and noise phobias.

During the physical examination, some neurological problems became evident. Rocky took longer to reposition his foot when it was placed upside down; he showed twitchiness when his skin was touched from the middle of his back to his tail; and the owner reported that Rocky showed signs of discomfort when he defecated. These signs all suggested that the tail chasing could be due to a neurological problem, so he was referred to a veterinary neurologist for further evaluation. A CAT scan showed a bulging vertebral disc and arthritic changes in his lower spine near his hip area, both of which resulted in pain. Two weeks after back surgery and pain medication, he stopped biting at his tail, had good tail movement, and could defecate normally.

How Do We Begin?

Compulsive disorders may look at first like the dog is having fun, but ultimately they can be frustrating for both the dog and the owner. Figuring out how to manage them often requires some detective work to identify possible medical issues that might be contributing. As illustrated with Rocky and Jasper, some medical issues can be hard to find and may need veterinary specialists or advanced testing to diagnose them. These problems call for veterinary intervention first and foremost.

Early intervention is extremely important. A study done by veterinary behaviorist Dr. Andrew Luescher has shown that the longer a compulsive disorder continues, the more difficult it is to treat. So for your dog's sake, do not think a compulsion will go away on its own over time. Seek help as soon as possible.

Management Interventions
In all cases, even when the problem is medical, redirecting a dog's attention away from the compulsive behavior is vital to managing the problem. Your timing for redirecting the dog is critical, to avoid acci-

dentally rewarding the dog for the compulsive behavior. If you wave a toy or a treat at the wrong time, you may be sending the message to the dog that you are rewarding the unwanted behavior. One option is to call the dog to you to perform a request, such as "sit," and *then* redirect him with a toy or other object after he is sitting.

Another option is to be prepared by safely having the dog on a leash or a long, light line that you can pick up when your dog is just starting the behavior. This option decreases the likelihood that you will also give the dog attention for the behavior — which he may consider to be a reward. Finally, interrupting the behavior with an abrupt noise such as a knock on a table or stomping your feet (no yelling!) and then asking for a "sit," which you reward, may work for some dogs.

Behavior Modification Tools

Behavior modification, which uses desensitization and countercondi- tioning (see chapters 10 and 11), can help normal behaviors to return. This intervention works to diminish the compulsive tendencies by gradually exposing the dog to the situation that triggered the onset of the compulsive behavior, while at the same time rewarding a competing and more-appropriate behavior, such as sitting or relaxing in a dog bed (see chapter 7).

Harley's veterinary behaviorist felt he would benefit from a behav- ior modification program of desensitization and counterconditioning. She set up a treatment plan to countercondition and gradually desensi- tize him to the lights and shadows. Rachel started by shining a flash- light onto the ground in a well-lit room, so that there was little differ- ence between the light and dark parts of the room. At that level, Harley got very tasty treats as long as he kept his attention on Rachel. When the flashlight was off, the treats went away. Rachel repeated this fre- quently, having subsequent sessions in darker and darker rooms.

They also added sessions designed to get Harley used to shadows. The veterinary behaviorist suggested using shadows from the ceiling fan. Over time, Rachel was to have the fan run at higher speeds, with the light gradually providing more contrast. Eventually, Harley's reac- tion to these triggers diminished so that he was less likely to engage in shadow chasing and spend more time in his normal play behaviors.

Environmental Changes

Environmental changes, such as decreasing the stressors in the environment and controlling where the dog displays the compulsive behavior, are helpful. This includes eliminating shadows and flashing lights or drawing curtains to prevent sunlight from creating shadows for dogs who chase them. For dogs who display compulsive behaviors after a stressful event, we suggest owners start by avoiding those events whenever possible, then eventually work on desensitizing and counterconditioning the dog to those triggers.

Identify and Treat Medical Issues

Veterinary behaviorists often see cases that at first seem similar but are actually quite different. The earlier cases of Rocky and Jasper illustrate how a medical problem can look quite similar to a compulsive disorder. When your pet has a sudden onset of the problem, especially in middle age, with no apparent triggers, a full medical workup is the next step. You can't treat all the symptoms without an accurate diagnosis.

Table 13.2: Possible Medical Causes of Repetitive Behaviors

Repetitive Behavior	Possible Medical Causes
Light and shadow chasing	Ophthalmologic problem, neurological problem (seizures, tumor)
Acral-lick dermatitis	Infection, allergies, abnormal nerve sensation, orthopedic problem or pain
Tail chasing	Neurological problem (spinal nerve problem), inflamed anal sacs, allergies, injury to tail
Excessive licking of objects or air	Gastrointestinal disease
Flank sucking	Gastrointestinal disease
Circling (walking in circles)	Neurological problem, ophthalmologic problem
Pacing	Pain or discomfort that decreases time spent lying down

Identify and Treat Other Behavior Problems

Some cases are combinations of a medical condition and an underlying behavioral problem. To properly treat the dog, you have to address *both* the medical and the behavioral problem.

Dan brought Daisy, a six-year-old Beagle, to see a veterinary behaviorist because she licked her front leg and created a very large, infected sore. Daisy was stressed and anxious whenever Dan and his wife left the house. She would bark and howl, and began to chew up the door frame. She licked her leg while they were gone and also when they were home with her. Daisy's history pointed to a behavioral explanation.

However, since Daisy focused her licking on just one leg, a closer look was needed. Daisy's skin infection was deep, and X-rays showed that the infection went down to the bone. Clearly pain and irritation contributed to her licking.

But why did she start? Dan remembered that Daisy's leg was shaved when she had blood drawn for a heartworm test a few months before it all began. This could have irritated her skin and started the process. Why did she continue? Once a dog starts licking excessively, the irritation can persist and get worse, causing a deep infection.

In addition to the heartworm test, Daisy's problem also started when Dan began working longer hours. So what came first, the separation anxiety or the lick lesion? It's hard to say, but this really did not matter for Daisy, because she needed to have both her medical *and* her behavioral problems treated at the same time.

Treating Compulsive Disorders

- Avoid triggers as much as you can.
- Redirect the dog's attention so it is focused on you or on doing another appropriate behavior. After the dog is redirected, offer play or chew toys or a treat.
- Desensitize and countercondition the dog to the trigger stimulus.
- Use medications as necessary.
- Keep in contact with your veterinarian.

It's Important to Get the *Whole* Story

It is also important to recognize and treat other behavior problems that contribute to overall anxiety and the compulsive disorder. For a dog who develops an acral-lick dermatitis (overlicking his front legs) during separations from his owner, we must also target and treat the underlying separation anxiety. If tail chasing is elicited by encounters with things the dog is afraid of, we must teach the dog not to be afraid. An example is a dog who only chases his tail when unfamiliar people come up to try to pet him, chasing his tail instead of trying to run away. To successfully treat him, we need to address his fear of unfamiliar people.

With some patience and perseverance, a dog with a compulsive disorder can improve and lead a more comfortable life, once we determine the underlying cause of the behavior and address it, modify the pet's environment, work on desensitization and counterconditioning, and add medication when needed.

Medication Can Play a Role

Only licensed veterinarians can prescribe medications for pets. Medications that affect serotonin can help decrease the intensity of some compulsive disorders, so learning new behaviors can begin. The current hypothesis is that compulsive disorders may be related to serotonin levels in the brain, and in people with this disorder, medication that alters serotonin levels can be beneficial; we have utilized this information to treat dogs. Studies by veterinary behaviorists Drs. Andrew Luescher, Nicholas H. Dodman, and Kersti Seksel have shown that clomipramine or fluoxetine are beneficial in dogs who presented with spinning and tail chasing. Other medications affecting different neurotransmitters have been used but have had limited success.

No response, or limited response, to a medication in a dog with a suspected compulsive disorder may suggest that there is a medical component to the problem. When a medication does help, a pet may continue on medication for months to years, depending on the nature of the problem, the environment, and his response to therapy. Withdrawing medication is an extremely gradual process that should take place over several months, while the dog is monitored for the return of symptoms.

Can I Prevent Compulsive Disorders?

Preventing compulsive disorders is difficult because their exact mechanisms aren't well understood. Not playing with flashlights or laser lights may help avoid shadow or light chasing. However, it has never been proven that these games actually cause compulsive behaviors.

Avoiding Pitfalls and Staying on Track

As with any aspect of animal behavior, and despite everyone's best efforts, there are concerns and misconceptions about treating compulsive disorders that can derail owners, their pets, and their relationships. Table 13.3 (opposite) lists some of the common misconceptions about treatment. The key to avoiding and working through them is to keep in contact with your veterinarian to make changes sooner rather than later.

Another useful tip is to keep a journal of your pet's behavior changes. Sometimes when the change is slow, or when the problem is not completely resolved, it's hard to see the progress. By keeping track of such changes, like "He only spins for five minutes instead of ten minutes" or "She can walk by shadows unless they are very dark," you can see that there is progress. A 50 percent improvement is by no means a cure, but the problem is only half as bad as it was when you started. Additionally, the journal helps you identify where some of the sticking points may be in the treatment plan.

(*Text continues on page 294.*)

Table 13.3: Common Misconceptions About Treatment

Misconception	Reality
Expecting a quick diagnosis	Sometimes we can quickly get to the root of the problem, while in other cases we have to dig deeper to find out what is going on, especially if we are trying to rule out underlying medical conditions.
Expecting a quick recovery	Changes in brain chemistry play a role in compulsive disorders. While the underlying process in the brain can be changed with behavior modification and medications, it will take time, sometimes weeks or months, before you see progress. It can take several more months to completely resolve these problems.
Blaming yourself	While human involvement may play a role in these problems, it rarely is the only cause.
Expecting drugs alone to cure the problem	Medications are often useful, but behavior modification is what makes the lasting change. Additionally, it may take time to find the right medication and treatment plan for your individual pet.
Punishing the dog	Punishment usually adds to the dog's anxiety and can perpetuate the problem or make it worse and may cause the dog to distrust family members.
Using a physical impediment to stop the behavior	While often we use such things as Elizabethan collars to stop dogs from further damaging their skin, this does nothing to address the underlying cause.
Believing the dog behaves this way because he seeks to be dominant	There is absolutely no truth to the theory that the behavior of a stressed dog has anything to do with being "dominant" over people or other dogs.

The initial treatment plan for Harley included exercise and household enrichment, maintaining a strong relationship with Rachel through attention and training, avoiding flashes of light and shadows, then desensitization and counterconditioning to the triggers of shadows and lights, and adding a serotonin-enhancing medication, such as Prozac (fluoxetine).

These interventions resulted in a dramatic change in Harley's behavior. At a follow-up appointment, Rachel reported that Harley was about 70 percent improved, especially when he was outside the house and actively engaged in a sport or training. He resumed running on hikes and playing with his toys and ignored such things as reflections off hubcaps and shadows on the ground. Through planning and care, Harley was on his way back to his normal self.

The take-home message? If you suspect your dog has a repetitive behavior in general, or more specifically a compulsive behavior, don't give up! There are so many things you can do to improve life for you and your pet.

What Did We Say?

- A compulsive disorder is a group of behaviors that appear to arise from normal activities, such as moving, grooming, eating or licking objects, or vocalizing. But in this case, the behavior occurs at continuously high levels and it often appears that the dog has no control over the beginning and continuation of the behavior.
- In some dogs, frustration or conflict (the inability to do what the dog wants to do) seems to trigger the compulsive behavior.
- These same behaviors can be due to underlying medical problems.
- They can also serve as attention-seeking behaviors or as ways to cope with another problem behavior or stressor.
- It is important to recognize and treat all behavior problems that are present and that contribute to overall anxiety and to the compulsive disorder.
- Treatment focuses on avoiding triggers, redirecting the dog's attention, teaching new behaviors, and counterconditioning and desensitization.

- Medications that enhance serotonin can be useful to help decrease the intensity of the compulsive behavior, so that learning new behaviors can begin.
- Behavior changes slowly, so patience and constant contact and follow-up with your veterinarian are necessary to help your pet get better.

14

Dogs with an AARF Card: Growing Old with Grace

Old Dogs Should Learn New Tricks

Gary Landsberg, DVM, DACVB, DECAWBM (Behavior)

About fifteen years ago, the behavior of our twelve-year-old Nova Scotia Duck Tolling Retriever, Grace, began to change. Up to that point in her life, Grace had a regular daily routine of morning and evening meals and spent most weekdays with me at my veterinary office, where she received social time and play in the yard several times a day. On weekends Grace was just like one of our kids — sleeping until well past noon. Although she generally waited for us to take her outdoors to eliminate, Grace would sometimes whine at the back door when she needed to use the yard, and she would also stand over her food bowl and whine if we were late for her meals. She was a laid-back dog for a working breed but got quite excited about walks, treats, play, and meals.

Over a period of several months, though, Grace became less interested in physical activity and play, and it was getting more difficult to get her to rise in the morning to go to work. She also became much less responsive to requests to perform certain behaviors. Was this a case of selective hearing? Grace's hearing did not seem to be significantly affected, since she was alert, aware, and responsive whenever food was being prepared. In addition, she was beginning to occasionally urinate indoors, even if she had recently been outdoors to eliminate.

Facts, Not Fiction

With advances in veterinary care, nutrition, and behavioral care, many dogs are now living longer lives. However, with increasing age, organs begin to fail, tumors become more common, the immune system weakens, and the ability to handle stress is greatly reduced. All of these physical changes can contribute to changes in behavior. That's why behavior changes in senior pets should not be attributed to pets just "getting old."

On the outside, old dogs may show very few signs of age. However, it's what's inside that counts. Often the first or only sign of underlying health problems is a change in behavior. That's why you play a critical role in early identification of health issues. The earlier the diagnosis, the earlier treatment can be implemented and the better the chances of a positive outcome. For example, diabetes and thyroid disease can be controlled if they are diagnosed before complications develop. In fact, the health of any organ might be maintained or improved with early diagnosis and treatment. For example, dogs with kidney failure do not display outward signs or changes in their blood and urine tests until 66–75 percent of kidney function is lost. Cases diagnosed early might

It's what's inside that counts! Millie (right) is twelve years old, and her daughter, Peach, is four. Even though Millie appears healthy and alert, the gray on her face and neck are obvious signs of aging. Less obvious changes are mild muscle loss on her face and the loss of dark coloring on the end of her nose. However, to detect cognitive dysfunction, it is up to her owners to recognize and report any changes in her behavior.
Photo provided courtesy of Theresa DePorter and Judy Merians

be controlled with dietary therapy for years. For this reason, twice-a-year examinations and regular blood and urine screenings are advisable even in healthy senior pets; these tests can detect problems even before there are outward signs.

The same is likely true for the brain, where early intervention, including environmental enrichment and nutritional supplements, might help to maintain or even improve the health of brain cells. A recent focus of veterinary research has been on the effects of aging on the brain. We now know that with increasing age, some dogs develop a condition similar to human Alzheimer's disease, known as cognitive dysfunction syndrome (CDS). Signs of CDS in dogs are known by the acronym DISHA (see table 14.1 on page 304). The letters in DISHA stand for the following:

- D: disorientation
- I: changes in social interactions
- S: changes in sleep-wake cycles
- H: house soiling
- A: changes in activity levels

Anxiety or agitation may also be signs of CDS; these symptoms are also common in some humans with Alzheimer's.

To determine if a dog's problem is CDS, other medical causes must first be ruled out. This is particularly important in senior pets because an increasing number of health issues, including tumors, organ decline, hormone imbalances, and a greater susceptibility to infection are more common.

So what happened with Grace? Grace's blood and urine tests were normal, except for a low thyroid value. On examination, Grace had no abnormalities except a decline in vision, due to retinal degeneration and cataracts, and some stiffness in her left hind leg. X-rays revealed arthritis in her left tarsal (ankle) joint from a previous injury. The only other problem was that Grace was overweight.

Since a decrease in activity and playfulness could be related to pain, low thyroid, excess weight, or a combination of these, we first placed Grace on pain-control medication, a thyroid supplement, and a stricter weight-control program. After two months of treatment, there was no improvement in Grace's behavior, although she appeared more comfortable when walking. Her behavior signs included a decreased interest in social interactions, a decrease in activity, decreased responsiveness to our requests, and continued house soiling.

However, our biggest issue was that Grace had begun to whine and whimper for no apparent reason, even if she had finished her meal and had been outdoors to eliminate. The final straw came one evening when my wife and I were watching television and Grace began to whine incessantly. My wife turned to me in frustration and said, "What does your dog want?" It was clear that something had to be done — for Grace and for the family.

In fact, Grace had all of the signs of DISHA. Her persistent whining for no obvious reason was due to disorientation and confusion (D). She was less interested in play and interacting with family members (I). She could no longer sleep until noon, slept more during the day, and was more difficult to wake (S). She was house soiling (H). And her activity level was dramatically reduced (A).

Cognitive Dysfunction Syndrome

Brain aging is a degenerative process that leads to loss of learning, memory, attention, and awareness. Although mild cognitive decline might be expected with increasing age, once one sign of brain aging appears, it often progresses to multiple signs of CDS, including changes in interactions with family members and daily functions, such as sleep and elimination. In fact, there are many similarities between CDS in dogs and Alzheimer's disease in humans. Drugs, diets, and supplements are now available that might improve the signs and possibly slow the progress of CDS. As in Alzheimer's disease in humans, it's not necessary to have a brain scan to identify CDS. Behavioral signs indicate that there is a problem.

What Causes CDS?
Although the causes of CDS are the subject of ongoing studies, the damage done by toxic free radicals and a decline in oxygen flow to the

brain may be factors. The effect of age on any organ, including the brain, is cell loss, cell death, and a decline in organ function.

What Does That Mean?

Neurons: Neurons or nerve cells make up the nervous system and transmit impulses in the brain, spinal cord, and nerves.

Beta-amyloid, senile plaques, and tau proteins: Proteins that are toxic to nerve cells and that develop in the brain in humans with Alzheimer's disease. Some of these proteins can also be found in senior dogs.

Free radicals: Chemicals released during cell metabolism. An excess of free radicals due to aging or environmental toxins can cause damage to cells, especially those in the brain.

Antioxidants: Substances that decrease damage from toxic free radicals

Neuroprotective: Any intervention that serves to protect nerve cells from damage

Neurotransmitters: Chemicals produced in the body, such as dopamine, serotonin, acetylcholine, and noradrenaline, which affect mood and behavior

Cognitive decline: A deterioration in cognitive function — the normal decline associated with age — leads to increasing difficulty in speed of learning and processing, which may progress to impairment or dysfunction.

Both in dogs and humans, brain cells (neurons) are lost with increasing age, there is a decline in neurotransmitters, and beta-amyloid is deposited in the brain — a protein that is toxic to brain cells. The beta-amyloid in dogs with CDS has the same chemical structure as that in humans with Alzheimer's. In addition, in dogs and humans, the greater the amount of beta-amyloid, the greater the dementia. However, the damage in dogs does not progress to the same degree of severity as it does in humans with Alzheimer's. That's because humans develop more dense plaques and accumulations of a protein known as tau.

What Are the Behavioral Signs?

As in humans, dogs have well-developed social relationships that can be dramatically affected by aging. A decreased interest in social interactions, increased irritability and aggression, or an increase in clinginess and increased attachment behaviors have been reported in dogs with CDS. Altered day-night schedules (including waking at night) and an increase in anxiety or agitation are some of the signs common with CDS.

Are There Changes in Learning and Memory?

In humans, the earliest and most dramatic changes of Alzheimer's disease are those associated with loss of memory or language skills.

One of these objects is not like the others. In this attention task, a twelve-year-old Beagle has not yet learned that the food is under the empty soda can. *Photo by Gary Landsberg; copyright CanCog Technologies*

However, to assess learning and memory in dogs, tests had to be developed that do not require the dog to use language. In one test, the dog is presented with an object that has food hidden underneath (such as the soda can in the photograph on the previous page). Once the dog learns that this is the "correct" object, she is presented with the correct object and up to three additional objects that are incorrect (the dark blocks in the same photo). The more incorrect objects presented, the harder it is for old dogs to learn. With these types of tests, we see that dogs with CDS develop deficits in learning and memory with age. In fact, this decline in learning and memory begins several years before signs of cognitive dysfunction become apparent to owners.

Dogs with the most severe impairments in these tests also exhibited alterations in activity levels, decreased interest in social interactions with humans and new toys, and altered day-night schedules. Although it is not possible to take our companion dogs for memory evaluation tests (at least at the present time, because these are performed only in laboratory settings), there are behavioral signs that might tell us they are experiencing memory loss, such as the inability to remain housetrained.

Neuroscientists studying human Alzheimer's have found that dogs *do* have brain changes, *do* have changes in behavior, and *do* have deficits in learning and memory that resemble the early stages of human Alzheimer's disease. However, dogs *do not* progress to the same level of cognitive impairment (loss of mental skills, including the ability to eat) or the same intensity of beta-amyloid and tau protein damage associated with advanced human Alzheimer's.

How Common Is CDS?

Signs of CDS become increasingly more common with advancing age. In fact, once a dog demonstrates one sign of CDS, she is likely to progress to additional signs. Based on behavioral signs alone, in a survey conducted in Australia and New Zealand by Dr. Hannah Salvin and others in 2009, the overall prevalence of CDS in dogs over ten years of age is approximately 14 percent, ranging from 5 percent of ten-to-twelve-year-old dogs to 41 percent of dogs over fourteen years of age. However, 85 percent of these cases had not been diagnosed. In a 2000 Hill's Pet Nutrition study, only 12 percent of pet owners had reported these signs to their veterinarian.

What Are the Most Common Behavior Problems in Old Dogs?

Behavioral problems in senior dogs can be looked at in two ways. The first group comprises the most common behavior problems reported by owners of senior pets. These are the behavioral issues that are serious enough for owners to seek a professional diagnosis and intervention, because they are causing problems for the owner, the pet, or both. Either medical problems or CDS could cause these signs, or they could have other behavioral causes.

The second group of signs is related to CDS. These signs are likely to be much more common in older dogs, but they may be so mild or subtle that pet owners may not report them to their veterinarian or may assume they are just hallmarks of old age. In addition, many pet owners are not aware that treatment options are available that might improve the signs and possibly slow the progress of the disease. Signs of CDS can be far more subtle and most often go unreported and therefore untreated. That's why it's so important to be on the lookout for any of these signs and *report* them to your veterinarian for early diagnosis and treatment.

As you can see in table 14.1 (overleaf), there is some overlap between reported behavior problems and signs of CDS. This makes it challenging to determine the cause of the behavioral change. So what should you do? Be proactive; report any change in behavior or the appearance of new behavioral signs to your veterinarian as soon as they appear. Most important, *don't ignore subtle changes in behavior!* These may be the first signs of a medical problem or of CDS. Either way, early identification provides the best chance to resolve the problem or slow its progress and improve the health and welfare of your senior pet.

Table 14.1: Commonly Reported Behavior Problems and Signs of Cognitive Dysfunction

Behavior Problems Most Commonly Reported by Pet Owners*	Signs Associated with CDS (DISHA)
Aggression	Disorientation (confused, gets lost, forgets) • Gets stuck, ends up on the wrong side of door, lost in the yard or home • Stares blankly; drops food and can't find it • Does not recognize familiar people or pets • Less responsive or overreactive to sounds, sights, smells
Waking and anxious at night	Interactions (altered social relationships) • Less interested in greeting, petting • More irritable, aggressive with people or other pets • More clingy
Anxiety, fears and phobias, including separation anxiety	Sleep-wake-cycle changes • Wakes at night • Sleeps more during day
Vocalization	House soiling (in dogs previously housetrained) • Indoor soiling • Loss of signaling the need to go out
Compulsive behaviors, including repetitive circling, snapping at air, licking	Activity changes (decreased or increased) • Increased wandering, pacing, repetitive behaviors such as licking • Decreased interest in play, more sleep
Destructive behaviors	Anxiety (including phobias and separation anxiety) • Fears, phobias of sights or sounds • Separation anxiety
House soiling	Learning and memory (forgets learned tasks) • Impaired ability to do work or tasks for which the dog is trained • Less responsive to requests for learned behaviors

*Source: Behavior referral practices of Dr. Debra Horwitz and Dr. Gary Landsberg, and Veterinary Information Network

How Do We Begin?

We begin with an accurate diagnosis. When a dog has behavior signs that might be due to CDS, other causes must first be ruled out. However, even if a medical problem is the cause (such as when kidney failure or diabetes leads to house soiling), the behavior problem may persist even after the medical problem is treated, because new behaviors can be learned. Therefore, both medical and behavioral treatments may be required. It is also important to consider the possibility that as pets get older, they may develop multiple health problems.

Diagnosis involves the following:

- **History:** Does the dog have any other medical or behavioral signs? Is the pet taking any medications or supplements that might affect behavior? Does the dog have any signs that might indicate pain, a loss of sight, or a loss of hearing? Was there a change in the household when problems first appeared?
- **Tests:** A physical examination and blood and urine tests are needed to rule out internal health problems that might cause behavioral signs. If abnormalities are found, additional tests might be needed.
- **Treatment:** In cases where it is difficult to pinpoint a specific cause, sometimes the best option is to try the treatment that appears most likely to be effective and see how the pet responds.

Medical Conditions and the Behavior Signs They Cause

- **Brain:** Diseases of the brain or a decline in any of the senses can lead to a change in personality, ranging from aggression to dullness, increased fear and anxiety, vocalization, house soiling, and repetitive behaviors, such as circling, licking, or air snapping.
- **Hormones:** A decline in thyroid hormones (hypothyroidism) can cause lethargic behavior and decreased activity or even increased

irritability. Tumors of the testicles or ovaries might cause sexual behaviors such as mounting, urine marking, or increased aggression. An increased production of cortisone in Cushing's disease could lead to house soiling, increased appetite, and night waking. Diabetes may cause increased drinking, increased appetite, and house soiling.

- **Organ failure:** Kidney failure can lead to house soiling and night waking. Heart failure can lead to panting, night waking, and decreased interest in exercise.
- **Pain:** Often the only sign of pain is behavioral. In fact, decreased interest in play and greeting, decreased response to behavior requests, avoiding contact, and increased irritability and aggression can all be due to pain.
- **Digestive tract:** Stomach and intestinal problems might cause increased licking of objects, decreased appetite, house soiling with stool, night waking, or eating stools (coprophagia) and nonfood items (pica).
- **Urinary tract:** Problems such as infections can cause house soiling and can lead to waking at night.

Crystal, a twelve-year-old female Bichon Frise, began waking at night and house soiling near the back door and in a guest bedroom when her owners were away from home. She had recently also begun to soil even when her owners were at home. From the time she was six months old, Crystal was housetrained, even when the owners were away from 9:00 A.M. to 5:00 P.M.

They reported that Crystal was now drinking and urinating more frequently. Blood and urine tests confirmed a diagnosis of diabetes, and after four weeks the disease was well controlled with insulin injections and diet. However, the night waking and soiling continued.

Dogs with CDS who forget their housetraining are more likely to soil in random locations rather than in specific spots. Therefore, Crystal's blood and urine tests were repeated, and this time a bladder infection was found (which is common in dogs with diabetes). After treating the bladder infection, the frequency with which Crystal urinated returned to normal and she no longer soiled as long as her owners were at home. However, she continued to soil at the back door when the owners were out. It was suspected Crystal had learned that urinating on the mat was a good way to relieve herself while the owners were out all day. The owners hired their neighbor's teenage son to walk Crystal during his lunch break from school, and the problem was solved. Crystal's case demonstrates the need to first rule out possible medical causes for sudden changes in behavior.

Treating Behavior Problems in Senior Dogs

Some of the most common behavior problems in senior pets are aggression, night waking, increased fears, anxiety and phobias, and house soiling. Of course, beyond addressing any medical problems, there may be limitations on what can be achieved with a senior dog, and the dog's schedule or environment may have to be modified.

The environment may need to be modified to help pets overcome their limitations, such as adding steps so that this twelve-year-old Westie, Oscar, can get to his favored sleeping spot.
Debra Horwitz

For example, dogs with kidney failure need to urinate more often. Therefore, more frequent trips outdoors or perhaps an indoor toilet area will be needed. As the pet's sight, hearing, mobility, or cognitive function decline, new odors, sounds, and surface textures or improved lighting might help the dog navigate better at home. Pets who have lost their hearing may need to learn hand signals or wear a leash all day to facilitate communication. Ramps, dog steps, and physical support, such as lifting, may be necessary to help pets who can no longer jump or climb, or the dog's bed may need to be moved to the floor.

Dogs Who Wake at Night

One problem that is of particular concern is a senior pet who wakes her owners during the night. Medical problems such as pain, high blood pressure, or any condition that causes an increased frequency of urination must be ruled out before any behavioral plan begins.

When dealing with night waking, try the following approaches:

- Reestablish a normal day-night schedule by providing increased exposure to daylight, including outdoor activities if possible, and increased daytime enrichment (see chapter 9).
- Even if a dog has medical problems that limit her ability to exercise, activities can be modified to include short walks; more opportunities to sniff and explore; play sessions of such activities as retrieving, chase, or tug games; reward-based training sessions; and social times with other animals.
- Another approach to enrichment is to make feeding more mentally and physically challenging by switching from food-bowl feeding to stuffing food in toys, placing food in puzzle toys, hiding or spreading food around the home or yard for hunt-and-search games, and using food as rewards for training.
- Not only does enrichment help keep the dog more active and stimulated during the day, but it also has been shown to improve brain health. (Use it or lose it!)
- At bedtime, take your dog to her bed or sleeping area. If she wakes at night, attempts to calm her will only reward the behavior. On

the other hand, punishment and frustration add to the dog's anxiety. The best approach is to ignore the dog until she is quiet, or to use basic requests such as "sit" and "lie down" to calm and settle the pet.

- Combine the previous approaches with drugs, diets, or supplements for CDS. In addition, natural supplements such as pheromones, L-theanine, melatonin, or lavender oil might really help to reduce anxiety. Your veterinarian might also consider drug therapy to help the pet sleep through the night.

Junior, a fifteen-year-old neutered male mixed breed, was waking and barking in the middle of the night. He also slept more during the day, was less interested in play, and was increasingly seeking attention from his owners. When Junior woke at night, the owners tried to comfort him, took him outdoors to eliminate, and eventually resorted to offering food to quiet him. He was then presented to a veterinary behaviorist.

After a thorough examination and laboratory tests, it was determined that Junior's signs were likely due to CDS, since his only health problems were a decline in vision due to cataracts and possibly a decrease in hearing. In addition, the attention, walks, and feeding at night were rewarding Junior's behavior.

Junior was started on Anipryl (selegiline hydrochloride), a medication that increases dopamine in the brain and increases alertness each morning. His owners gave him a heated dog bed in the corner of the bedroom and placed a humidifier in the room during the winter and a fan during the summer to provide comfort and to mask any outside noises that might disturb Junior. A program of increased enrichment included walks in the morning, afternoon, and before bedtime to give him regular outdoor aerobic activity. Social time with the owners, and a predictable daily routine were also implemented. He also started getting a portion of each meal inside toys for further enrichment.

The veterinary behaviorist set up a training plan that focused on rewarding settled behaviors and a structured program in which all affection, toys, food, and treats were given only when Junior lay down or relaxed. At bedtime, the owners took Junior to his dog bed, had him lie down and relax, and gave him his favorite food puzzle toy. If Junior awoke during the night, they either ignored him or immediately took him back to his bed and told him to relax. They also plugged in a pheromone diffuser (see chapter 5) in the bedroom to help him settle.

After one week, Junior was more alert during the day and was less needy for affection. He went calmly to his bed but continued to wake each night. The owners took him back to his bed and ignored him until he fell back asleep. In the second week a CDS supplement, Senilife, was added to the treatment and a leash was left attached to Junior's harness so he could be immediately returned to his bed if he woke. By the fourth week, Junior slept through the night.

Use It or Lose It: The Benefits of Enrichment

Recent studies in dogs (done to assess the efficacy of a senior diet) have shown that mental stimulation and enrichment in the form of training, play, exercise, and novel toys can help maintain cognitive function. On the other hand, inconsistency and change can be particularly stressful to senior dogs and negatively affect their health and behavioral well-being.

Enrichment should focus on social interactions in the form of play, reward-based training, exercise, and new and varied opportunities to explore and find food and treats. Food toys that require rolling, lifting and dropping, tugging, or other forms of manipulation to release food can make feeding more enriching and stimulating for a senior dog. Owners can initiate these opportunities by scattering food, playing toss-and-retrieve or hide-and-search food games, providing food mazes, and stuffing food into toys to create more challenging ways for pets to acquire food.

Drugs, Diets, and Natural Supplements

CDS cannot be cured, but deterioration may be slowed and clinical signs improved with treatment. Since damage to brain cells caused by toxic free radicals and a decline in blood flow to the brain may be factors in CDS, antioxidant products that improve blood flow to the brain and products that improve neurotransmission may be effective. To date, the following drugs, supplements, and diets have been studied and shown to have some value in improving learning, memory, or clinical signs of CDS in dogs.

Drugs

Selegiline (brand name Anipryl, made by Pfizer Animal Health) is the only drug licensed in North America to treat CDS in dogs. It may act to enhance neurotransmitters such as dopamine, and might also have neuroprotective effects. (See the website www.cdsindogs.com for additional information.) In some countries outside North America, propentofylline (Vivitonin, Karsivan) is licensed for treating dullness, lethargy, and depressed demeanor in old dogs. Propentofylline may act by improving blood flow through the brain and may also have neuroprotective properties.

Diets

Hill's Prescription Diet b/d Canine, a special diet developed by Hill's Pet Nutrition to treat cognitive aging in dogs, has been demonstrated to improve the clinical signs of CDS and slow cognitive decline. However, the combined effect of the diet and environmental enrichment provides the greatest benefit.

A diet containing medium-chain triglycerides (MCTs) from vegetable oil (Purina One Vibrant Maturity 7+ Senior Formula, Nestlé Purina PetCare) was shown to significantly improve performance on a number of learning and attention tasks.

Nutritional Supplements

Supplements that have demonstrated improvement in clinical trials or tests of learning and memory include Senilife (made by Ceva Animal Health), Aktivait (made by VetPlus), S-adenosyl-l-methionine (also known as SAMe, available from a variety of sources), S-adenosyl-l-methionine-tosylate (available as Novifit from Virbac Animal Health), and apoaequorin (available as Neutricks from Quincy Animal Health).

Table 14.2: Natural Therapeutics for CDS

Product	Ingredients	Suggested Methods of Action
Senilife	Phosphatidylserine, ginkgo biloba, vitamin B6, vitamin E, resveratrol	Improve neuron transmission and nerve cell health, antioxidant
Aktivait	Phosphatidylserine, omega-3 fatty acids, vitamins E and C, L-carnitine, alpha-lipoic acid, coenzyme Q^{10}, selenium	Improve neuron transmission and nerve cell health, antioxidant
Novifit	S-adenosyl-l-methionine-tosylate disulfate (SAMe)	Improve neuron transmission and nerve cell health, antioxidant
Neutricks	Apoaequorin	Protection against calcium damage to neurons
Hill's Prescription Diet b/d Canine	Fruits and vegetables, vitamins E and C, beta-carotene, selenium, L-carnitine, alpha-lipoic acid, omega-3 fatty acids, and many more	Antioxidant, improve neuron transmission
Purina One Vibrant Maturity 7+ Senior	Medium chain triglyceride oils (from vegetable oil)	Alternative source of energy (ketones) for aging brain cells

Is That Really True?

Sam, a Shetland Sheepdog, was owned by a trainer and dog walker. Sam went for walks with the other dogs and joined in play sessions at off-leash parks. Sam was well trained to immediately come when called. When he was nine years old, his owner reported that he stopped responding to her commands and was less interested in play. An examination, urinalysis, and blood tests, including thyroid, were all normal.

A loss in hearing, vision, or both was suspected. Sam's owner made an appointment with a neurologist to test Sam's hearing and an ophthalmologist to evaluate Sam's vision. At the same time, he was started on Hill's Prescription Diet b/d Canine. The ophthalmologist found no problems with Sam's vision. And before the appointment to test Sam's hearing, he actually began responding to the owner and was more playful and alert. What happened? Sam's new diet may have been the cause. In fact, we have now discovered a number of dogs with what *seems* to be improved hearing or vision after treatment for CDS. This may have been because the dogs' hearing or vision was still working, but the dogs were unable to respond normally because of the CDS.

What Happened to Grace?

Fortunately for Grace, research into CDS in dogs, its relationship to Alzheimer's in humans, and the development of new therapeutic options was being studied by the Department of Life Sciences (now the Department of Pharmacology and Toxicology) at the University of Toronto. This provided an opportunity to learn firsthand about the latest in brain aging in dogs. When the first drug for treating CDS, L-deprenyl (now known as selegiline), was ready for testing, I was given the opportunity to take part in the initial trials and then to treat Grace when the product was launched.

Within weeks of starting treatment, Grace's transformation was remarkable. We also had the opportunity to put her on Hill's Prescription Diet b/d Canine. Grace was more mellow and relaxed. She went back to her regular schedule of waking for work on weekdays and sleeping in on weekends, stopped all house soiling, and was more alert and responsive. Most important to my wife and family is that Grace's incessant whining and whimpering was gone. Her biggest admirer, our youngest son, Jordan, was especially pleased that he could once again play with his Gracie.

Grace's behavior remained calm and relatively stable for four more years. Grace lived to a happy and healthy sixteen years, thanks to advances in health care for the aging brain and ongoing medication for pain management. For our family, the improvement in Grace's mental health was critical for reestablishing and maintaining a healthy and happy relationship.

Avoiding Pitfalls and Staying on Track

Report any change in behavior or new behavior problems, no matter how subtle or mild, to your veterinarian. These may be the first or only signs of pain, medical problems, or cognitive dysfunction syndrome. Your dog's health and well-being depend on you noticing changes and speaking up.

Even when medical problems and cognitive dysfunction are treated, behavior signs may persist after they have been learned. Therefore, you may also need guidance in environmental management and behavioral modification to improve problems such as aggression, phobias, or house soiling.

In senior pets, health problems, pain, and cognitive dysfunction might be improved but not cured. Therefore, discuss with your veterinarian how much improvement you can expect and what modifications may have to be made to provide the "assisted living" your dog may need.

What Did We Say?

- Behavioral signs that arise in senior pets are often due to health problems.
- Cognitive dysfunction syndrome (CDS), a brain-aging disease in dogs, is similar to Alzheimer's disease in humans — although it does not become as severe as Alzheimer's.
- Most cases of cognitive dysfunction go undiagnosed because owners do not report the signs to their veterinarian. Be proactive! It is important to report any change in behavior to your veterinarian, since it could be the first sign of CDS or another underlying medical problem.
- Signs of CDS include disorientation, altered social interactions, waking at night, house soiling, change in activity, and agitation.

- When signs of CDS are identified, a diagnosis involves ruling out other possible medical causes.
- Treatment of CDS includes environmental enrichment, drugs, supplements, and diets. Treatment can improve clinical signs and possibly slow the progress of the disease.

CONCLUSION

This book has been a very long time in the making. In creating *Decoding Your Dog*, we, the members of the American College of Veterinary Behaviorists, have worked diligently to offer a never-before-published view of dog behavior, one based on experience, science, and ongoing collaboration with other experts in the field. With so much misinformation out there endangering both pets and their owners, we want to set the record straight and offer strategies that work and improve the dog-owner relationship.

Every day offers challenges but also new insights into the behavior of these wonderful creatures we choose to share our lives with. Central in understanding dogs is the realization that dogs are not out to dominate us, control us, or make us angry; they want to be our companions and helpmates. Dogs try to speak to us the only way they know how: with their eyes, ears, tail, and body. When they choose a behavior, it is because they think it is the right thing to do at the time. We hope we have taught you how to listen to your dog and clearly interpret what he is saying — and that you use this information to take your relationship with your dog to another level.

Getting a puppy or a dog and keeping him for a lifetime is not the same thing. You need to use the tools here to choose the right dog or puppy for you and your family, to make that relationship work for the long term. You must also troubleshoot the inevitable problems that crop up along the way, from house soiling to barking, jumping, and other nuisance behaviors. And when the problem behaviors become more serious, such as with aggression, separation anxiety, noise and storm phobias, or aging changes, we hope this book will help you avoid or manage them and utilize resources that are available for hands-on help. Keep in mind that besides veterinary behaviorists (www.dacvb .org), there are other qualified behavioral professionals, such as Certified Applied Animal Behaviorists (www.animalbehavior.org/ABS AppliedBehavior/caab-directory), who can also help you and your dog and we hope you will use the resource section to find them.

To have longevity, of course, a dog needs to be healthy, both medically and behaviorally. Raise your puppy or dog for optimum behavioral health. And always remember: medical health and behavioral health are linked. If you notice a sudden change in your pet's behavior, always get him examined by your veterinarian to make sure all is okay.

We, the editors, want to share a special word about what this book means to us. For us this was a labor of love. Whether it is by maintaining the wonderful relationship you already have with your dog, or repairing the damage to that relationship that can occur with behavior problems, keeping dogs and people together is our ultimate goal. So, as we go about our lives and see happy people and happy dogs, we will hope we've had a little something to do with it.

DEBRA F. HORWITZ, DVM, DACVB
JOHN CIRIBASSI, DVM, DACVB

APPENDIX

Crate-Training Tips

Many dogs love their crate right from the start. But some are reluctant or even afraid to enter the crate. When first introducing your dog to a crate, encourage her to go into it by tossing treats in or smearing the back wall with soft treats such as spray cheese or peanut butter. Leave the crate open and available to your dog at all times.

If you have a dog who is reluctant to enter, *do not* force her in. This just makes the crate even scarier. Here's a cool trick instead: Play Hansel and Gretel. Set up a trail of treats leading into the crate. At this stage, you don't have to do anything else. As your dog gets bolder and takes

a step toward the crate, she will be remotely rewarded for her efforts by the treats you left. Eventually, she will walk right into the crate following the treat trail.

Use a trail of treats to encourage your dog to get into the crate. *Lori Gaskins*

When she is willingly running into the crate to see if there are treats, toss a few in, wait until she is inside, and then close the door for a few seconds and continue to hand treats in to her through the grate in the door. Do this for just a few seconds; let her out while she is still happy. Increase the time the door is closed by a few seconds each time you play this game.

When you leave her in the crate for any length of time and you are not there to toss in treats, give her a long-lasting yummy such as a piece of rawhide or a food puzzle toy. When it's time to release her, make sure she is calm by tossing in a few treats before opening the door. Do not take the long-lasting treats out of the crate until the dog is safely behind a closed door, in case your dog might aggressively guard those items.

It is important to remember that not all dogs like to be confined. If your dog refuses to go into the crate or gets extremely agitated or aggressive when you try to put her in the crate, stop immediately and seek additional veterinary advice on confinement techniques for your dog.

GLOSSARY

Aggression: Behavior that harms or threatens to harm another individual. Because aggressive behavior bears a cost to the aggressor (who might get hurt as well), the function of aggression is often to increase the distance between the aggressor and the target.

Antioxidants: Substances that decrease damage from toxic free radicals.

Anxiety: Apprehensive anticipation of dangerous, dreaded, or fear-inducing situations. Anxiety is usually recognized in dogs by signs of hypervigilance (the dog is easy to startle and is excessively watchful), restlessness, increased muscle tension, and trembling.

Appeasement behaviors: Behaviors that a dog may perform in an attempt to diminish what she perceives as a threat. For example, if an owner is angry and reaches for the dog's collar, the dog may roll over in an attempt to appease or stop the owner from taking hold, because she feels threatened by the action.

Attachment behaviors: A desire to be physically close to a member of the social group (person or pet). With overattachment disorders, the dog is overly anxious or distressed when separated.

Attention-seeking behaviors: Those behaviors exhibited in the owner's presence or in an attempt to get the owner to interact with the dog.

Avoidance behaviors: Avoidance behaviors are usually exhibited by a dog when she is afraid of a particular stimulus and would like to escape it if she can. She may lower her head, flatten her ears, lower her body, and then actively try to back away from or completely leave the area where the scary stimulus is present. If a dog leaves the room every time a particular person or animal enters, she may be demonstrating avoidance behavior.

Avoidance learning: Learning that occurs when a stimulus becomes associated with something a dog would like to avoid.

Beta-amyloid, senile plaques, and tau proteins: Proteins that are toxic to nerve cells and that develop in the brain in humans with Alzheimer's disease. Some of these proteins can also be found in senior dogs.

Casual breeder: People who are selling or giving away puppies who were born either from an unregistered mother or in a nonprofessional breeding setting. Often these are accidental breedings or families who want to experience having one or more litters from their family dogs. These people may be less well informed and put less planning and care into the health and behavior of the puppies.

Chew toy: A long-lasting edible treat (such as rawhide) or an inedible toy that is filled or smeared with food that a dog has to work to obtain.

Classical conditioning: Learning in which the presence of one event becomes associated with another event that naturally elicits the desired response.

Cognitive decline: A deterioration in cognitive function; the normal decline associated with age leads to increasing difficulty in speed of learning and processing, which may progress to impairment or dysfunction.

Compulsive disorder: A group of behaviors that appear to arise from normal activities, such as moving (spinning, tail chasing, fence running, pacing, light or shadow chasing), grooming (licking or sucking an area of the body), eating or licking objects or air, or vocalizing, and which seem to occur at continuously high levels. It often appears the dog has no control over the beginning and continuance of the behavior. Compulsive disorders can also be self-injurious.

Conflict-related aggression: Aggression directed toward owners (and family members) in contexts that create conflict between the dog's drives and his ability to inhibit the behavior. Triggers can include threatening postures by (often unaware) owners, punishment, physical manipulation, and other interactions.

Counterconditioning: The process of changing the animal's perception or underlying emotional state by teaching a new behavior that is fun and is incompatible with exhibiting the undesirable behavior. Counterconditioning goes hand in hand with desensitization.

Cowering: A body posture that a fearful or anxious dog may show by tucking her tail, flattening her ears, dropping her head, and lowering her body toward the floor. It is as if the dog is trying to make her body look smaller to avoid the attention of someone or something that seems threatening.

Crate: An enclosed container for confining a dog, usually made of molded plastic or wire.

Defensive aggression: A nonspecific term that describes aggressive behaviors motivated by self-defense, territorial defense, and defense of resources.

Desensitization: The process of exposing the animal to the stimulus of which she is fearful in a manner that is the least threatening and incites no or minimal fearful response (such as playing recordings of fireworks or storms at a very low volume).

Deterrent: Something aversive added in response to a dog's behavior to decrease the likelihood that the dog will repeat that behavior or frequent an area again. A remote deterrent allows the dog to make a choice and when used properly may diminish the possibility of a fearful or aggressive response.

Distress: A behavioral and physiological response that has harmful effects on an animal's welfare, both physiologically and emotionally.

Dominance: In a relationship between two dogs, the dog who more often than not controls access to valuable resources is considered to have dominance over the other dog. Dominance does *not* equal aggression. Dominance can also depend on context; one dog may be the winner in one context but not in another. Dominance is only expressed within that specific relationship and that context. The idea of possessing the dominant position in any relationship or hierarchy has inappropriately been applied to dog training, based on faulty research on wolf behavior. That idea has now has been disproved by research on free-ranging wolves, and with that in mind, certainly does not apply to dogs.

Elimination: Urination and defecation.

Enrichment: Providing objects or having interactions with your dog that occupy and stimulate his thinking and/or physical activity. Proper enrichment techniques allow the animal to make some choices and be an active participant in these activities. The overall goal is to help your dog use these activities to dissipate stress and relieve boredom.

Environmental enrichment: Providing new objects and other variations in the environment that encourage investigation and allow the animal to have a choice of activities. In some cases, environmental enrichment also includes enabling the animal to be alone, if that's what he wants. Enrichment can limit boredom, encourage thinking, and aid the animal in coping with mild stresses (such as being left alone or ignored by a working owner, or the presence of potentially frightening things, such as loud noises or young and active children).

Escape behaviors: Anything a dog does to try to get away from something she perceives as dangerous or threatening or to be reunited with a person. These behaviors may occur in dogs with separation anxiety, during storm or noise events, when an owner punishes or tries to punish the dog, or when someone reaches for the dog.

Exercise: The physical activity part of stimulation, such as a dog running on leash alongside a running, biking, or skating human, with no opportunity to investigate the environment.

Extinction: The disappearance of a learned response because it is not rewarded or reinforced. We say the response has been *extinguished*.

Extinction burst: A sudden display of a behavior that was going away after you stopped rewarding it. Sort of like your dog saying, "Was she *really* serious about that?"

Fear: An emotional response that begins when an animal perceives a threatening stimulus. That emotional response is important because it tells the body to begin physiological and behavioral responses that protect the animal from the threatening stimulus. When the stimulus can be identified, the fear can be normal and appropriate in certain situations.

Fear-related aggression: Aggression used as self-defense. Such aggression may be a "last resort" in dogs who otherwise cannot escape, or it can also be a preemptive behavior when a threat is anticipated.

Fear response: Fear is a feeling of apprehension about a situation or object. The fear response is the behavior shown by an animal experiencing fear. The response also includes physiological changes, such as increasing heart and respiration rates, visual cues such as flattening the ears and/or lowering the head and tail, and avoidance behaviors.

Food puzzle toys: Toys that require a dog to manipulate them to get the reward inside.

Free radicals: Chemicals released during cell metabolism. An excess of free radicals due to aging or environmental toxins can cause damage to cells, especially those in the brain.

Generalize: To learn that after a behavior is established in one particular environment, it should also occur in all other environments.

Habituation: The process by which a dog stops responding to a situation just by being exposed to it many times. The response to this can depend on the intensity of the stimulus.

Highly invested breeder: This type of breeder strives to produce puppies who best represent the ideal health and behavior profile of a given dog breed. Reputable breeders should be able to provide information on the behavior of both parents, the conditions during pregnancy, and the behaviors of previous litters, as well as the standard physical health certifications known to be important for that particular breed.

Housetraining: The process by which a puppy learns to urinate and defecate when and where you designate.

Housetraining accident: Eliminating in what you consider to be the wrong spot.

Interactive play: Play involving social interaction.

Intermittent reinforcement: Rewarding a behavior only on occasion, instead of every time it occurs.

Irritable aggression: Aggression associated with disease but not directly a result of pain.

Marker signal: A unique sound, such as a clicker, whistle, or special word or noise that is used to aid the training process. Initially, the sound you choose is always followed by a high-value reinforcer (usually a special treat), and this is repeated over and over until your dog learns to anticipate the treat after hearing the sound. At this point you can use the sound to mark the moment when the dog does the desired behavior.

Mental stimulation: The thinking part of stimulation. These might be activities in which a dog works out a problem, hones her social abilities or physical coordination, or investigates her environment.

Motivation: The underlying reason a dog may perform a behavior. It can be anything dogs want: food, treats, attention, praise, a belly rub, balls thrown, doors opened, the leash snapped on for a walk or taken off at the park, coming along for a car ride, or the need to escape danger or an uncomfortable situation, etc.

Negative reinforcement: Something you keep doing to the dog that is unpleasant, until he does what you want. For example, you pull on the leash until he moves toward you. His reward is that you stop pulling. You are then removing something unpleasant (that's the negative part) to increase the likelihood that the dog will move toward you again (that's the reinforcement part). Your pulling should increase the probability that he will approach you when he feels the tension on the leash increase.

Neurons: Neurons, or nerve cells, make up the nervous system and transmit impulses in the brain, spinal cord, and nerves.

Neuroprotective: Items, products, or interventions that serve to protect nerve cells to avoid damage.

Neurotransmitters: Chemicals produced in the body, such as dopamine, serotonin, acetylcholine, and noradrenaline, that affect mood and behavior.

Operant conditioning: Learning that occurs when a particular behavior produces consequences, either reinforcement or punishment.

Overstimulation: Too much stimulation. Just as there can be a problem with lack of stimulation, there can also be excessive stimulation. Dogs can become overwhelmed when they have too much to deal with. This can lead to exaggerated reactions to benign events.

Pain-related aggression: Aggression that occurs directly as a result of pain.

Panic: A sudden, intense feeling of terror, accompanied by strong physical signs, such as a racing heart, agitation, stomach upset, escape behaviors, and panting. Panic may occur even if there's no specific, identifiable trigger.

Phobia: A persistent, abnormal, intense fear of a stimulus that is out of proportion to the stimulus.

Physical stimulation: A good daily workout and, if the dog is social, regular play sessions with other dogs.

Pica: Eating nonfood items.

Positive punishment: Adding something to decrease the frequency of a behavior. Of course, it's most effective if it's something the dog doesn't like. Using positive punishment effectively poses some serious timing issues.

Positive reinforcement: Delivering something the animal desires in response to a behavior, so that the behavior is more likely to be repeated in the future.

Predatory behavior: Behavior that is motivated by the instinct to detect, pursue, and kill for food. Unlike overtly aggressive behaviors, the objective of predatory behavior is *not* to increase the distance between the aggressor (dog) and the target (prey).

Punishment: Any change in an animal's surroundings that occurs after a behavior or response and reduces the likelihood of that behavior occurring again. Punishment can be positive (something is added to the situation) or negative (something is taken away from the situation).

Puppy mills: High-volume breeding facilities. Usually, a broker purchases large numbers of puppies at once and sells or distributes them to local pet stores. The breeding animals are typically confined to cramped and solitary living spaces with limited or no social or physical stimulation and little or no regard for their physical and behavioral health.

Puppy socialization: Arranging pleasant, safe introductions of puppies to people and dogs as well as to other types of animals. A well-socialized puppy is better equipped to take life's experiences in stride because she has already seen it all and has learned that other living beings are nice to be around. Ideally, these activities should occur between six and fourteen weeks of age.

Puppy socialization classes: Classes specifically designed to facilitate socialization. Although some basic skills may be taught, obedience is not the focus. The purpose of a puppy socialization class is to offer puppies the opportunity to meet other puppies and their families.

Puzzle toy: A toy that requires a dog to think and try different strategies to obtain a reward. A food toy may be a puzzle toy if the dog must work out how to get the food. There are also puzzle toys that don't involve food; for example, some toys can be disassembled or have smaller toys inside the larger toys, which the dog has to figure out how to extract.

Reinforcement: The presentation of a stimulus following a response that increases the frequency of subsequent responses. Reinforcement can be positive (something is added to the situation) or negative (something is taken away from the situation).

Reinforcers: Anything dogs want and will work for: food, treats, attention, praise, a belly rub, balls thrown, doors opened, the leash snapped on for a walk or taken off at the park, coming along for a car ride, etc., which increases the likelihood that the behavior will be repeated.

Remote deterrents: Tools that add something aversive to the environment in response to a dog's behavior and so decrease the likelihood the dog will repeat that behavior. Veterinary behaviorists recommend using remote deterrents to reduce the likelihood of the dog engaging in the problem behavior when not supervised, and to prevent the dog from associating the owner with the deterrent. It is important to also give the dog the option to choose to do a desired behavior once deterred from engaging in the problem behavior, and to reinforce the right choice with a reward.

Rescue groups: Typically, nonprofit organizations that take in and rehome pets. Some rescue groups obtain their pets directly from families who wish to rehome their pets, while others pick up from local municipal shelters dogs who might otherwise be euthanized. Most of these pets then stay in temporary foster homes until they are matched with an adoptive family. There are breed-specific rescues for most dog breeds.

Resource guarding: Defending resources perceived by the aggressor as having high value. Examples are food, toys, resting places, and even owners.

Safe refuge: A safe haven for a dog, which can be anywhere in the home where the dog can go to avoid situations that induce fear or anxiety.

Selective breeding: A process by which breeders select a set of characteristics (behavioral, physical, or both) that they find desirable and then choose to breed animals who have those characteristics so that they will be more likely to pass them on to their offspring.

Sensitization: An *increased* response to a stimulus after repeated exposure. This is usually an undesirable response that occurs when, instead of habituating, a puppy becomes more and more frightened with each exposure.

Separation anxiety: Significant distress that accompanies a dog's anticipation of being separated from family members and that continues when she is left alone. Many of these dogs exhibit clinical signs of panic when they are left alone.

Snarl: A canine facial expression that involves pulling up the lips and exposing the teeth and that is usually associated with an aggressive threat.

Social enrichment: Opportunities provided for animals to interact with people or other animals and to develop social relationships.

Socialization: A special learning process occurring in a young animal during which an individual learns to accept close proximity to various other species or to individuals of her own species.

Sound sensitivities: Anxieties, fears, and phobias associated with sounds.

Status-related aggression: Aggression between household dogs related to resources, social and physical access to desired locations, and postural provocations.

Stereotypic behaviors: Behaviors very similar to compulsive ones, in that they seem to occur without the animal being able to stop the behaviors. Often stereotypic behaviors are characterized by uniform, ritualized (very repeatable pattern of activity), and species-typical (normal behaviors for the species) behaviors.

Stimulation: A type of enrichment; stimulation is the opportunities for thinking or physical activity that are available to a dog.

Stimulus: A thing or event that elicits a specific reaction from an individual.

Stress: A condition that is broad and nonspecific. Most behaviorists agree that the basic function of stress is to maintain a physiological and psychological balance so that individuals can react in a healthy, normal manner to life's changes and stressors. Stress becomes counterproductive when the physiological response is sustained or activated too often.

Submissiveness: In a relationship between two individuals, in this case, dogs, the dog who more often than not relinquishes things of value or defers to the other dog is considered to be submissive. This may not be the same in all contexts between the same two dogs.

Systematic desensitization: A treatment process that is meant to be gentle and gradual and to incorporate learning. This technique involves exposing a dog to the situation that causes fear or distress, but at such a low level that the dog does not react with distress, and then gradually increasing some aspect of the exposure the dog finds distressing while rewarding calm behavior. This process goes hand in hand with counterconditioning.

Temperament test: Also known as a behavior assessment or behavior evaluation, this process includes a series of standardized interactive tests, typically performed on shelter dogs, to assess the behavior and personality of the dogs. Most temperament tests assess dogs for social interest in people, compatibility with other dogs, physical handling issues, and potential for resource guarding and some other aggressive behaviors.

Territorial aggression: Defensive aggression associated with the arrival of an intruder in or near the house, yard, car, or other area perceived by a dog as his territory. Territorial aggression is usually facilitated — worsened — by the presence of other household members. It is most common for territorial aggression to be associated with fear.

Tether: A leash or line that is used to secure a dog to something or someone. These must always be used with caution and supervision, because the dog could get tangled or tighten the collar and choke off her own air supply. Must always be used with direct supervision.

Threat: Something that is perceived as dangerous by an individual.

Tie-down: A leash used to secure a dog to a specific location. To avoid injury, a tie-down should only be used under direct supervision.

Trigger: A thing or event that causes a specific response.

Variable ratio of reinforcement: A reinforcement or reward schedule in which the number of responses necessary to get a reward varies.

RECOMMENDED RESOURCES

Professional Organizations

American College of Veterinary Behaviorists
www.dacvb.org

The American College of Veterinary Behaviorists (ACVB) is a professional organization of veterinarians who have achieved board certification in the specialty of veterinary behavior. Board-certified specialists are known as Diplomates. These specialists do research and work with individual pet owners, other animal professionals, and facilities that care for animals to manage behavior problems and improve the well-being of animals. The authors of this book and all the other members of the college are listed at the end of the book; they are also listed on the website, so you can locate a veterinary behaviorist near where you live.

Academy of Veterinary Behavior Technicians
www.avbt.net

The Academy of Veterinary Behavior Technicians (AVBT) certifies qualified veterinary technicians as Veterinary Technician Specialists (VTS) in the field of behavior. A VTS in behavior has demonstrated superior knowledge in scientific and humane techniques of behavior health, problem prevention, training, management, and behavior modification.

American Animal Hospital Association
www.healthypet.com

The American Animal Hospital Association accredits small-animal hospitals throughout the United States and Canada for achieving excellence in pet health care. The site includes pet news and information with articles written by experts, helpful videos, and activities for children.

American Humane Association
www.americanhumane.org

Since 1877, the American Humane Association has been at the forefront of every major advancement in protecting children, pets, and farm animals from abuse and neglect. Their mission is to unleash the full potential of the bond between humans and animals, including protecting pets and children in emergencies, through the Red Star Animal Emergency Services program, and the "No Animals Were Harmed" certification program in film productions.

American Society for the Prevention of Cruelty to Animals
www.aspca.org

The American Society for the Prevention of Cruelty to Animals (ASPCA) website includes updates on legislative matters, animal shelter support, as well as general information about animal welfare, including the National Animal Poison Control Center.

American Veterinary Medical Association
www.avma.org

The American Veterinary Medical Association site includes podcasts and the latest news in veterinary medicine that may affect your pet — everything from pet food recalls to information about preventing dog bites.

American Veterinary Society of Animal Behavior
www.avsabonline.org

The American Veterinary Society of Animal Behavior (AVSAB) is a group of veterinarians and research professionals who share an interest in understanding animal behavior. AVSAB is committed to improving the quality of life of all animals and strengthening the bond between animals and their owners. The site offers several expert position statements on important issues, and a locator to help you find a veterinarian with an interest in behavior in your area.

Animal Behavior Resources Institute
www.abrionline.org

Legendary veterinary behaviorist Dr. R. K. Anderson created this site to not only write about behavior but, through videos, to demonstrate how to deal with a range of behavioral problems. Veterinary behaviorists, Certified Applied Animal Behaviorists (CAAB), and well-known dog trainers participate in these demonstrations, and they include many contributors to *Decoding Your Dog*.

Animal Behavior Society
www.animalbehaviorsociety.org

The Animal Behavior Society is an organization devoted to the scientific study of animal behavior, including applied animal behavior, which studies the behavior of companion animals and of farm, zoo, laboratory animals, and wild animals as it applies to their management. The site also includes a list of Certified Applied Animal Behaviorists (CAAB) and Associate Certified Applied Animal Behaviorists (ACAAB) who have met the society's requirements for certification, and these individuals provide behavior consulting services to the public as well as to other professionals.

Association of Pet Dog Trainers
www.apdt.com

The Association of Pet Dog Trainers (APDT) is a professional organization of individual trainers who are committed to becoming better trainers through education. The site includes a trainer locator as well as general dog care and training tips and other information.

Certification Council for Professional Dog Trainers
www.ccpdt.org

The Certification Council for Professional Dog Trainers (CCPDT) is the international testing and certification resource for dog training and behavior professionals. The site has information on how to obtain help for your dog and on becoming certified through the CCPDT. Dog owners, veterinarians, and shelters or rescue organizations can locate certified animal training and behavior professionals through the search function and find other valuable resources on the site.

Pet Partners
www.deltasociety.org

Pet Partners, formerly the Delta Society, is a nonprofit organization that brings individuals together who share a common passion — a love of animals and people — often in the realm of animal-assisted therapy and other activities.

Society of Veterinary Behavior Technicians
www.svbt.org

The Society of Veterinary Behavior Technicians (SVBT) promotes scientifically based techniques of training, management, and behavior modification. SVBT connects veterinary technicians around the world, sharing their knowledge and experience to enhance the role of veterinary technicians in veterinary medicine and animal welfare.

Books on Choosing a Dog

American Kennel Club. *The Complete Dog Book*. 20th ed. New York: Ballantine Books, 2006.

Coren, Stanley. *Why We Love the Dogs We Do: How to Find the Dog that Matches Your Personality.* New York: Fireside Books, 1998.

Hart, Benjamin L., and Lynette A. Hart. *The Perfect Puppy: How to Choose Your Dog By Its Behavior.* New York: W. H. Freeman, 1988.

Tortora, Daniel. *The Right Dog for You.* New York: Simon & Schuster, 1983.

Walkowicz, Chris. *Choosing a Dog for Dummies.* New York: Hungry Minds, 2001.

ABOUT THE EDITORS

Dr. Debra F. Horwitz is a graduate of Michigan State University College of Veterinary Medicine, and a Diplomate of the American College of Veterinary Behaviorists. She has been in behavior referral practice for more than thirty years, working with thousands of owners and their pets. Her practice is located in St. Louis, Missouri. In 2012 she received the Veterinarian of the Year award from Ceva Animal Health and was voted North American Veterinary Conference 2012 Small Animal Speaker of the Year.

An active lecturer, she speaks worldwide to veterinarians and pet owners on companion-animal behavior and has served as adjunct faculty at the University of Missouri College of Veterinary Medicine. She is a frequent guest on radio and television. Teaching veterinarians is a passion; she serves as a behavioral consultant for the Veterinary Information Network, a teaching and clinical resource for veterinarians, and has taught online behavioral courses as well.

Debra Horwitz, DVM, DACVB
Eugene Horwitz

Her book *Blackwell's Five-Minute Veterinary Consult, Clinical Companion: Canine & Feline Behavior*, (with Dr. Jacqueline C. Neilson) was published in June 2007. She is an editor and contributor to the *BSAVA Manual of Canine and Feline*

Behavioural Medicine, 1st and 2nd editions. She is the behavior section editor for *Blackwell's Five-Minute Veterinary Consult: Canine and Feline,* 3rd, 4th, and 5th editions, and has written several book chapters on behavior as well as the LifeLearn behavior handouts (with Dr. Gary Landsberg) for veterinarians to give to pet owners.

Dr. Horwitz serves on numerous committees for the American College of Veterinary Behaviorists and is a past president. She has also served on the Committee for the Human-Animal Bond of the American Veterinary Medical Association. She is a member of the Greater St. Louis Veterinary Medical Association, the Missouri Veterinary Medical Association, and the American Veterinary Medical Association.

She would like to thank Houghton Mifflin Harcourt for the opportunity to share behavioral advice with so many veterinarians and pet owners. She hopes this book will help keep pets in their home and create lasting and satisfying bonds between them and their human family.

Dr. John Ciribassi was born and raised in Jersey City, New Jersey. Living in an urban area, his interest in animals was fueled by television programs like *Mutual of Omaha's Wild Kingdom.* After working summers at a veterinary hospital, he realized that veterinary medicine offered him the chance to combine his interests in animals and in medicine. After graduating from the University of Illinois College of Veterinary Medicine in 1984, along with his wife, Elise, who is also a veterinarian, he moved to north central Pennsylvania, where he worked with dairy cattle. Four years later, Elise and he moved to the Chicago area and began a small-animal practice in Carol Stream, Illinois. It was here that he developed his interest in animal behavior.

In 1998 he began working with Dr. Andrew Luescher of Purdue University to achieve certification as a specialist in animal behavior and became board certified with the American College of Veterinary Behaviorists in 2006. He now owns and operates a behavior specialty

John Ciribassi, DVM, DACVB
David Bader

veterinary practice in the Chicago area, and helps run, along with Elise, the Carol Stream Animal Hospital. He has two daughters, Danielle and Rebekah, a graying Boxer named Tyson, and a constantly purring cat named Abbey.

Dr. Ciribassi was president of the Chicago Veterinary Medical Association in 2000 and president of the American Veterinary Society of Animal Behavior from 2006 to 2008.

Steve Dale, a Certified Animal Behavior Consultant, writes a twice-weekly syndicated newspaper column (Tribune Media Services). He's a contributing editor at *USA Weekend* and host of two nationally syndicated radio shows, *Steve Dale's Pet World* and *The Pet Minute*, and is a program host at WGN Radio (Chicago). He's also a columnist for *Cat Fancy* magazine. His blog can be read at www.chicagonow.com/steve-dales-pet-world, and he contributes to blogs on various other websites, including for Victoria Stilwell and "Petphoria!" for *USA Weekend*. Steve's national radio website is www.petworldradio.net, and his personal site is www.stevedale.tv.

Steve Dale
Glenn Kaupert; reprinted with permission from Tribune Media Services, Inc. © 2012

Steve has appeared on *The Oprah Winfrey Show; National Geographic Explorer; Pets: Part of the Family* from PBS; various Animal Planet shows; and many others. In print, he's been quoted in the *Wall Street Journal, USA Today, Los Angeles Times, Redbook,* veterinary publications, and dozens more. Among Steve's books are two recent e-books, *Good Dog!* and *Good Cat!* He's written introductions or contributed chapters to more than a dozen books.

Steve serves on the board of directors of the Winn Feline Foundation and of the Tree House Humane Society in Chicago. He's a national ambassador and former board member at the American Humane Association.

Among Steve's many awards are the AVMA Humane Award and *Editor & Publisher* syndicated newspaper Feature Writer of the Year Award. Steve is a regular speaker at veterinary and shelter conferences around the world, shelter fundraisers, and special events. He was inducted into the Dog Writers Association of America Hall of Fame in 2012.

ABOUT THE AUTHORS

Melissa Bain, MS, DVM, DACVB

Dr. Melissa Bain is board certified by the American College of Veterinary Behaviorists and is the chief of service of the Clinical Animal Behavior Service at University of California–Davis School of Veterinary Medicine. She received her DVM from the University of Illinois in 1994. After graduation she worked in an exclusively small-animal veterinary practice in the Chicago suburbs before moving to a veterinary practice in Wisconsin. In 2007 she received a master's degree in Advanced Clinical Research from the UC–Davis School of Medicine. She has served as president of both the American College of Veterinary Behaviorists and the American Veterinary Society of Animal Behavior. Dr. Bain enjoys spending time with her husband, son, and four-legged family members, which currently include Thumper the Wonderdog and Charlie-Annoying-Kitty.

Jeannine Berger, DVM, DACVB

Dr. Jeannine Berger is board certified by the American College of Veterinary Behaviorists. She obtained her veterinary degree in 1991 in Zurich, Switzerland. After graduation, she worked at the University of Zurich, where she completed her doctoral thesis. She then worked in private practice before moving to Davis, California, in 1998. Dr. Berger is currently the director of Behavior Resources at the San Francisco SPCA. She focuses on strengthening the human-animal bond by helping owners modify and manage their animals' unwanted behaviors. Her interests include behavior modification and specialty training for dogs, cats, and horses.

E'Lise Christensen, DVM, DACVB

Dr. E'Lise Christensen is board certified by the American College of Veterinary Behaviorists and has a behavior practice in New York City. While in veterinary school, she researched separation anxiety in shelter dogs, was an assistant trainer at an animal shelter, and studied with numerous board-certified veterinary behaviorists. She entered the Behavior Residency Program at Cornell University in 2004, during which she did research and treated behavioral problems in a number of different species. Her most cited research involved evaluating the efficacy of canine temperament tests in animal shelters. Dr. Christensen enjoys lecturing internationally on an array of behavior topics, including but not limited to small animal behavior, public health, and animal sheltering.

Leslie Larson Cooper, DVM, DACVB

Dr. Leslie Larson Cooper graduated from the University of California at Davis School of Veterinary Medicine in 1980, and became board certified in the American College of Veterinary Behaviorists in 1995. During her career, Dr. Cooper has worked in general practice, as a resident and instructor in the Behavior Service at UC–Davis, and as a specialist in several private specialty practices. Along the way, her family has shared lives and living space with two Siberian Huskies and four cats.

Gerrard Flannigan, MS, DVM, DACVB

Dr. Gerry Flannigan counsels owners with dogs and cats who have behavior problems at Carolina Veterinary Specialists. He received his DVM from the Ontario Veterinary College at the University of Guelph in 1991 and a master's degree from the Western College of Veterinary Medicine, University of Saskatchewan. Dr. Flannigan completed a residency in clinical veterinary behavior at Tufts University School of Veterinary Medicine (2000) and became a Diplomate of the American College of Veterinary Behaviorists in 2003. He is an adjunct assistant professor with the North Carolina State University, College of Veterinary Medicine. Dr. Flannigan is past chair of the American Veterinary Medical Association's Committee for the Human-Animal Bond. Dr. Flannigan has a long history of competing in American Kennel Club events and is a member of local and national Golden Retriever breed clubs.

Lori Gaskins, DVM, DACVB

Dr. Lori Gaskins is board certified by the American College of Veterinary Behaviorists. She grew up in North Carolina and went to undergraduate and veterinary school at North Carolina State University. She was in private practice for many years in Hawaii, and then returned to UC–Davis in California to do a residency in behavior. She currently teaches animal welfare and behavior at St. Matthew's University on Grand Cayman Island. She has always had dogs in her life, both as pets and as patients. She has taught them many things, but not as much as they have taught her.

Lore I. Haug, MS, DVM, DACVB

Dr. Lore Haug is board certified by the American College of Veterinary Behaviorists. She graduated from Texas A&M College of Veterinary Medicine in 1993 and completed a one-year internship in small animal medicine and surgery at Louisiana State University School of Veterinary Medicine. In 2002, she finished a master's degree and residency program in animal behavior at Texas A&M College of Veterinary Medicine. She is also a certified professional dog trainer through the Certification Council for Professional Dog Trainers and is a Certified Animal Behavior Consultant through the International Association of Animal Behavior Consultants. Dr. Haug has a special interest in aggression problems and the neurobiology of behavioral disorders and learning principles. She has been involved in dog sports for three decades. Dr. Haug is also an avid equine enthusiast and spends many hours training and riding her Polish Arabian gelding.

Meghan Elaine Herron, DVM, DACVB

Dr. Meghan Herron is a clinical assistant professor and head of the Behavioral Medicine Clinic at The Ohio State University Veterinary

Medical Center. Dr. Herron graduated from Arizona State University with a degree in zoology in 1999 and is a 2005 graduate of The Ohio State University College of Veterinary Medicine. She worked in small animal general practice, and also as a clinical instructor in the Shelter Medicine and Surgery Program at Ohio State. She completed a residency program in behavioral medicine at the University of Pennsylvania's School of Veterinary Medicine in 2009, followed by board certification as a Diplomate of the American College of Veterinary Behaviorists. Dr. Herron has been published in the *Journal of the American Veterinary Association* and in *Applied Animal Behaviour Science, Topics in Companion Animal Medicine,* and *Compendium,* including studies evaluating the effect of confrontational training techniques.

Katherine Albro Houpt, VMD, PhD, DACVB

Dr. Katherine Albro Houpt is board certified by the American College of Veterinary Behaviorists and is professor emeritus of behavioral medicine at Cornell University, where she mentored a half dozen residents who became Diplomates of the American College of Veterinary Behaviorists. She now lives in Michigan, where, instead of retiring, she opened Animal Behavior Consultants of Northern Michigan. She shares her home with Denver, her Cairn Terrier, an Arabian horse, and a Swedish Gotland pony.

Mary P. Klinck, DVM, DACVB

Dr. Mary Klinck graduated from the University of Prince Edward Island Veterinary College (Canada) in 2001. She completed her residency training in veterinary behavioral medicine at the University of Pennsylvania in 2008. In addition to her work as a behaviorist certified by the American College of Veterinary Behaviorists, she has worked in general veterinary practice with small and large animals, and she has worked with shelters to improve behavioral management of dogs and cats. She currently resides in Montreal, Canada, with her dog, Meike, who frequently shows off what she knows to students.

Gary Landsberg, DVM, DACVB, DECAWBM (Behavior)

Dr. Gary Landsberg works at the North Toronto Animal Clinic in Thornhill, Ontario, and is a 1976 graduate of the Ontario Veterinary College. He is board certified by the American College of Veterinary Behaviorists (ACVB) and the European College of Animal Welfare and Behavioural Medicine (ECAWBM). He is a former president of the Toronto Academy of Veterinary Medicine, American Veterinary Society of Animal Behavior, and ACVB. He is an adjunct professor of the Ontario Veterinary College, a behavior consultant for the Veterinary Information Network, and is director of Veterinary Affairs for CanCog Technologies. Dr. Landsberg is coauthor of *Handbook of Behavior Problems of the Dog & Cat,* as well as numerous journal publications and chapters in veterinary texts. He's a coauthor of client-behavior handouts, one set from the American Animal Hospital Association, and a book of behavior handouts from LifeLearn. Dr. Landsberg is a frequent speaker at veterinary conferences around the world as well as at events for pets owners and has hosted his own TV and radio shows in Canada.

Emily D. Levine, DVM, DACVB, MRCVS

Dr. Emily Levine is a veterinary behaviorist board certified by the American College of Veterinary Behaviorists, with a referral practice at Animal Emergency and Referral Associates in New Jersey. She is a graduate of the College of Veterinary Medicine at Mississippi State University. After graduation she spent an additional year in general practice in Arizona before entering a behavioral residency program at Cornell University under the mentorship of Dr. Katherine Albro Houpt. She continued her studies after her residency program, traveling to the United Kingdom to work with Dr. Daniel Mills at the University of Lincoln. Dr. Levine lectures internationally and has written several chapters on behavioral topics for textbooks. Dr. Levine currently lives in Roseland, New Jersey, with her husband, David, her daughter, Anya, her twelve-year cancer-surviving cat, Little Casanova (AKA L.C.), and Henry, her eight-month-old mixed-breed dog.

Ellen M. Lindell, VMD, DACVB

Dr. Ellen M. Lindell graduated from the University of Pennsylvania School of Veterinary Medicine in 1983. After working in general veterinary practice, Dr. Lindell began her residency in behavior at Cornell University College of Veterinary Medicine. Dr. Lindell is board certified by the American College of Veterinary Behaviorists. She owns a specialty practice in which she treats pets with behavioral concerns. Dr. Lindell also enjoys lecturing and writing about animal behavior, consulting with veterinarians through the Veterinary Information Network, an Internet resource for veterinarians. Recent publications include chapters in *The Five-Minute Veterinary Consult,* the *BSAVA Manual of Canine and Feline Behavioural Medicine,* and *Caring for Family Pets.* In her spare time, Dr. Lindell trains and shows her dogs in assorted dog sports.

Patrick Yves Melese, MA, DVM, DACVB

Dr. Patrick Melese is a Diplomate of the American College of Veterinary Behaviorists and director of Veterinary Behavior Consultants, a southern California specialty veterinary practice dedicated to preventing and solving behavior problems in animals. Dr. Melese was in general private practice for thirteen years, in San Diego, before accepting a three-year appointment as clinical faculty specialist in behavioral medicine with the UC–Davis School of Veterinary Medicine. Dr. Melese's training includes a master's degree from UC–Davis in 1980 and a DVM from UC–Davis in 1986. He has been active in the field of clinical animal behavior, including providing regional and national veterinary continuing-education programs, publications, and clinical research. Dr. Melese also serves regularly as an expert witness in animal injury cases in superior court.

Jacqueline C. Neilson, DVM, DACVB

Dr. Jacqueline Neilson earned her DVM from the University of Florida and completed a residency in animal behavior at the University of California–Davis School of Veterinary Medicine. She is a Diplomate of the American College of Veterinary Behaviorists. She owned and practiced at the Animal Behavior Clinic in Portland, Oregon, from 1997 to 2011.

She has served as a visiting instructor at the University of Florida and Oregon State Colleges of Veterinary Medicine. She is past president of the Oregon Veterinary Medical Association, 2011–2013 president of the American College of Veterinary Behaviorists, and is a member of the Board of Trustees of the Oregon Humane Society and of the Feral Cat Coalition of Oregon. She has published several papers and book chapters and is coauthor (with Dr. Horwitz) of *Blackwell's Five-Minute Veterinary Consult, Clinical Companion: Canine & Feline Behavior.* She frequently lectures to veterinarians, their staff, and the public about animal behavior. In 2011 Dr. Neilson joined Elanco Companion Animal Health as a senior veterinary technical consultant.

Karen L. Overall, MA, VMD, PhD, DACVB, CAAB

Dr. Karen Overall is a Diplomate of the American College of Veterinary Behaviorists (ACVB) and is certified by the Animal Behavior Society (ABS) as an Certified Applied Animal Behaviorist (CAAB). Dr. Overall has a long association with the University of Pennsylvania, at one time running the behavior clinic, and currently does research in the medical school at Penn. She has lectured extensively both nationally and internationally and authored more than one hundred scholarly publications and dozens of textbook chapters. Her textbook, *Clinical Behavioral Medicine for Small Animals,* was published in 1997. Her new book, *Manual of Small Animal Clinical Behavioral Medicine,* is soon to be published and will include an instructional video. Dr. Overall is the editor in chief for the *Journal of Veterinary Behavior: Clinical Applications and Research.* Dr. Overall resides with her husband and collaborator, Dr. Art Dunham, outside Philadelphia, where they share their lives with the resident wildlife and their rescued Australian Shepherds.

Marsha Reich, DVM, DACVB

Dr. Marsha Reich is a Diplomate of the American College of Veterinary Behaviorists. She is the owner of a house-call behavior practice that gives her the opportunity to evaluate and treat the behavior problems of pets in their own home. A 1989 graduate of Virginia-Maryland Regional College of Veterinary Medicine, she worked in small-animal veterinary practice for eight years. In 2000, she completed a three-year behavioral medicine residency at the University of Pennsylvania and became board certified in 2001. Dr. Reich lectures both nationally and internationally and has contributed to textbooks on pet behavior. She also consults with local animal rescue groups. She lives in Maryland with her Wheaten Terrier mix, Shandy. In her spare time she enjoys baking, biking, and racing sailboats on Chesapeake Bay.

Ilana Reisner, DVM, PhD, DACVB

Dr. Ilana Reisner received her DVM from Oregon State University and Washington State University Schools of Veterinary Medicine, and a PhD in behavioral physiology from Cornell University. Dr. Reisner is a Diplomate of the American College of Veterinary Behaviorists. She currently runs a companion-animal behavior referral practice in the Philadelphia region and consults with veterinarians, educational groups, and industries on dog-bite safety. Dr. Reisner has published and spoken extensively on clinical animal behavior topics, with particular attention to canine aggression and the safety of children and their family.

Stefanie Schwartz, MS, DVM, DACVB

Dr. Stefanie Schwartz is board certified by the American College of Veterinary Behaviorists and has been in veterinary behavior practice since 1984. She has an undergraduate degree in psychobiology/animal behavior from McGill University, and both a master's degree (in ethology) and a DVM from the University of Montreal. Dr. Schwartz works at California Veterinary Specialists in Carlsbad, California, and at the Veterinary Neurology Center in Tustin, California. She is a clinical adjunct professor at the Virginia-Maryland Regional College of Veterinary Medicine. Dr. Schwartz has appeared on television (including *Swift Justice*, *NOVA*, and *CNN Headline News*) and radio.

Valarie V. Tynes, DVM, DACVB

Dr. Valarie Tynes is a native of Fort Worth, Texas. She attended Texas A&M University and received her doctor of veterinary medicine degree in 1987. After several years in private practice, she completed her residency in clinical animal behavior at the University of California at Davis in 2003. Her special interests include animal behavior problems, miniature pigs, and other exotic pets. She is a Diplomate of the American College of Veterinary Behaviorists and a frequent speaker at professional meetings around the world. She has written numerous articles and chapters on a variety of other behavior-related topics. She is the editor of the recently published book *Behavior of Exotic Pets.* She currently provides consulting services for zoos, pharmaceutical companies, veterinarians, and pet owners. Dr. Tynes gratefully acknowledges the assistance of Jennifer Shryock, BA, CDBC, and Laurie Bergman, VMD, DACVB, in preparing her chapter.

MEMBERS OF THE AMERICAN COLLEGE
OF VETERINARY BEHAVIORISTS

(as of May 2013)

Dr. Julia Albright
Dr. R. K. Anderson (deceased)
Dr. Melissa Bain
Dr. Bonnie V. Beaver
Dr. Sara Bennett
Dr. Jeannine Berger
Dr. Laurie Bergman
Dr. Walter F. Burghardt Jr.
Dr. Gabrielle Carter
Dr. E'Lise M. Christensen
Dr. John Ciribassi
Dr. Leslie Larson Cooper
Dr. Sharon Crowell-Davis
Dr. Terry M. Curtis
Dr. Sheila D'Arpino
Dr. Nicholas H. Dodman
Dr. Margaret Duxbury
Dr. Gerrard Flannigan
Dr. Diane Frank
Dr. Lori Gaskins
Dr. Martin Godbout
Dr. Margaret Gruen
Dr. Benjamin L. Hart
Dr. Lore Haug
Dr. Meghan Herron
Dr. Debra Horwitz
Dr. Katherine Albro Houpt
Dr. Mami Irimajiri
Dr. Soraya V. Juarbe-Diaz

Dr. Mary Klinck
Dr. Gary Landsberg
Dr. Emily Levine
Dr. Ellen M. Lindell
Dr. Scott W. Line
Dr. Andrew Luescher
Dr. Rachel Malamed
Dr. Patrick Melese
Dr. Petra Mertens
Dr. Alexandra Moesta
Dr. Kelly Moffat
Dr. Jacqueline C. Neilson
Dr. Niwako Ogata
Dr. Karen L. Overall
Dr. Christopher Pachel
Dr. Patricia Pryor
Dr. Lisa Radosta
Dr. Marsha Reich
Dr. Ilana Reisner
Dr. Stefanie Schwartz
Dr. Lynne M. Seibert
Dr. Kersti Seksel
Dr. Barbara L. Sherman
Dr. Carlo Siracusa
Dr. Meredith Stepita
Dr. Karen Sueda
Dr. Vint Virga
Dr. Victoria L. Voith
Dr. Thomas Wolfle (deceased)

INDEX

Page numbers in italics refer to illustrations and tables.

accidents defined, 61
acepromazine, 276
acetylcholine, 300
acral-lick dermatitis, *289, 290,* 291
Adaptil, 271
adoption. *See* dog adoption/selection
Afghan Hounds, 164
aggression
    anxiety and, 1–2, *1, 2,* 5, *5,* 13–14, 49,
        202–3, 211, 213
    avoiding pitfalls, 232–33
    behavioral repertoire and, 200
    costs of, 200
    defensive reasons, 116, 201, 202, 203, 204,
        205
    definition, 200
    dog fights/stopping, 205, 213–14
    dogs having no agenda, 206
    dog's right to say no and, 229–30
    dominance myth and, 201–2
    examples, 1–2, *1,* 2, 199–200, 209–10
    fear and, 201, 202, *203,* 204, 205, *212*
    genetics and, 230–31
    keeping/not keeping aggressive dog,
        231–32
    "meanness" and, 217–18
    miscommunication between dogs/
        humans, 213, 214
    misconceptions, 108–9
    mismatches and, 231–32
    moving your dog and, 203
    muzzle use and, 89, 100, 225
    myths on, 207–9, *208*
    normal vs. abnormal aggression,
        209–11
    physical problems and, 205, 209, 210–11
    protecting you and, 207, *208*
    punishment/problems, xvi, 202–3, *203,*
        205, 206, 223–24
    "rage syndrome," 210
    redirected aggression, 210
    resource guarding, 153, 204, 209, 218
    serotonin dysfunction and, 210–11
    signals of, 1–2, *1,* 2, 207–8, *208,* 212–13,
        212, 214–17, *215*
    sleeping in human bed and, 207
    summary, 233–34
    taking food/toys away and, 116, 203
    territory and, 204
    triggers overview, 205, 218
    types/overview, 203–5
    uncertainty and, 205
    unsafe situations, 225–26
    veterinary visit and, 211
    See also children and dog bites;
        communicating with dogs/dog
        aggression; dog bites
aggression/behavior modification
    control devices and, 225
    counterconditioning, 226–27
    desensitization, 226–27
    example, 226–27
    overview, 224–27
    summary guidelines, 224–25
aggression management
    "curing" vs., 227, 229
    dog behavioral maturity and, 220
    dog parks and, 213, 226, 233
    dogs signaling and, 207–8, 220
    force-free training and, 206
    medication and, 227–29
    moving a dog, 222
    overview, 100, 218, 219–24
    predictability for dog and, 223

aggression management (*cont.*)
    punishment/problems, 223–24
    resource-guarding dog, 221–22
    safe refuge and, 223
    triggers and, 220, 221
    understanding provocations, 220–21
agility, *190, 192*
aging dogs. *See senior dogs*
Akita, 216
Aktivait, 311, *312*
alprazolam, 276
Alzheimer's disease/CDS comparisons, 298,
    299, 300–301, 302, 313, 314
American College of Veterinary
    Behaviorists (ACVB), xvii
    See also specific individuals; veterinary
      behaviorists
American Kennel Club (AKC), 21, 23, 30,
    31, 36
Anderson, R. K., xxii
Anipryl (selegiline), 309, 311
anogenital reflex, 60
anti-bark collars, 93–94, 102
anti-pull harnesses, 89
antioxidants, 300
anxiety
    aggression and, 1–2, *1, 2,* 5, *5,* 13–14, 49,
      202–3, 211, 213
    antianxiety devices, 95–96
    becoming sedate and, 107–8
    cognitive dysfunction and, *304*
    definition, 4, 243
    misbehaviors and, 49
    pheromones use, 95
    signs of, *5,* 107–8
    See also separation anxiety
Anxiety Wrap, 95, 102
apoaequorin (Neutricks), 311, *312*
Assess-a-Pet, 34
attention-seeking (behavior), 131, *284*
avoidance behaviors
    around children, 150, 155, 157, 161, 163
    definition/description, 154

barking
    anti-bark collars, 93–94, 102
    cause and, 47, 101, 102
    changing behavior, 101–2, *133, 135*
basket muzzles, 90, *90*
Basset Hounds, 39
Beagles, 25, 39, 209, 290, *301*
behavior
    common behavior repertoires, 110, 200
    definitions, 4
    flexibility of dogs, 119

    See also normal behaviors; *specific*
      behaviors
behavior problems
    dogs' social maturity and, 111–13
    getting help, xviii, 104–5
    human-dog bond and, xviii
    main problems, 99–102
    reinforcing the right things, 104
    See also normal behaviors/changing;
      specific problems
behaviorists. *See* American College of
    Veterinary Behaviorists (ACVB);
    veterinary behaviorists
belly bands, 63
beta-amyloid, 300, 302
Bichon Frise, 306–7
Biology of Animal Stress, The (Moberg), 30
Blackwell, Emily, 96
Blue Dog, The (CD/American Veterinary
    Medical Association), 160
body carriage and body language, *9*
body harnesses, 89, *89,* 103
body language of dogs
    summary, *9*
    See also specific behaviors
body wraps, 95, 102, 277, *277*
Border Collies
    adopting/activity and, 22–23, 164
    herding/activity and, 22, 179
    light/shadow-chasing example, 281–83,
      282, 284, 288, 294
    as "smartest"/most trainable breed, 29, 39
    variations within breed, 24–25, *25*
    word memory/associative learning, 39
boredom. *See* lack of stimulation/results
Bradshaw, John, 45
breeding/breeder types, 17–18
breeds of dogs
    fads, 31–32, 37
    groups overview, 23
    information sources, 21–22, 24
    overview, 23–24
    smartest breeds, 29, 39
    trainability and, 39
    variations within breeds, 22, 24–25, 39
    working purpose and, 137–38
    See also specific breeds
buckle collars, 83, 85, 86, *86*
Bulldogs, 216
Buster FoodCube, 42, 93

Calming Caps, 95, 100
Canine Eye Registration Foundation
    (CERF), 30
canine freestyle, *189*

casual breeder, 18
CDS. *See* cognitive dysfunction/syndrome (CDS)
Centers for Disease Control, 200
chewing
    as normal behavior, 130
    preventing, *133*
Chihuahuas, 164
children and dog bites
    children's age and, 153
    example of child hurting dog, 157–58
    familiar vs. unfamiliar dogs, 153
    grandmother/grandchildren example, 13–14
    as preventable, 151, 153, 166, 219
    resource guarding and, 153
    situations to avoid, 13–14, 153, 219, *219*
children and dogs
    baby equipment/strollers and, 165–66, 167–68, 170
    baby odors and, 167, 169
    benefits to children, 151, 173
    children wanting pet and, 171–73
    dog adoption/selection, 34–35, 164
    dog avoidance behaviors, 150, 155, 157, 161, 163
    dog jealousy myth and, 151, 154
    dog running at child, 161–62, *162*
    dominance myth and, 152–53
    expectations and, 158–59
    games to play, 171, 174–75
    interaction examples, 171, 173–75
    myths on, 151–53, 154
    new baby example, 150
    older dogs and, 168
    summary, 175–76
    surrendering dogs/euthanasia and, 150, 152
children and dogs/preventing problems
    attention for dogs and, 170, 174
    avoiding pitfalls, 160–63
    bringing baby home, 169–71
    child/baby gates and, 155, 166, 170
    children approaching dogs, *159,* 161
    children eating and, 165
    children handling roughly/injuring dogs, 156–59, 164
    children under age of four/five and, 150, 156–57, 161, 208–9
    children's sounds/size and, 152, 155, 166, 167
    commercial baby recordings and, 167
    dog eating/resting and, 116–17, 153, 160, 168
    dog-human bond and, 150–51, 153

dog seeking attention and, 151, 168, 170
dog's health and, 156, 157
fear/signs and, 150, 151–53, 157, 161
forcing dogs and, 150, 155, 169
hugging and, 160
human bed and, 166–67
introducing dog to infants/children, 120, 169
miscommunication/results, 152–53
planning ahead, 164–65
predatory behavior and, 156, 169–70
preparing dog for new arrival, 165–66
punishment/results and, 156, 162–63, 169
puppy-raising and, 119–20, 154–55
resource guarding and, 153, 174
resources on, 160
safe refuge for dog, 153, 155, 163, 165, 166, 168
separation and, 157, 208–9, 225
socialization and, 119–20, 154–55, 164–65
staring at dogs and, *159,* 160, 161, 175
summary, 175–76
teaching children and, 151, 152, 159–60, *159,* 165
teaching dog/positive experiences, 155
toddlers and, 150
walking with baby/dog, 170
choke/slip collars, 83, 85, 86, *87*
Chow Chow, 216
Christensen, E'Lise, 34
circling (walking in circles), *289*
Ciribassi, John, xvii, xviii
classical conditioning, 41–42, 47
clicker training, 41–42, 50, 58, 91, *92*
clickers, 91, *92,* 143
Clomicalm, 259, 260
clomipramine, 276, 291
cognitive decline, 300
cognitive dysfunction/syndrome (CDS)
    Alzheimer's disease comparisons, 298, 299, 300–301, 302, 313, 314
    behavior and, *297*
    causes, 299–301
    diagnosis, 305–7
    diet, 311, *312,* 313
    DISHA/signs, 298, 299, 301, *304*
    learning/memory and, 301–2, *301*
    medications, 311
    nutritional supplements, 311, *312*
    other health issues and, 298
    overview, 299–303
    statistics on, 302–3
    tests and, 301–2, *301*
    treatments, 299, 310–11, 312–13, *312*

collars
    types overview, 86, 86–87, *87, 88*
    See also specific types
Collies (Lassie), 3, 32, 150–52
    See also Border Collies
"come" command
    teaching, 53–54
    uses, 51, 55, 56–57, 58, 91, 123, 168, *189,*
        222
communicating with dogs
    avoiding pitfalls, 14
    expectations and, 3, 12–14, 15
    learning dog language, 8–9
    listening with human eyes, 3, 10, 14
    miscommunication traps, 11–12
    summary, xviii–xix, 8, 14–15
    training and, 12, 15
    visual vs. verbal cues, 10–11, 14
communicating with dogs/dog aggression
    anticipating problems, 217
    breed physical differences and, 214, 216,
        218
    children and, 219, *219*
    congruent signals, 215
    importance of, 216–17, 218
    incongruent signals, 215
    preventing problems, 217, 220
    signals of, 1–2, *1, 2,* 207–8, *208,* 212–13,
        212, 214–17, *215*
Complete Dog Book (AKC), 31
compulsive behaviors
    acral-lick dermatitis, *289,* 290, 291
    causes, 283, *304*
    definition/description, *284*
    floor-licking example, 285–86, *286,* 287
    light/shadow-chasing example, 281–83,
        282, 284
    myths on, 283
    neurotransmitters involved, 283
    as redirection from normal behavior,
        282–83
    separation anxiety and, *284,* 287, 290, 291
    serotonin and, 283, 285, 294, 295
    summary, 294–95
    tail-chasing example, 286–87
    terms defined/described, *284–85*
compulsive behaviors management
    avoiding pitfalls, 292, 294
    counterconditioning, 289, 290, 294
    desensitizing, 289, 290, 294
    dominance myth and, *293*
    early intervention, 287, 292
    environmental changes, 289
    journal and, 292
    light/shadow-chasing example, 288, 294

    medical problems and, 285–86, 287, 289,
        289
    medication and, 285, 286, 291–92, 294
    misconceptions on treatment, *293*
    other behavior problems and, 290, 291
    prevention and, 292
    punishment and, *293*
    redirecting behavior, 287–88
    summary, 290, 294–95
conflict-related aggression defined, 205
conformation, 21, 24–25, *189*
Coonhounds, 285–86, *286,* 287
Coren, Stanley, 29
corticosteroids, 211
cortisol, 30, 269, 277
counter and food, 127, 129, 132
counterconditioning
    aggression and, 226–27
    compulsive behaviors and, 289, 290, 294
    separation anxiety and, 243
cowering, 154
crate training/housetraining
    alternative confinement options, 75, *75*
    benefits/uses, 36–37, 71, 90, 100
    crate dividers and, 72
    crate size and, 66, 71–72, *72*
    den concept and, 65–66
    items in crate, 71, *91*
    maximum time for puppies, 73, 76
    positive experience and, 74
    separation anxiety and, 75, 79, 80, 101,
        243–44, 245, 246, *246*
    tips, 74–75, 318–19, *318*
    training described, 71–72
crates overview, 90, *91*
Crowell-Davis, Sharon, 271, 276
"curbing" your dog, 70

Dale, Steve, xviii
Dalmatians, 32, 157–58
daycare for dogs, 196
Deerhounds, 164
defensive aggression defined, 204
desensitization
    aggression and, 226–27
    compulsive behaviors and, 289, 290, 294
    separation anxiety and, 243
designer dogs, 25–26, 30
diabetes, 227, 297, 305, 306
digging, *135*
DISHA/signs, 298, 299, 301, *304*
    See also cognitive dysfunction/syndrome
        (CDS)
displacement behavior, *284*
distress defined, 266

Doberman Pinschers, 43, 216
dock jumping/diving, *190*
Dodman, Nicholas H., 278, 291
dog adoption/selection
　behavior/temperament tests, 17, 18, 34–35
　behavior vs. appearance, 19
　breed dispositions and, 17
　childhood dog and, 19
　children and, 34–35
　definitions overview, 17–18
　first days and, 35, 36–37
　gender of dog and, 33
　hereditary physical conditions and, 16
　matching dog/humans, 16, 18–20
　mixed-breed vs. purebred dogs, 20–23
　multiple dogs and, 26, 35–36
　myths on, 35–36
　postadoption honeymoon period, 35
　private adoptions, 32
　puppy age and, 31
　puppy vs. adult, 32–33
　resident dog/cat and, 35
　sources overview, 16–17, 26–32
　summary, 37
dog bites
　fear and, 201
　punishment and, 202–3
　statistics on, 200
　See also children and dog bites
dog parks, 182, 213, 226, 233
dog shows, 21
dog trainers/consultants
　behaviorists vs., xv
　selecting/dos and don'ts, 105
dog walkers, 127, 196, 312
dominance
　aggression vs., 4
　definition, 4, 49, 131
dominance myth
　description, xv, 3–5, 48–49, 58, 114–15, 127–28, 131, 201–2
　dogs/wolves and, 48–49, 58, 201
　false basis of, 201–2
　problems from, xxii, 5, 201
　proponents of, xvi
　social hierarchy and, 201
　studies of feral dogs and, 201
　See also specific behaviors
door dashing, *135*
dopamine, 283, 300, 309
"down" command
　teaching, 50–51
　uses, 50–51, 52, 57, 91, 123, 134, *135,* 165, 174, *189,* 253, 268, 272, 274, 309

Dreschel, Nancy, 269
Duxbury, Margaret, 85

ears and body language, *9*
Easy Walk harness, *89*
electronic fencing, 47, 94, 226
elimination defined, 61
endorphins, 283
enrichment
　avoiding pitfalls, 197
　breeds/job examples, 178–79, *186–88*
　definition, 180
　determining type/amount, 181–83, 191–95
　dos and don'ts, 196–97
　evaluating dog's response, 194–95
　food puzzles/toys, 42–43, 71, 93, 101, 164, 170, *181,* 243, 251, 254, 255, 261, *273,* 308
　investigating environment, 179–80
　playing with other dogs, *185,* 193, *193*
　senior dogs and, 308, 309, 310
　solo activities/games, 183–84, *184–85*
　summary, 197–98
　toys, *184*
　undivided attention and, 196
　variety and, 195
　water activities, *190,* 193, *193*
　See also lack of stimulation/results; *specific types;* sports for dogs
environmental enrichment defined, 180
exercise
　definition, 180
　See also physical stimulation
extinction burst, 131, 136
extinguishing behavior, 43, 47–48, 48
eyes and body language, *9*

fear
　aggression and, 201, 202, *203,* 204, 205, *212*
　changing behavior, 92, 95, 102
　definition, 4, 154
　pheromones use, 95
fear-related aggression defined, 204
fear response, 154, 276
fencing, 47, 94, 226
fetch, 53, 134, *135,* 174, *185,* 193, 249, 270
fight-or-flight behavior, 211, 276
fireworks. *See* sound sensitivities
flank sucking, *289*
floor licking, 285–86, *286,* 287
fluoxetine (Prozac), 291, 294
flyball, *190*
flying disc/Frisbee, *190*

food allergies, 286
food puzzles/toys, 42–43, 71, 93, 101, 164, 170, *181*, 243, 251, 254, 255, 261, *273*, 308
foraging for food/treats, *184*
Frasier (TV show) and dogs, 24, 32
free radicals, 300, 310–11
Frisbee, *190*
Fuller, John L., 110, 111
furniture and puppies/dogs
    aggression and, 109
    deterrents, 93, 97
    normal behavior and, 114, 115

gates/uses, 75, *75,* 90, 155, 166, 170
generalizing behavior, 48, 50, 55, 58
Genetics and the Social Behavior of the Dog (Scott and Fuller), 110
Gentle Leader head collar, *88*
Granger, Douglas, 269
Great Danes, 216
greeting rituals, 11
grooming procedures. *See* maintenance procedures (body care); *specific procedures*
guilty myth
    description, 3, 61–63
    example, 6–8, *6,* 61–63
    housetraining and, 6–8, 61–63
    punishment/effects, 5–6, 62–63
    submission vs., 5–6, *6*
gunshots. *See* sound sensitivities

habituation, 109, 112, 251–52, 265
hand signals, 10, 50–51
Hare, Brian, 49
harnesses
    overview, 89, *89*
    positive associations with, 103
Hart, Benjamin L./Lynette A., 21, 81
head collars, 85, 86, 87, *88,* 100, 102–3, *102,* 225
Herron, Meghan, 5, 45, 97
hide-and-seek games, 131, *135,* 138, 171, 174–75, 185
"high five," *135*
highly invested breeders
    adopting puppy from, 30–31
    behavior information and, 30–31
    breeding dogs and, 21
    definition, 17–18
    health testing and, 30
Hill's Pet Nutrition study (2000), 302–3
Hill's Prescription Diet b/d Canine, 311, *312,* 313

Horwitz, Debra, xvii–xviii
Houpt, Katherine Albro, 94
housetraining
    adult dogs, 75–76
    bell-ringing use, 68
    carrying puppy, 67, 76
    cleaning up after your dog, 71
    "curbing" your dog, 70
    definition, 61
    den concept and, 59, 60, 78
    early learning problems, 79
    eliminating on request/human cue, 69–70, *70*
    example, 59, 80–82
    excitement/submissive behavior and urinating, 80
    external reinforcement/reward, 61, 68, 70
    human expectations, 69, 80
    importance of, 59–60
    indoor confinement size, 65–66
    indoor toilet systems, 73–74
    intrinsic rewards, 61, 68
    leash-belt system uses, 66, 77, 82
    marking, 63
    medical/physical problems and, 79–80
    myths on, 61–65
    newborns to nine weeks, 60
    preplanning and, 65
    preventing accidents overview, 60–61
    problem questions/answers, 76–78
    punishment/effects, 63–65, 69
    puppy elimination times/schedule, 66, 80
    responding to accidents, 68–69
    restricting water intake and, 66
    schedules/importance, 66–67
    smaller dogs and, 81
    substrate/location preferences, 60
    summary, 82
    teaching to signal, 67–68, 78
    treating problems (overview), 101
    See also crate training/housetraining
housetraining log/apps, 67
HPA axis abnormalities, 30, 211
Hurricane Katrina, 28
hypothyroidism, 305–6

insightful behavior, 39
intelligence
    smartest breeds, 29, 39
    trainability vs., 39–40
interactive play defined, 181
intermittent reinforcement
    changing normal behaviors and, 129–30

definition, 130
See also "variable ratio of reinforcement"
irritable aggression defined, 205

Juarbe-Diaz, Soraya V., 94
jumping up on people
    changing behavior, 54–55, 96, 120, *133*
    dominance myth and, 127, 129
    greeting ritual and, 96, 108–9, 115, 128–29
    intermittent reinforcement and, 130
    as normal behavior, 108–9, 115, 120–21, 127–29
    punishment effects, 120–21
    sit command and, 120, *133*, 134
    stay command and, 55

kidney failure, 297–98, 306
Kong Wobbler/toys, 42–43, 71, *91, 93*

Labradoodles, 25
lack of stimulation/results
    description, 180–81
    example story, 177, 178
    surrendering dogs and, 178
Landsberg, Gary, xxii, 277
language of dogs. *See* communicating with dogs
Lassie/*Lassie* (TV show), 3, 32, 150–51
leashes
    overview, 88–89
    retractable leashes/problems, 88, 89, 136–37
Levine, Emily, 272
licking (excessive), *289*
lifespan of dogs, 24
light/shadow-chasing, 281–83, *282, 284*, 288, *289, 294*
limited admission shelters/rescue groups, 27–28
"look" command
    teaching, 51–52
    uses, 49, 58, 134, 253
Luescher, Andrew, 287, 291

maintenance procedures (body care)
    distractions and, 142
    dog's "good"/"bad" side and, 144
    marker signals and, 143, 146, 147
    overview, 138–48, *143, 144, 146, 147*
    tips, 141–44
    tricking your dog and, 140
    See also specific procedures
Maltese, 59, 80–82
MannersMinder, 91–92
Marder, Amy, 34

Martingales/limited-slip collars, 86, *87*
massage for dogs, 253, 271, 274
Match-Up II, 34
medication. *See specific behaviors/issues; specific medications*
medium-chain triglycerides (MCTs), 311
Meet Your Match/SAFER (Safety Assessment for Evaluating Rehoming), 34
Mensa/dog, 38
mental stimulation
    definition/examples, 131, 138
    dog inactive/recovering and, 43, 183, 197
    importance of, 19, 23, 125, 138, 179
    See also enrichment
Miklosi, Adam, 49
Mills, Daniel, 264, 271
mixed-breed dogs
    adopting, 20
    DNA tests and, 20
    trait inheritance and, 40
Moberg, Gary, 30
motion-activated devices, 93
mouth and body language, 9
Mutt Muffs, 95, 102
muzzles/use, 89–90, *90*, 100, 103–4, 225
myths on dog behavior
    overview, 3–8
    See also specific behaviors; specific myths

nail trimming
    dog fighting/avoiding example, 138–39
    domination myth and, 139
    human anger and, 140
    miscommunication and, 139–40
    solving behavior problems, 140–41, 142, *143*
    tricking dog/effects and, 140
neck collars, 86
negative punishment defined, 46, 48
negative reinforcement, 46
Neilson, Jacqueline, 215
neurons defined, 300
neuroprotective interventions, 300
neurotransmitters, 283, 300
    See also specific neurotransmitters
Neutricks (apoaequorin), 311, *312*
noise sensitivities. *See* sound sensitivities
noradrenaline, 300
normal behaviors
    descriptions, 108–9, 110, 114–15, 120–21, 127–28
    dominance myth and, 114–15, 127–28, 131
    intermittent reinforcement and, 129–30

normal behaviors (*cont.*)
    punishment/effects, 131
    See also specific behaviors
normal behaviors/changing
    avoiding pitfalls, 148
    consistency and, 134, 137, 148
    goals, 134–35
    maintenance procedures (body care) and,
        138–48, *143, 144, 146, 147*
    management techniques summary, *133*
    managing, 132, *133,* 134
    summary, 148–49
    training alternate behaviors summary,
        135–36, *135*
    training and, 134–36, *135*
Novifit (S-adenosyl-l-methionine-tosylate
        disulfate), 311, *312*
nuisance behaviors. *See* normal behaviors

obedience/training, *189*
"off-label use" (medication), 228–29
101 Dalmatians (movie), 32
open admission shelters/rescue groups,
        27
operant conditioning
    convalescing dog example, 43
    definition/description, 42–43, 47
    See also positive reinforcement/training;
        punishment
Orthopedic Foundation for Animals
        (OFA), 30
overstimulation, 181

pacing, *289*
Pageat, Patrick, 96
pain-related aggression defined, 205
panic defined, 242–43
Pavlov, Ivan, 41
pawing at people, *135*
PennHIP, 30
"people dogs," 129
Perfect Puppy, The (Hart, Benjamin L./
        Lynette A.), 21, 81
Pet store puppies
    adopting, 28–30
    problems, 28–30
    puppy mills and, 29–30
pheromones
    definition, 95, 96
    natural pheromones, 95, 96
    synthetic pheromones/forms, 95, 96
    uses, 95, 96, 101, 260, 271, 274, 310
phobias
    changing behavior, 92, 95, 102
    definition, 265

pheromones use, 95
    See also specific phobias
physical stimulation
    definition/examples, 131
    importance/benefits, 137–38, 179
    overexercise/results, 196
    See also enrichment; sports for dogs
pica, 89
piloerection, 214, 216
"place" command, 54, 55–56
Pointer, English/mix, 199–200
Poodles
    designer dogs and, 25
    Miniature, 150, 154, 155
    raised hackles and, 216
    Standard, 25
    Toy, 164
    trainability/intelligence and, 25, 39
positive punishment defined, 46, 48
positive reinforcement/training
    benefits, xvi, xxii, 12, 15, 45
    definition, 4
    described, 12, 42
    studies overview, 45
predatory behavior
    children and dogs, 156, 169–70
    definition, 205
    human reaction and, 205
prong/pinch collars, 83, 85, 86–87, *87*
propentofylline, 311
Prozac (fluoxetine), 291, 294
Puggle, 25
Pugs, 25, 179, 216
pulling while walking
    with baby stroller, 168
    changing behavior, 46, *133, 137,* 168
    examples, 45, 83–84, 136–37
    as normal behavior, 108–9
    See also specific tools; tools of the trade
punishment
    definition, 44, 46, 48
    positive vs. negative punishment, 45–46,
        48, 96–97
    problems with, xv–xvi, 45, 96, 97, 206
    proponents of, xvi
    timing and, 44–45, 64
    See also dominance myth; *specific
        behaviors*
puppy mills
    AKC-registered papers and, 36
    definition, 18
    designer dogs and, 26, 30
    effects on puppies/breeding dogs, 18,
        26
    pet store puppies and, 29–30

puppy raising
avoiding pitfalls, 124–25
examples, 107–8, 117–18, 125
exposure to adults, 120–21
exposure to children, 119–20, 154–55
exposure to other dogs, 121–22, *121*
food-handling advice, 117
genetic/environmental factors and, 108
myths on manners, 114–15
owners' goals and, 119
sharing food and, 115–17
summary, 125–26
See also socialization
puppy socialization classes
definition/description, 109, 126
overview, 122–23
skills learned, 122–23
what to look for/avoid, 123
purebred dogs
adopting, 20–23
See also breeds of dogs; *specific breeds*

"rage syndrome," 210
rally obedience, *189*
Reconcile, 259, 260
reinforcement
definition, 48
See also specific types
reinforcers defined, 130
Reisner, Ilana, 153, 210, 232
relocating dogs, 28
request-response-reward, 98–99
rescue groups
definition, 18
See also shelter/rescue groups
resource guarding
definition, 153, 204
description/examples, 153, 204, 209, 218
managing, 153, 174, 221–22
Retrievers
behaviors, 23
Golden, 107–8, 117–18, 125, 210, 230
Labrador/mixes, 127, 129–30, 138,
158–59, 216, 226–27, 275
Nova Scotia Duck Tolling, 296, 298–99,
313–14
rolling on back, 207–8

S-adenosyl-l-methionine (SAMe), 311, *312*
S-adenosyl-l-methionine-tosylate disulfate
(SAMe) (also Novifit), 311, *312*
safe refuge
aggression management, 223
children/dogs and, 153, 155, 163, 165,
166, 168

definition, 153–54
description, 163
planning/training for, 163–64
sound sensitivities and, 271, 274
safety tips
dog fights/stopping, 213–14
dog running at you, 161–62,
162
resource guarding and, 221–22
See also specific behaviors
Salvin, Hannah, 302
SAMe (S-adenosyl-l-methionine), 311, *312*
Schilder, Matthijs, 85
Schnauzer, Giant, 199, 233
Schnoodle, 25
Scott, John Paul, 110, 111
seat belts for dogs, *44*
seizure
definition/description, *285*
medication for, 286
Seksel, Kersti, 291
selective breeding defined, 17
selegiline (Anipryl), 309, 311
senile plaques, 300
Senilife, 310, 311, *312*
senior dogs/problem treatments
enrichment, 308, 309, 310
environmental modifications and, 307–8,
307
examples, 298–99, 306–7, *307*, 309–10,
312–14
medications, 309, 310
overview, 310–11, *312*
pheromone use, 310
summary, 314–15
waking at night, 308–10
See also cognitive dysfunction/syndrome
(CDS)
senior dogs/problems
avoiding pitfalls, 314
babies/children and, 168
behavior problems overview, 296, 297,
303, *304,* 305–6
digestive tract overview, 306
early diagnosis/intervention and, 297–98,
303
examples, 296, 297, 298–99, 306–7,
313–14
medical conditions/behavior signs
summary, 305–6
pain and, 306
physical problems overview, 296–98, *297,*
305–6
summary, 314–15
urinary tract overview, 306

senior dogs/problems (*cont.*)
  vet routine exams and, 298
  See also cognitive dysfunction/syndrome
    (CDS)
sensitization, 109, 112, 116
separation anxiety
  abandonment/euthanasia and, 237
  anticipation and, 248
  behavior patterns and, 244
  behaviors with, 235–36, 238, 239, 244,
    248, 256
  bonding in dogs, 236–37
  breeds and, 241
  causes and, 241, 242
  definition/description, 237, 242
  detecting behaviors, 238
  examples, 235–36, 243–44, *246,* 257, 258,
    262
  facts on, 241–42
  MannersMinder system and, 92
  myths/conflicting opinions on, 239–40
  other household dogs/pets and, 35, 237,
    261
  punishment/problems with, 235, 242,
    245, 250, 258, 261
  puppy age at separating from parents/
    littermates, 245
  puppy normal behavior and, 244–45
  rescued dogs and, 237, 241
  "spoiling" your dog and, 240, 241
  "Velcro dogs," 237, 238
separation anxiety/behavior modification
  avoiding pitfalls, 260–61
  certified pet-trainer and, 258
  crates/possible problems and, 75, 79, 80,
    101, 243–44, 245, 246, *246*
  daycare and, 245, 249
  departure practice/steps, 254–56
  departure routine and, 251
  diagnosis and, 247
  early detection and, 239
  exercise and, 249–50
  expert help and, 92, 93, 258
  food puzzles/toys and, 101, 243, 251, 254,
    255, 261
  gates and, 245
  going too fast, 251–53, 256
  greetings/exits and, 249
  habituation and, 251–52
  medical problems and, 101, 259
  medication, 247, 257–60
  medication side effects, 258, 259
  neurochemical responses and, 246
  noise reactivity and, 246
  pet-sitter and, 248–49

pheromone use and, 101, 260
premedication laboratory work and, 259
quiet inside house and, 257
rewarding calm behavior, 250–51, 253–54,
  257
screening for other behavior problems
  and, 246–47
summary, 261–62
taking to work, 249
teaching dog to relax, 253–54
videotaping dog and, 235, 238–39, 242,
  246, 247, 253, 254, 256, 260, 261
serotonin
  compulsive behaviors and, 283, 285, 294,
    295
  function/dysfunction, 210–11, 300
Serpell, James, 31
sertraline, 285
Sex and the City (TV show) and dogs,
  32
Shar-Peis, 216
Sheepdog
  Old English, 216
  Shetland, 312–13
shelter/rescue groups
  adopting from, 27–28
  housetraining problems and, 60, 63–64
  types of, 27–28
Sheltie, 182–83
Shepherd
  Australian, 22
  German, 216, 286–87
  mix, 136–37
Sherman, Barbara L., 26
Shih Tzu, 13–14, 263
shock collars, 84, 85, 87
Shore, Elsie, 99–100
sighthounds, 164, *187*
"sit" command
  teaching, 50
  uses, 49, 53, 58, 91, 120, 123, *133,* 134–35,
    135, *135, 165, 168, 171, 174, *189,*
    253, 272, 274, 309
Skinner, B. F., 43
Skinner box, 43
snarl defined, 4
social enrichment defined, 180
social hierarchy
  feral dog studies and, 201
  See also dominance myth
socialization
  advice sources, 124
  age/bonding with owners, 108
  definition, 109
  dogs learning from other dogs, 212–13

genetics and, 212
guidelines, 113
importance of, 119–20, 154–55, 164–65
learning and, 212–13
misconceptions on, 108–9
orphan puppies and, 213
overview, 110–14, *111*, 124–25
owner guidelines, 124–25
rewards and, *111*, 112, 113
sensitive (critical) period, 110–11
summary, 126
timing/periods, 110–11
vaccinations and, 113–14, 122
socialization classes, 109, 117–18
See also puppy socialization classes
sound sensitivities
adopting another dog and, 269
behaviors, 266–67
causes, 264
common triggers, 244, 246, 264, 265
cortisol and, 269
definition, 265
dominance myth and, 268–69
escape behavior, 267
evolution/biological processes and, 264, 265
example, 263, 275
genetics and, 264, 279
"growing out of," 268
healthy vs. abnormal noise responses, 264–65
intelligence and, 267–68
learning while scared and, 275–76
myths on, 267–69, 279
owner's fears and, 269
punishment and, 268–69
self-injury, 267
storms/thunderstorms and, 244, 246, 263, 264, 265, 271
training and, 268–69
when to seek help, 270
sound sensitivities/treatment and management
avoiding pitfalls, 278–79
body wraps/Thundershirt, 277, *277*
counterconditioning, 272
crate and, 274
desensitization, 272
exposure to sounds/CD recordings, 270–73
habituation, 265
massage, 271, 274
medication to avoid, 276
medications and, 271, 275–77
music and, 274, 278

pheromones use, 271, 274
rewards and, 270, 272, 273, *273*, 274
safe havens and, 271, 274
summary, 279–80
throughadogsear.com, 274, 278
thunderstorms, 273–75, 277–78, *277*
Spaniels
Cavalier King Charles, 31
Cocker, 116
signaling and, 216
traditional jobs, *187*
sports for dogs
considerations, 188, 194
examples, *186–88, 189–91*
status-related aggression defined, 205
stay command
teaching, 55–56
uses, 51, 53, 54, 55–56, 58, 91, 134, 165, 168, 171, *189*, 253, 272
stereotypic behavior, *284*
stimulation
definition, 180
See also enrichment; *specific types*
Storm Defender (cape), 278
storms/thunderstorms
body wraps, 95, 102, 277, *277*
electrostatic changes and, 278
sound sensitivities and, 244, 246, 263, 264, 265, 271
stress
definition, 266
effects on dogs, 30, 266
normal vs. abnormal, 266
submissiveness defined, 4
Sundgren, Hal, 31
systematic sensitization
definition, 109–10
description/tips, 112–13

tail and body language, *9*, 11–12, 152
tail chasing, 286–87, *289*
tau proteins, 300, 302
terriers
Boston, 216
Cairn, 44, *44*, 53–54
Jack Russell, 23–24, 32, 62, 199
mix, 107–8, 117–18, 125
Westie, 38–39, *307*
Yorkshire, 137–38, 164
territorial aggression defined, 204
therapy dog work, 194
threat defined, 4
throughadogsear.com, 274, 278
Thundershirts, 95, 102, 277, *277*

thyroid problems
early diagnosis/intervention, 259, 297
hormone decline/effects, 305–6
supplements, 298–99
tie-downs
cautions with, 61, 66, 77, 101
definition, 61
uses, 66, 77, 82, 101
toileting area defined, 61
tools of the trade
avoiding pitfalls, 102–4, *102*
behavior problems and, 99–102
behavioral deterrents, 93–94, 97
creating positive associations with, 99,
102–4, *102*
humane vs. cruel tools/methods, 84–86,
93–94, 96–97, 106
keeping dogs off furniture, 93
preventing behavior problems, 98
pulling on leash example, 83–84, 85
reinforcement devices overview, 90–93,
92
reinforcing the right things, 104
request-response-reward, 98–99
summary, 106
See also specific tools
toothbrushing
steps in, 144–47, *144, 146, 147*
tips on, 142
toothpaste type, 146
tracking, *191*
trainability vs. intelligence, 39–40
training dogs/learning
age and, 38–39
attention and, 54
avoidance learning, 47
avoiding pitfalls, 57–58
avoiding word confusion, 52
classical conditioning, 41–42, 47
clicker training, 41–42, 50, 58, 91, *92*
"come," 53–54
consistency and, 49
definitions overview, 47–48
distractions and, 50, 57
as enrichment, *185*
extinguishing behavior, 43, 47–48, *48*
generalizing behavior, 48, 50, 55, 58
hand signals and spoken word, 50–51
hand signals/importance, 50–51
human anger and, 57
jumping on people, 54–55
learning definition/description, 40–41
"look," 51–52

looking to humans for help, 49, 51–52
matching to sample, 40
mental maps, 40
operant conditioning, 42–43, 47
"perfect dog" and, 38
"place," 54, 55–56
request-response-reward, 98–99
reward value, 53–54
"sit," 50
"stay"/"place," 55–56
summary, 58
timing and, 51
tone of human voice and, 53
"variable ratio of reinforcement," 43–44,
44, 48, 57–58, 129–30
See also dominance myth; punishment;
specific training types; tools of the
trade
trash eating, 127, *135*
treibball, *191*
tricking dog/effects, 140
Tug-a-Jug, 43, 71, 93, 138, 164
tug games, 99, 121, *121, 185,* 270, 272,
308

United Kennel Club (UKC), 21

"variable ratio of reinforcement"
training dogs/learning, 43–44, *44,* 48,
57–58, 129–30
See also intermittent reinforcement
veterinary behaviorists
board certification requirements, xxi
science and, xv, xxi, xxii–xxiii
trainers vs., xv
See also American College of Veterinary
Behaviorists (ACVB)
Voith, Victoria L., 207

Wan, Michele, 10
water hose and dogs, *133*
Weimaraner, 177, 178–79
Wilson, Bob, 31
wolves
dogs vs., xv, 48–49
dominance myth and, 48–49, 201–2
intelligence, 49
social hierarchy myth and, 201, 202
Wrubel, Kathryn, 26

Yin, Sophia, 45, 92

Zantac, 286